The Bullish Thinking Guide for Managers

The Bullish Thinking Guide for Managers

HOW TO SAVE YOUR ADVISORS AND GROW YOUR BOTTOM LINE

Alden Cass
Brian F. Shaw
Sydney LeBlanc

WILEY

John Wiley & Sons, Inc.

Published by John Wiley & Sons, Inc., Hoboken, New Jersey.
Published simultaneously in Canada.

Photo credits: Photo of Alden Cass, page xv, copyright © Chris Casaburi, all rights
reserved. Photo of Brian F. Shaw, page xvi, by Ian Leith. Photo of Sydney LeBlanc,
p. xvii, by James Kydd.

For general information on our other products and services or for technical
support, please contact our Customer Care Department within the United States at
(800) 762-2974, outside the United States at (317) 572-3993, or fax (317) 572-4002.

Wiley also publishes its books in a variety of electronic formats. Some content that
appears in print may not be available in electronic formats. For more information
about Wiley products, visit our web site at www.wiley.com.

Library of Congress Cataloging-in-Publication Data:

Cass, Alden, 1975–
 The bullish thinking guide for managers : how to save your advisors and grow
 your bottom line/Alden Cass, Brian F. Shaw, Sydney LeBlanc.
     p. cm.
  Includes bibliographical references and index.
  ISBN 978-0-470-13769-7 (cloth)
    1. Investment advisors—Psychology. 2. Stockbrokers—Psychology.
 3. Financial services industry—Personnel management. I. Shaw, Brian F.,
 1948– II. LeBlanc, Sydney, 1947– III. Title.
 HG4621.C376 2008
 332.6068'3—dc22

                                                              2007040685

Printed in the United States of America.

10 9 8 7 6 5 4 3 2

To the memory of my grandparents, Elizabeth and Adolph Mezei, who gave me the gift of a college education, and fostered the development of my strong work ethic and passion for life.—Alden Cass

To our families, friends, and colleagues who inspired us to take this rewarding journey, and who continue to remind us of what is meaningful at the end of our long days.—Brian F. Shaw, Sydney LeBlanc

Contents

Preface

WHY WE WROTE THIS BOOK

B*ullish Thinking* is designed to help branch managers who are dealing with the numerous challenges of operating a smooth-running office: hiring and retaining top-achieving advisors, staying in compliance, and abiding by the rules and regulations of the business. These challenges are difficult for you as well as for your advisors, and may result in problems of stress, anxiety, and depression. You may be one of the many managers who also work double-duty as watchdog of the branch and your brokers, *and* produce your own book of business.

Bullish Thinking will serve as a personal resource for you in helping you avoid and alleviate your own emotional distress in addition to serving as an educational tool for recognizing symptoms of emotional distress in your advisors. You will read about the problems and learn the solutions that will help your brokers return to the top of their game. The hard-hitting true stories illustrate the threats to their mental health, identify their problems, and discuss the process of getting help. The in-depth case studies and real-life examples we provide exemplify the challenges your brokers face on a daily basis, and how these challenges lead to emotional breakdowns. We'll identify skills and strategies, including *Bullish Thinking* exercises, which teach mastery over the volatility and unpredictability of their jobs. The book also shows you how to help manage and balance your advisors' personal lives while working in this rapidly changing and demanding industry.

This book offers immediate solutions for short- and long-term help. We, authors Dr. Brian F. Shaw, one of the developers of Cognitive-Behavioral Therapy, and Dr. Alden Cass, specialize in working with financial services executives suffering from job burnout and behavioral paralysis, or depression. We offer a variety of ways for individuals to proactively reduce their job stress through proven techniques, including the *Bullish Thinking* strategies, which are an important theme throughout the book.

The Bullish Thinking Guide for Managers underscores the importance of emotional discipline in the face of potential indulgences, emotional highs, and crushing defeats. It also offers information from the landmark broker study,* including the alarming industry statistics, and both Dr. Cass's and Dr. Shaw's warning signals, case studies, treatments, and solutions. *Bullish Thinking* is an easy, practical, and palatable way of teaching the cognitive therapy skills introduced to the world of psychology by Dr. Brian F. Shaw. Dr. Cass pioneered research on brokers' and traders' behavior, and counsels those in distress.

Who Should Read the Book

Branch managers, regional sales managers, offices of supervisory jurisdictions (OSJs), national sales managers, executive managers at retail brokerage firms, owners of small- to mid-sized broker-dealers, and owners of Registered Investment Advisers. Anyone who is in a position of overseeing or supervising securities industry professionals such as financial advisors, stockbrokers, commodities and options traders, financial planners, wealth managers, investment management consultants, wholesalers, and others, will benefit from this book. Managers supervising bank brokers, insurance planners, and professionals working at financial supermarkets, who are in emotional distress on the job, will also be helped by the *Bullish Thinking* strategies and case study solutions.

The bottom line is: If emotional distress is not addressed, there may be adverse or harmful consequences not only to your advisors, but also to your branch office and the firm in general. Here's a case in point: Our research* indicates that "stockbrokers are not utilizing effective coping skills for the purpose of alleviating their work-related stress, and consequently, are developing the debilitating symptoms of burnout, anxiety, and depression. It is our contention that negative personal outcomes will be associated with these mental health concerns, and will consequently lead to negative organizational outcomes such as absenteeism, and a decreased quality of life for

---

*"Casualties of Wall Street: An Assessment of the Walking Wounded," by Alden Cass, John Lewis, Ed Simco, Catalyst Strategies Group, catsg.com/casualties.asp.

employees and their families. Additionally, if the early warning signs of burnout, depression, and anxiety continue to remain unnoticed by stockbrokers, as well as their employers, their overall productivity and commitment to the organization may wane over time, leading to an increase in turnover. This may cost brokerage houses additional money for training replacement brokers, who will more than likely suffer the same fate as their predecessors."

That being said, we believe that our research, and ongoing experience of working with managers and financial advisors, lends credence to the importance of preventing mental and physical illness from infringing upon the lives of these individuals. Because these illnesses affect them, they will eventually affect you, the branch manager, and the growth of your firm. Costly personal and organizational outcomes may result from ignoring the need for stress management for yourself and your advisors.

The goal of the book is to generate awareness and a better understanding of clinical depression, which is nothing to be ashamed of, and to help everyone connected to the financial services industry recognize the emotional and physical signs of this potentially devastating illness.

ALDEN CASS
BRIAN F. SHAW
SYDNEY LEBLANC

Acknowledgments

A labor of love, a team of dedicated professionals breathed life into this book and watched over it until it became a reality. We would like to thank this group of individuals for their tireless work and exceptional guidance throughout the entire process. Special thanks go to Marnie Shaw, a dedicated rookie in this business, for her wisdom and guidance. Thank you to Miriam and Renny Cass for teaching the values of persistence, courage, and love; and to Joe Santoro and Al Bergman for taking a chance. We would also like to thank Diane Bartoli of Artist Literary Group and Lorin Rees of the Helen Rees Agency for their initial input and feedback when the book was still a concept. Our deep appreciation goes out to our team at John Wiley & Sons: Editorial Director Pamela van Giessen, for believing in the project; Associate Editor Jennifer MacDonald, Editorial Assistant Kate Wood, and Senior Production Editor Mary Daniello, for their excellent direction and handling of our manuscripts and for making our project a reality. Thanks to Mary Welsch for hours of transcribing and proofreading, making our chapters flow smoothly. Thank you Gil, Ernie, and Montgomery, for the silent comfort you brought to us.

Our most important thanks goes to our readers, the hard-working advisors and managers, who face each day not knowing which stresses and problems will meet them head on, but who nonetheless, accept the challenges with fierce determination. We hope you find this book meaningful and that it will help you through periods of emotional distress, guiding you back to better productivity, more happiness, and a clear balance in your personal and professional life. Thank you for allowing us to know you, work with you, and help you.

A. C.
B. F. S.
S. L.

About the Authors

Dr. Alden Cass is a licensed clinical psychologist and performance enhancement coach in New York City. He is the President of Catalyst Strategies Group, a team of psychologists and performance coaches specializing in coaching financial services executives to become more productive and disciplined during market downturns and other stressful times. He works with both individual advisors and teams to overcome their skill deficits and to hone their strengths. He has been a consultant for branch managers on Wall Street to help improve the performance and problematic behaviors of the branches' top producers. Dr. Cass conducted the nation's first clinical investigation in 25 years on the mental health of Wall Street stockbrokers. His astonishing findings were presented at both international and national research conventions and have received a tremendous amount of attention from the business and financial trade media.

Dr. Cass teamed up with the Securities Industry Association after the World Trade Center attacks of September 11, 2001, to create a symposium that targeted the coping skills of Wall Street executives. He presented his "Bullish Thinking" paradigm to executives to help them deal with depression, burnout, and grief. He later developed "Bullish Thinking and Subtle Sales Training" workshops presented at three Investment Management Consultant Association Conferences (IMCA), at the Money Management Institute (MMI), the London Bullion Market Association Convention, and the Wall Street Branch Managers meeting, held at the Federal Reserve Bank in New York City.

Dr. Cass's coaching and profiling services are currently being used by various mutual funds as a value-added service that is delivered to the top broker-dealers nationwide. Dr. Cass sits on the board of the National Association of Investment Professionals and is a Research Committee member of the Financial Services Policy Institute. He is on the advisory board for a not-for-profit charity called FM World Charities, which focuses on preventative medicine initiatives for those less fortunate. He writes two weekly columns for The Street.com, a monthly Internet column called "The Mental Edge" for *Trader Monthly*, and a bimonthly column for *On Wall Street* magazine.

In his practice, he has spearheaded a campaign to support the wives and significant others of high-powered executives through his new weekly group, "The Wall Street Wives Club," and has developed a "Divorced Male Executive Support Group." He has also initiated a new research project focusing on empowering female investors while helping advisors understand how to cater to this existing target population.

 **Dr. Brian F. Shaw** is one of the originators of applied cognitive-behavioral psychology for clinical practice, the performance of elite athletes, creativity, health promotion, and coping with significant illness. He is an expert on how the mind works, how it gets derailed, and how to get it back on track. More important, he understands how people refresh their thinking to gain new perspectives on their life, their world, and their future.

He is the principal of BFS Consulting, a sports and entertainment consulting firm based in Toronto, Canada. As one of the developers of Cognitive-Behavioral Therapy (CBT), a psychological treatment for depression, anxiety, and substance abuse, Dr. Shaw has adapted this technology to help those suffering from serious medical illness (cancer, heart disease, eating disorders, pain syndromes, and transplantation). Over the past 15 years, he has taken this research and adapted it to the everyday world, where people strive for health and peace of mind.

Dr. Shaw has developed a cognitive behavioral approach to help individuals in the financial sector manage the demands of a career in their high stress industry. He has counseled brokers, securities litigators, traders, and others on Wall Street for more than 20 years.

He developed, with Bruce Ferguson at the Hospital for Sick Children in Toronto, Canada, a province-wide initiative to help children and youth with mental health and addiction. This work has affected mental health, juvenile justice, and educational approaches to children and youth.

In sports, Dr. Shaw is well known for his work as the co-director of the NHL/NHLPA Substance Abuse and Behavioral Health Program. He also co-directs the behavioral health program for Major League Soccer (MLS/MLSPA). He is responsible for the educational program for all NHL and MLS players. Dr. Shaw is the psychologist for the Toronto Blue Jays and several other professional and Olympic-level athletes. He was recently a featured speaker at the player development forum hosted by the NBA, NFL, and the NHL on the topic "Managing Anxiety in Athletes" and at the 2007 seminar hosted by the Los Angeles Police Department (LAPD) on "Teen Addiction."

Scientifically, Dr. Shaw is one of the 50 highest-impact authors in psychology. He is the author, with Paul Ritvo and Jane Irvine, of *Addiction and Recovery for Dummies* (Wiley, 2004) and *Cognitive Therapy of Depression* (Guilford, 1979, with Aaron Beck, John Rush, and Gary Emery).

He is a professor at the University of Toronto. Dr. Shaw received his Ph.D. in clinical psychology at the University of Western Ontario in 1975 following a B.S. degree at the University of Toronto.

Sydney LeBlanc is a 30-year financial services industry veteran, journalist, author, and publisher. She was the co-founder and editor-in-chief of *Registered Representative* magazine, the nation's first trade magazine for stockbrokers, in 1976. Later, as editor-in-chief, she led the development of *Securities Industry Management* magazine, the first publication for branch managers.

Sydney helped launch and promote the Institute for Certified Investment Management Consultants (now IMCA) in the mid-1980s. A writer for such industry organizations as the Money Management Institute, International Association of Advisors in Philanthropy, and Success Continuing Education, LLC, she is also a writing coach and marketing consultant for industry trainers, financial advisors, broker-dealers, and money managers. Sydney is the author of *Legacy: The History of Separately Managed Accounts; Wealth Management Teams; Independent Business Ownership;* and the co-author of *Streetwise Investor; The Wealth Factor; The World of Money Management; Happily Ever After; Stop and Think;* and *PR Savvy for the Financial Professional.*

She is the recipient of several awards for her work, including the Ozzie Award for Excellence in Design, the *FOLIO:* Magazine Editorial Excellence Award for *Securities Industry Management* magazine, the 2007 Managed Accounts Pioneer award from the Money Management Institute, and First Place for Signed Editorial from the American Society of Business Press Editors. Her articles have appeared in *On Wall Street, Broker/Dealer, Financial Advisor, Global Investing,* and *Research* magazines, among others.

Co-director of Fisher LeBlanc Group, a financial publishing, marketing, and communications firm, she is also the managed accounts editor for *Financial Advisor* magazine and consulting editor for *Senior Consultant News Journal.* Sydney is an officer and board member of the Washington, D.C.–based Wealth Advisor Institute and is actively involved on the Marketing and Communications committee. She is also on the board of the National Association of Investment Professionals and is a research committee member of the Financial Services Policy Institute.

The Bullish Thinking Guide
for Managers

INTRODUCTION

Wall Street's Walking Wounded

Are your high-achieving producers depressed or anxious? Does it matter if your highest achievers are the most troubled? It does when it begins to affect your branch's bottom line and the morale and behaviors of others in the office. Would you be shocked to learn that an astounding 23 percent of the stockbrokers and financial advisors who participated in a landmark study* (by Dr. Alden Cass) had clinically significant symptoms of depression? Not only that, but the most significant finding of the study was that *brokers who were making the most money were the most dysfunctional when it came to their mental health.*

Million-dollar producers were the most dysfunctional? How could that be? They are at the top of their games, successful in their careers, and have earned the respect of their colleagues. It is difficult to comprehend that your superstars could let anything get them down or get in their way of their success. While all of this may be true, behind the scenes many of these individuals have the heavy burden of battling their demons in silence out of the fear of appearing weak. Think about this: Your high achievers are living and working in a fiercely competitive environment. They constantly struggle to win and keep clients, while trying to differentiate themselves from their competition. The market is a major concern for many, especially your transaction-oriented brokers or traders. Industry regulations continue to tighten and morph into complicated rules almost impossible to decipher and faithfully follow.

---

*Alden Cass, John Lewis, Ed Simco, "Casualties of Wall Street: An Assessment of the Walking Wounded." See Appendix A.

1

Your superstars (and prospective achievers) must respond quickly to their clients and, at the same time, attempt to stay in compliance. Because of these and other daily issues, these individuals will exhibit higher levels of emotional exhaustion, higher levels of depression and anxiety, and display the poorest coping skills. According to the study, "Casualties of Wall Street," the highest earners also used the most drugs and consumed alcohol to excess. As a result, we are witnessing a generation of brokers and advisors who are trading money and affluence in exchange for their mental health.

But, you say, you are not a psychologist, doctor, or nursemaid. Understood. That's not in your job description. But what *is* in your job description is to recruit, train, retain, and (at times) terminate producers so you can maintain a profitable, smooth-running branch. Retention is a vital part of the equation. Not only is it expensive to have turnover in your office, it is also stressful, time-consuming, and disruptive to the environment of your branch. Something to consider about the retention of high achievers and depression: In an eight-month follow-up survey to the study, nearly 25 percent of the brokers who made the most money were *no longer employed by their firms.* They had been fired, changed jobs, or just burned out and dropped off the radar. While they might have been riding a wave of success, their earning potential for the long haul was hampered by their need to distance themselves from experiencing painful internal emotions such as disgust, guilt, remorse, shame, and inferiority.

Take Stock of Your Advisors Today

Are your advisors controlling huge assets and great wealth while struggling with overwhelming mental distress? How would you know? As we have already mentioned, some individuals have a talent for keeping things inside, so it will take keen observation on your part. In *Bullish Thinking,* we illustrate helpful strategic observation techniques and what you can do once you have determined an advisor has a problem. Coming to his or her aid *before* they make serious mistakes on the job and in their personal lives is your goal. It is heartbreaking for some brokers and advisors to accept that their decisions can potentially ruin a client's life. It is even more sobering when some of the outcomes of their decisions are affected by external factors beyond their control, for example, market volatility, world events, the weather. Sometimes all they need to hear is "It's not your fault. What else is going on in your life that is troubling you?"

These are the types of questions you might consider asking yourself:

- Why are my top producers burning out, plateauing, or disengaging?
- Why are their numbers down?
- What can I do to bring my star producers back to emotional health?
- How can I avoid having my brokers and advisors fall in to this vicious trap?
- What can I do to make them more comfortable in discussing their challenges with me?

Increasingly, as managers ask these questions, many are attempting to answer them and take the necessary action. But you must *first* address and understand the challenges, fears, and taboos of the serious emotional demons your advisors are facing every day on the job. You already know the many threats of this high risk and reward business, and how critical it is to help your producers keep their focus, balance work productivity with their personal lives, and . . . maintain their sanity. But you may need help in learning the necessary skills and navigating through their emotional challenges and needs.

Is There Any Doubt This Book Can Help You and Your Advisors?

Let's make this simple and direct: Immediately addressing potential (or ongoing) problems in your branch that are a direct result of stress, anxiety, burnout, or depression is not only necessary from a mental health perspective, it also makes good business sense from your firm's point of view. Do you, as a manager of a branch or a corporate executive at a retail brokerage firm want to continue spending time and money constantly recruiting and hiring new brokers, while never questioning your age-old broker turnover problems? As with any problem, getting to the root cause, eliminating or fixing it will ensure that most, if not all, of the problems will be solved. If you are the kind of manager who can manage emotions, who is comfortable feeling, and who can relate to clients, you will be more successful in helping your advisors in the long run.

It is our goal—no, it is our responsibility—to teach you the warning signals and dangers of depression, to uncover the myths, offer practical solutions, and lead the investment professional back to a healthful emotional and physical state of mind. And we want to do this in a nonthreatening, empathic, and positive manner. So, we are offering you positive ways of coping with the numerous challenges you and your advisors face on the job; ways that allow changes in patterns of thinking and behaving; ways that provide relief, which will result in the achievement of a healthy mindset. Our hope is that we will encourage countless advisors (and managers like yourself) to seek the coaching or counseling they may need to improve their lives and businesses; those who might not otherwise come forward to ask for help. The payback for everyone is that the industry will see that psychology and business can coexist.

The stories and solutions inside this book bring to life the debilitating symptoms of mood disorders like clinical depression, burnout, anxiety, and substance addiction, to show that it is nothing to be ashamed of and to help you and other managers recognize the emotional and physical signs of these potentially devastating problems. The heart-wrenching case studies of individuals whose lives have been uprooted and disrupted are presented in full detail to show you that you and your advisors are not alone, there is a light at the end of the tunnel, and that it is never too late to reach out for help.

Bullish Thinking Strategies for Positive Change

The concept of Bullish Thinking, designed by Dr. Alden Cass, was created to meet the needs of individuals who need help managing the daily volatility and stress of work, but who don't want to feel like a patient on a psychiatrist's couch. Bullish Thinking allows one to achieve emotional discipline regardless of the stressor, and is an easy, practical, and palatable way of teaching the cognitive therapy skills introduced to the world of psychology by co-author Dr. Brian F. Shaw. We are dedicated to the mission of countering the misunderstanding and stigma that we observe every day in the financial services industry. These are the conditions that we label as mental illness and addiction, but that we know even better as human tragedy. We are dedicated to preventing the tragic mental and physical casualties proliferating in the industry today.

This book is the first step in that direction.

1

Stop the Dance

ARE YOU TURNING A BLIND EYE
TO PROBLEMS IN YOUR OFFICE?

On Monday morning, manager Jim Smith's branch office was humming with activity. Jim hired the million-dollar producer sent over by his industry recruiter, and the firm's bottom line—as well as Jim's own compensation—would quickly begin to grow by a robust margin. Jim was happy, relieved, and satisfied that his regional manager would now cool down for a while and allow him to manage his advisors.

Manage? No, according to Jim, that was impossible. You can't *manage* million-dollar producers. Instead, you *support* them. You *encourage* them. And you *thank* them. Jim truly believed he was, in essence, the Advisor Dad.

But, there was a flaw in his thinking and in his methods. Because if this was the case, why didn't Mr. Advisor Dad—the intuitive, kind, billion-dollar supportive manager—spot at least one or two of the looming warning signs and symptoms of emotional distress that were quietly eating away at some of his top producers? Was he afraid of how they would react if he confronted them? Was he too caught up in red tape to be aware? Did his advisors feel that he was unapproachable? Did he choose to ignore them or did he not have the skill to recognize and identify the signals? Or was it simply that he did not have the tools with which to rescue them?

Shouldering the largest office in the firm's network, with more than 30 advisors each producing in excess of $2 million in gross commissions annually, Jim boasted he had seen it all in his 35-year career of managing successful brokerage offices. But was he turning a blind eye to some of the most damaging elements affecting (or potentially affecting) his branch office, his producers, the firm, and, ultimately, himself?

For Jim to really *see* if emotional distress was either preventing his advisors from moving to a higher production (or asset) level, or causing his advisors to act out aggressively toward colleagues, clients, and others, he needed to stop and reflect on the external, as well as the internal, influences on these individuals. He needed to step back, release himself from the stresses of being sandwiched between advisors and management. He needed to stop running from unsolved problem to unsolved problem.

He needed to stop the dance.

Unsung Heroes: Kicking or Kissing Butt?

You know who you are. You are the juggler, the watchdog, the psychologist, the businessman, the recruiter, the meatloaf in the middle of the sandwich. You're being eaten alive by your advisors and upper management. So, stopping the dance is easier said than done.

Simply put, you're under significant stress. Stress, in plain English, is the wear and tear our minds and bodies experience as we adjust to our continually changing environment. And there is much to be stressed about in this industry, which seems to change daily. Stress is an unavoidable part of life. On the positive side, challenges caused by stress can help us develop new skills and behavior patterns. The problems occur, however, when stress becomes excessive. It can become destructive and can turn into *dis*tress. Too much stress on your mind and body can make you feel miserable, sad, angry, anxious, and depressed.

As we mentioned, the heavy demands and responsibilities you have can be internal as well as external. Internal, meaning self-generated demands such as personal standards or expectations of control; and external, meaning such things as your firm's culture, corporate and economic shifts, needy clients and advisors, market volatility, and so forth. But they are terribly hard to handle. Every day, managers like you face more information than they can effectively process; it's all part of the information overload crisis. Typically, with information overload you experience a crisis management mindset. Dealing with paperwork and administrative excess is the easy part—it's a cakewalk compared to the overwhelming emotional ups and downs that managers deal with today. You are constantly in a battle to get time just to be able to think and process important issues like compliance, making sure that the regulations are being met, and that all of your advisors are in line. So, the tendency then is to get irritable if your advisors aren't doing what they should be doing. That's called the *tyranny of the shoulds.*

The tyranny of the shoulds happens when you actually get into a mindset of thinking: "If my advisors would only think about *what they should be doing,* and then do it, then I wouldn't have to be dancing so much." The tendency is to get out there and kick butt just to get people to do *what they should be doing* and that makes you appear to be authoritative, demanding, and hard to deal with. Some of the more experienced advisors shrug it off, but when a lot of the younger, less experienced advisors are looking for support, coaching, and skill-building, that type of attitude has the potential to make or break a rookie advisor.

Finding Your Inner Coach

It can be very difficult for a manager to find the middle ground, without crossing the lines: To get out and kick butt, and thereby develop the reputation of being a control freak, or to balance that with being the type of manager who has an open door policy and is ready to talk to his advisors about the problems they are facing.

Managers usually have their own style of managing, coaching, and running the office. (We discuss the four styles of management and five styles of advisor personalities in depth in Chapters 3, 4, and 5.) But, let's use a football example for our purposes now: Tony Dungy, who won the Super Bowl with Indianapolis, is a guy who never raises his voice and never swears. If we compare coaches like Vince Lombardi, Bill Belichick, Lovie Smith, and other well-known coaches to one another, we all get images of what a leader should be like. So, Dungy is really surprising because when he first pulls his team together, he doesn't raise his voice. Instead, he says, "Gentlemen, I'm going to tell you about this coming year and this is the loudest I am going to speak to you all year." He is like Superdad.

Tony Dungy and Lovie Smith are similar types of leaders. Whereas many NFL coaches instill fear into their teams with their demeanor, both Smith and Dungy use a different route to command respect.

That's what the great coaches do, and that's what great managers do: Command respect. But we ask ourselves: How can a manager persuade grown men (and women) to sacrifice themselves to a common goal? The cynic would say advisors and brokers have infinite reasons to want to win. But the crucial difference is that true leaders, including all of the coaches named above as well as successful branch managers, have high, but reasonable, expectations for each individual and hold them accountable to those standards. The end result, no matter what the leadership style in football and in business, is that the leaders learn to listen and to command respect. That being said, the manager must also hold himself to the same standards. Those standards, however, are sometimes difficult to uphold if that individual is also in an emotional crisis, not to mention if the *advisors* are also in emotional crisis.

Help Yourself First; Then You Can Help Others

Before you can effectively recognize, understand, and help emotionally distressed advisors, it's important to recognize how your own emotional state can influence the way in which you treat them. If you are irritable, overwhelmed, depressed or frustrated, it comes across immediately to others. Conversely, if you are feeling great and are in good spirits, you can deal with problems in the office in a more supportive, caring way. It is the zigzagging moods, the inconsistency, and the never knowing what frame of mind you are in that day that advisors have trouble with, because if you're always a kick-butt manager, then your advisors can count on you to be a kick-butt manager. If you're a superdad, then they count on you to be just that. Managers who are hot today and cold tomorrow are the ones who leave their advisors and their staff feeling helpless because they can't predict the manager's mood or how he is going to treat them. They wonder which manager is going to show up: Dr. Jekyll or Mr. Hyde. When a manager is perceived as having a Jekyll-or-Hyde type of personality, advisors tend to avoid asking for help. They often walk the other way, because they believe that you won't want to talk with them. It is important for advisors to be assertive in asking for your time, but the onus should not fall just on them.

Life experience also has a big impact on a manager's attitude and behavior and how she treats advisors. Some managers feel compassion toward those struggling with emotional, addiction, or life problems like divorce, while others are hostile or rejecting. We learn more about emotions in Chapters 2 and 3. For now, think for a moment. How are you feeling? Are you relaxed, happy, content, irritable, sad, afraid, guilty? Check the temperature of your emotions and take an inventory of your attitude(s). What kind of attitude do you have? Are you open or closed to new information? Do you believe in people's ability to learn and change or are you cynical and pessimistic? Are people with mental health or addiction problems weak, lazy, stupid? Or are they in a temporary downturn in their lives? Would your advisors agree with your assessment?

Facing the Hard Issues on Your Desk

Now that you've checked the temperature of your emotions and have taken an inventory of your attitude, this is a good time to examine the challenges on your desk as well as those of your advisors. Most managers would agree that managing the egos, helping teams develop or merge, dealing with office competition (which can be a positive if structured correctly; for example, wealth management teams), jealousy, and aggression are major potential problems. These are the symptoms of deeper issues that you will be called upon to deal with as astute, open-minded, and dedicated to solving these problems, thereby creating a smoother-running office. You can deal with these issues on a one-to-one basis with your advisors, or, sometimes even as a group effort.

Lest we forget other major stressors in your life, we should mention hiring and retaining top-producing advisors or those who have significant assets under management. You are called upon to mentor recruits or team them up with suitable veterans who can train them. You also are a sales manager, a coach and motivator, and a team organizer. Often unannounced, your regional or national sales manager checks in on other issues such as legal and compliance matters, sales quotas, supervision, and client oversight. Are there any other hats that you should be wearing? Oh, yes, you are a time management expert, a psychologist to your advisors whose personal lives may be affecting their performance on the job, and you are also in charge of continuing education training, as mandated by the regulators.

Now that we've pinpointed most of your areas of responsibility and, hence, areas of potential stress, we give you help on alleviating it so you can do a more effective job as manager but, most important, we give you insight and solutions to help your advisors identify and eliminate the emotional barriers to their mental health and, ultimately, to their success.

But, how can you do this effectively? The quick and dirty answer is: By using an action-oriented self-monitoring intervention that allows individuals to transcend any work stressor with perseverance, giving them a sense of control over their jobs. We call it *Bullish Thinking*.

The concept of Bullish Thinking was created to meet the needs of financial professionals who need help managing the daily volatility and stress of work but don't want to feel like a patient on a psychiatrist's couch. Bullish Thinking allows one to achieve emotional discipline regardless of the stressor, and is an easy, practical, and palatable way of teaching cognitive-behavioral therapy skills.

The concept, as well as solutions and case studies, are explored in more detail in the next chapter and those that follow. You will learn how to recognize warning signs of serious *Bearish Thoughts* (yours and your advisors), how to manage conflict in the office and at home, why and when treatment is necessary, dispelling the myths of psychological treatment, and the Bullish Thinking solutions to crisis management. We'll use examples of monitoring logs—real scenarios of advisors suffering from Bearish Thinking and how to turn them around with the positive, reinforcement actions of Bullish Thinking. Learning these skills will be a challenge for you, but one we believe you are ready to undertake.

Ready to get started?

CHAPTER 2

Bullish Thinking

HOW TO CHANGE NEGATIVE BEHAVIOR
AND DESTRUCTIVE THOUGHTS

In the previous chapter we discussed the significant stressors you have while trying to juggle your work and supervise the personalities and individual challenges of the advisors in your office. We also described a few personal and professional difficulties that can potentially add to your being an ineffective manager, as well as creating an unhappy environment in your private life.

Let's discuss the concept of Bullish Thinking now and how it can help you achieve emotional discipline, and how to recognize Bearish Thoughts or negative behavior in your advisors so you can help them, too.

Designed by co-author Dr. Alden Cass, Bullish Thinking is an innovative and action-oriented way of maintaining emotional discipline. Its theory is rooted in the principles of Cognitive-Behavioral Therapy (CBT), as developed by co-author Dr. Brian F. Shaw, and is based on the assertion that our perceptions of stressful or negative events—whether they are Bullish (positive) or Bearish (negative)—can actually affect how we handle ourselves in reaction to them. To clarify further: *How we perceive a negative event* is directly linked to *how we respond to it* from a physiological, performance-based, and emotional standpoint. Additionally, these perceptions will affect how much we feel in control of ourselves within the context of work.

Bullish Thoughts are defined as rational, positive, and based on personal historical evidence. *Bearish Thoughts* are often irrational predictions, expectations, and beliefs about ourselves, others, and our future. This type of perception is often based on exaggerated or black and white thoughts, or beliefs about reality. For example, your advisors may say, "I lost my client's money, so I must be incompetent as a financial advisor," or "I will never overcome this bad month because of a terrible mistake I made." Bearish Thoughts are cyclical and tend to predominate our thinking during the course of an overwhelming week. Spending more time thinking and obsessing about recent failures or setbacks rather than about successes and achievements is a good example. Typically, negative or stressful events are more salient than positive ones. As humans who want to survive as part of evolution, we are highly attuned to threats in our environment. We have a threat detection system that is sophisticated and constantly scanning for trouble. We also have a startle response that pushes us into action in less than a second. Consequently, we sit with losses much longer than we savor successes. This type of negative focus is part of human nature. When the mind goes into overdrive and the threat system won't turn off, we have to apply Bullish Thinking strategies to bring it under control and calm it down.

The helpful thing about Bullish Thinking intervention is that it teaches the power of how just one realistic thought that has the ability to wipe out an entire army of negative ones often hampers your or your advisors' moods and productivity at work. It uses familiar industry language to minimize the negative stigma associated with receiving cognitive-behavioral therapy in business. It places the responsibility on the advisor to take charge of her thought patterns to improve her productivity and emotional state. In a job where control and uncertainty can be a commodity, this level of control over some aspect of one's life is usually perceived as reassuring and stabilizing.

Before we begin discussing Bullish Thinking strategies and solutions and how they can help you and your advisors, let's discuss the various ways to recognize the symptoms of emotional distress in your advisors (or in yourself—you have feelings too). This is the first step in preventing the escalation of an underlying emotional problem.

You may already have noticed from time to time that some of your advisors are suffering from—or exhibiting signs of—burnout. It's a common syndrome and one that has been discussed openly since the early 1970s. But emotional illnesses such as depression, anxiety, and addiction are rarely talked about. The important thing to remember is that, oftentimes, burnout is just one step before clinical depression or anxiety disorders.

Let's look at it as a continuum. If normal, everyday stress is a 5 on a 1–10 scale (10 being the most stressful), and most people perform at an optimal level at a 5 or 6, we can safely assume that advisors are forced to work very hard at keeping their anxiety level from reaching a level of 7 or above.

If the stress, frustration, or disillusionment facing the advisor are not corrected or challenged, and subsequently, brought down to levels that are in alignment with reality, then burnout rears it head. And it can be ugly. If you or one of your advisors are experiencing burnout, or have a genetic predisposition toward depression or anxiety and it is left unchecked, prominent symptoms of major depression may emerge that may require medication and intensive therapy.

Some of the initial symptoms of burnout are abrupt episodes of agitation, fatigue, and poor concentration. It can feel like being trapped in quicksand, and an individual often perceives any efforts to change his or her work situation as being futile. An individual may suddenly become irritable, insensitive to others' feelings, snappy, and overreactive to even the most trivial of things. Depending on what the perceived threat is, an advisor may try to hold it together for the sake of clients and then dump on everyone else—you (her manager), her spouse, family members, friends, and significant others.

Advisors who are skilled at projecting confidence will do everything in their power to *keep their frustrations hidden* from you, their clients, and others. It's rare when an advisor will openly admit to uncertainty, fear, worry, or anxiety. It's uncommon and a well-kept secret. This is where you can help them feel more comfortable in confiding in you. (We discuss these techniques in depth later in the book.)

Self-defeating thoughts and pessimism about her future will hamper an individual's performance whether she is in the financial services industry or playing in a sports arena. For advisors, the heat is on every day. In sports, it's game seven of the league championship series; in law, it's the high profile case. In the world of finance, it's hunting the "big elephants" (or the affluent individuals) and bringing them on as clients. It's managing clients' life savings, building, preserving, and distributing their wealth. At the same time, they are trying to make a living, building their book of business, capturing more assets, targeting the high net worth investor, staying in compliance, and on and on.

What can wreck the train for your advisors are the variables they can't control, or don't anticipate. Nassim Nicholas Taleb (*The Black Swan,* Random House, 2007) referred to these events as *Black Swans:* events that are highly improbable, outside the realm of normal expectations that, nonetheless, have an extreme emotional and economic impact. Volatile markets, terrorism, corporate scandals, tsunamis, foreign crises, and war are obvious examples. Inevitably, as advisors continue down their career paths, capture larger assets, and manage money—whether retail or institutional—many tend to think of their clients as numbers—or situations or problems—and the day-to-day business of working with them becomes less personal and more technical.

In essence, these advisors become depersonalized, creating an emotional distance from their clients, their colleagues, and their manager. To avoid experiencing painful emotions like sadness, frustration, worry, or anger, they begin treating their clients as though they were useful only for monetary gain. Much like a nightclub promoter who counts heads at the door to anticipate his take for the night, many times the advisor's clients similarly become just "heads." You know that your high achievers like to solve problems, the bigger the better. They love the challenge, the action. Once they have landed a client and the challenge has been overcome, however, some advisors have a tendency to move them to the back of their priority list. Consequently, their servicing mentality will apply only to novel and prospective clients. But these very characteristics may make it difficult for them to understand the thoughts, feelings, and needs of others, including those sitting right across from them at work, and those of their family.

Are You Listening to Their Silent Cries for Help?

Depression and anxiety are common mental health syndromes that have serious negative physical, emotional, and behavioral implications. These syndromes can rob one of needed sleep and pleasure, cause early morning awakening, or a feeling of dread, thus wracking a person's nerves to the point of collapse. Let's discuss the definitions and feelings of *helplessness, hopelessness,* and *worthlessness,* how these symptoms affect your advisors, and also read examples of monitoring logs we mentioned—real scenarios of advisors suffering from Bearish Thoughts. (See Figures 2.1 and 2.2.)

Helplessness

A state of mind, defined by an inability to perceive any control over the events in one's life—and, even worse, the inability to predict when future negative events may emerge. If one of your advisors is in a situation where stress is unrelenting (pretty much every day on Wall Street), he may begin to question his competence. "What am I doing? I can't compete, can't keep up. I'm getting hammered here. I don't know what to do. There is no way out of this situation." The achievements of his colleagues may make this individual feel like a total loser. "How do they keep up? How do they do it? I can't believe it! No matter what I do, I screw it up. I can't win."

These thoughts drive one's mind into a state of paralysis and shock. At this point, your advisor may retreat to a protective passive stance, lying in bed wishing that life's responsibilities would stop weighing down on them, if only for a moment. In a crippling state, the advisor is frozen while the world spins past.

Now here's the real kicker. The perfectionism and fear of failure turns into hostility; a self-hatred for being weak that drives him into further despair. The highly self-critical and harshly judgmental attitude that fuels his ambition and blind courage works against him as he tries to understand why he can't impose his will on the work environment. He believes that no matter what he does, he can't change or control the situation or circumstance. He knows that something is wrong with him, but doesn't know what it is. Tragically, this scenario continues to drive such advisors down in the same way that our immune system—which is designed to fight off infection—can turn on us. Both conditions can be costly if they aren't treated effectively and quickly.

Hopelessness

Adopting a helpless stance in managing our emotional states accelerates and perpetuates a sense of hopelessness, a belief that failure and loss is inevitable, so giving up is the only course. Hopelessness is best seen as a flood of negative predictions. Your advisor might say things like "I am doomed. This strategy will never work." "Life isn't worth

CATALYST STRATEGIES GROUP

BULLISH THINKING *MONITORING LOG*

WORK EVENTS Describe two situations, events, or interactions that lead to specific consequences.

1. David the Financial Advisor:

"A client gives you an ultimatum 'You have 2 strikes left' when you were a day late in organizing the transfer of his funds."

2. Jim the Financial Advisor:

"Facing a protracted market downturn. Many of my clients' profolios are hurting. A new client calls at 9:00 A.M. to tell me that I am incompetent because he has been losing money and his friend has done better with his investment."

PERCEPTION OF EVENT Stream of positive, rational thoughts, and/or self-statements

BULLISH THINKING	BEARISH THINKING	BULLISH THINKING	BEARISH THINKING
1a. "I'm going to take things one step at a time and write everything down. I will follow through with a 'To Do List' and maintain an organized and disciplined practice!"	**1a.** "I'm too distracted. I screwed up and he will take his money elsewhere."	**2a.** "My strategy has been effective in the past. I will not second-guess my decisions or the money managers who work for me. We will stick to our long-term investing strategy. I will help my client understand the realities of investing and remind him of his stated risk tolerance and the long-term expectations that are required to minimize risk over time."	**2a.** "I must be doing something wrong with my strategy. My money mangers are obviously not doing their job and I'm going to lose more soon."
1b. "I have a proven track record in this business and I developed a solid relationship with this client. He will leave his money with we to ensure positive returns down the road."	**1b.** "I'm going to lose all my clients if I keep making simple mistakes. This will be a domino effect. I will lose my solid reputation and my business."	**2b.** "I will stay disciplined and focused on my investment strategy. I will not be swayed by short-term market gyrations because the investor is bombarded by so much recent information. I will keep my clients grounded in reality and help them manage their reactions to short-term loss. I will make them money over the next 3 years."	**2b.** "I should revamp my strategy and replace my poorly performing money managers. If I don't act quickly, I will lose this new client as well as others who are nervous about this downturn in their investment."

CONSEQUENCES

BULLISH OUTCOMES	BEARISH OUTCOMES	BULLISH OUTCOMES	BEARISH OUTCOMES
Physiological **increased** – energy, healthy sleeping **decreased** – heart rate, blood pressure, sweating, headaches	Physiological **increased** – heart rate, blood pressure, sweating, headaches, muscle tension, insomnia, fatigue	Physiological **increased** – energy, healthy sleeping **decreased** – heart rate, blood pressure, sweating, headaches	Physiological **increased** – heart rate, blood pressure, sweating, headaches, muscle tension, insomnia, fatigue
Performance **increased** – confidence, discipline in strategy focus, retention of clients, clients centered and managing their reactivity	Performance **increased** – hesitancy, second-guessing distractibility, isolation, loss of clients **decreased** – discipline, client-centered service, ability to handle short-term issues & manage clients' emotions	Performance **increased** – confidence, discipline in strategy focus, retention of clients, clients centered and managing their reactivity	Performance **increased** – hesitancy, second-guessing distractibility, isolation, loss of clients **decreased** – discipline, client-centered service, ability to handle short-term issues & manage clients' emotions
Emotional low ①②③④⑤⑥⑦⑧⑨⑩ high frustration, worry, anger	Emotional low ①②③④⑤⑥⑦⑧⑨⑩ high anxiety, frustration, anger	Emotional low ①②③④⑤⑥⑦⑧⑨⑩ high frustration, worry, anger	Emotional low ①②③④⑤⑥⑦⑧⑨⑩ high anxiety, frustration, anger
Sense of Control less ①②③④⑤⑥⑦⑧⑨⑩ more	Sense of Control less ①②③④⑤⑥⑦⑧⑨⑩ more	Sense of Control less ①②③④⑤⑥⑦⑧⑨⑩ more	Sense of Control less ①②③④⑤⑥⑦⑧⑨⑩ more

Figure 2.1   Sample Monitoring Log

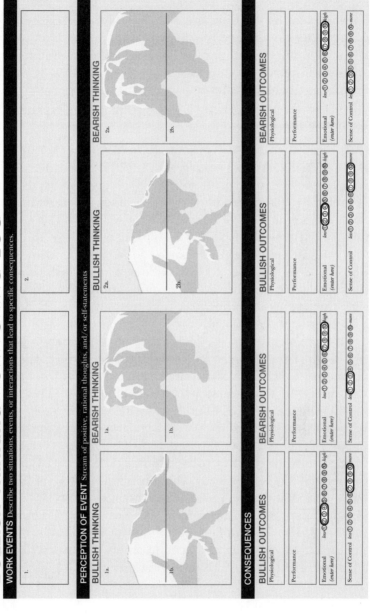

BULLISH THINKING MONITORING LOG

WORK EVENTS Describe two situations, events, or interactions that lead to specific consequences.

1.

2.

PERCEPTION OF EVENT Stream of positive, rational thoughts, and/or self-statements

BULLISH THINKING

BEARISH THINKING

BULLISH THINKING

BEARISH THINKING

1a.

1b.

2a.

2b.

CONSEQUENCES

BULLISH OUTCOMES

Physiological

Performance

Emotional *(enter here)*   low ① ② ③ ④ ⑤ ⑥ ⑦ ⑧ ⑨ high

Sense of Control   low ① ② ③ ④ ⑤ ⑥ ⑦ ⑧ ⑨ more

BEARISH OUTCOMES

Physiological

Performance

Emotional *(enter here)*   low ① ② ③ ④ ⑤ ⑥ ⑦ ⑧ ⑨ high

Sense of Control   low ① ② ③ ④ ⑤ ⑥ ⑦ ⑧ ⑨ more

BULLISH OUTCOMES

Physiological

Performance

Emotional *(enter here)*   low ① ② ③ ④ ⑤ ⑥ ⑦ ⑧ ⑨ high

Sense of Control   low ① ② ③ ④ ⑤ ⑥ ⑦ ⑧ ⑨ more

BEARISH OUTCOMES

Physiological

Performance

Emotional *(enter here)*   low ① ② ③ ④ ⑤ ⑥ ⑦ ⑧ ⑨ high

Sense of Control   low ① ② ③ ④ ⑤ ⑥ ⑦ ⑧ ⑨ more

CATALYST STRATEGIES GROUP, INC.

Figure 2.2   Blank Monitoring Log

living; nothing ever goes right for me; I can't stand it anymore," and a feeling that he can't see anything bright in the future. His stream of thoughts are filled with black and white words like *never, anymore, doomed,* or other examples like *always* and *impossible.* In essence, the advisor will see a black, foreboding, cloudy sky instead of the cracks of sunshine peeking through.

Worthlessness

Over time, this advisor might ask, "Why? Why me? Why is everything going so badly? What's wrong with me?" She usually comes to one conclusion: She is the problem. She is so tough on herself, using self-deprecating statements like "I am worthless, a loser who can't compete; can't take care of business. I am washed up, a has-been who might as well check out now. I am a piece of garbage and am flooded with my past memories of failure and loss." On occasion, individuals who feel this way may actually sabotage relationships with people they care about because they feel guilty about bringing others down with them. Furthermore, they may also avoid loved ones because they no longer feel worthy of being around them.

It hurts so bad that they ache; they physically ache with the belief that *they and they alone* are the cause of their own misfortune. There is no one else to blame. Not their manager, not the firm, not their spouse, kids, or dog. They've known it for a long time. They've been living a lie, making those they care about feel like they have brought them down. Who are they kidding? These advisors are some of the world's great imposters, right? Losers who have fooled everyone . . . right?

See the power of negative thinking? It is paralyzing and gut-wrenching. There seems to be no way out. But there is! Our research has shown that this powerful triple threat to sanity of "helplessness, hopelessness, and worthlessness" (known as the Cognitive Triad)* can be beaten. It is, in fact, based on major errors in thinking and significant biochemical changes in brain chemistry. To help your advisors, you can learn how to identify this Cognitive Triad—*the*

---

*Cognitive Triad: When a depressed individual harbors negative feelings about the future, the self, and the world. These feelings are automatic results of depression. From Aaron T. Beck, A. John Rush, Brian F. Shaw, and Gary Emery, *Cognitive Therapy of Depression* (New York: Guilford Press, 1987).

sense of helplessness, hopelessness, and *worthlessness* that consumes their thinking much like fire consumes oxygen, sucking the life out them—and learn how to combat it.

The Symptoms Emerge

When our job is going well, we are expansive and euphoric. We have a sense of being in control and may believe we can actually predict certain events. We start to feel invincible, almost like we have the Midas touch. You've probably noticed many of your advisors tend to feel this way. Oftentimes, risk-taking comes more easily and a thirst for indulgences becomes insatiable. In this scenario, one must watch out for the negative consequences, both financial and personal, when "irrational exuberance" starts to appear. When things are going badly, the thinking flips, and anxiety sets in, and the blame game begins. Initially, these advisors might point the finger at everything and everyone *except* themselves for their failure. Blame may be placed on specific members within the team, the branch manager, or even their spouse!

After a while, these advisors begin to believe that it is, in fact, their decisions and judgments that are wrong. They have failed. The blame lies within themselves. Unfortunately they may have lost so many friends, colleagues, or loved ones in the wake of this blaming. It is a vicious cycle perpetuated by a lack of emotional insight, and a tunnel-vision focus on achieving material wealth and even more important to some, status and power.

To understand it fully, it's important to know that this pattern springs from a *fear of failure.* An advisor may be afraid that if he fails, he will be exposed for his weaknesses. This type of thinking is characterized by actual fear. "What if I can't recover my position?" "If only I hadn't put everything on the line." "What if I lose my clients—they might see through me." "What is Mr. Smith going to say?"

In the healthy advisor, the thought process goes like this: "OK, I made some serious mistakes. I screwed up. I'll take responsibility. Everybody fails from time to time and I just have to tolerate it, get through it, and move on. This is a temporary setback, and my past performance of choosing the most appropriate money managers and helping my clients to achieve their short-term and long-term goals will repeat itself this year. What can I learn from this experience? I'll be fine if I accept my mistakes and learn from them."

But what begins to happen in the earlier-mentioned situation, if it is not corrected, and with any fear, is that anxiety-based physiological symptoms surface. Known as the *fight or flight response*, one may become fearful or aggressive or, at the very least, irritable. Muscles tense, blood pressure goes up, the heart rate gets faster, and breathing gets shallow. This individual is ready to fight. She is waiting for the next threat or challenge to rear up so she can blast off against all comers. One can't sustain this state for very long. Adrenaline is surging through one's veins and in time, fatigue sets in. If a person remains wired, her sleep will be disrupted, perhaps with the dreaded early morning awakening (up at 3 or 4 A.M., and ready to go—this is the path to exhaustion).

These physiological symptoms are the same that advisors will experience when faced with anxiety. Anger, fear, and anxiety have the same physiological symptoms based on the adrenaline response. The difference is that anxiety is fueled by the mindset of threat or danger, and anger has the mindset of frustration, perceived injustice, or being wronged or hurt. In both cases, the adrenaline kicks in and prepares the individual for fight or flight. We call this state of mind being *tired and wired;* you are ready to explode.

> **Anger.** Anger can be divided into two themes, or components (states of mind, really). The first component is *frustration—* when an individual feels stifled or restricted because he knows he has been blocked from a desired goal. "They can't do that to me—that's not fair—I won't stand by and watch while they screw me."

> **Resentment.** The second anger-driven mindset is a deep sense of having been wronged, or having been used or abused or deceived and taken advantage of. It is hard for this individual to see what role she may have played in the outcome. She "knows" what is going on and concludes (often erroneously) that she has been conned. It is likely she is viewing her world through distorted lenses colored by her strong emotions. Resentment is the foundation of the blame game. This individual is so angry that she *has to understand* what went wrong. It can't be her fault—someone else did it to her. "I'm getting screwed." This resentful person has trouble taking responsibility. The anger only really abates once it converts to another emotional state. These angry states are maintained

until the individual starts to identify and challenge the faulty and irrational thought patterns that caused her temperature to rise, and takes responsibility for her own actions and decisions.

Let's take a look at Ned, a transaction-based stockbroker, who was filled with guilt, grief, worry, and anxiety and almost allowed his emotional state to completely override rational thought and almost ruin his career and his life. It's what we call Bearish Thinking.

A Wall Street Tragedy: The Descent of Ned

Veteran Wall Street reporter Landon Thomas Jr. covered depression in an in-depth article for the *New York Observer* several years ago. With the title "To Live and Throw Up on Wall Street: Diagnosing Brokers' Depression," Mr. Landon discussed the challenges that depression caused for Wall Street professionals, including suicide, and included a case study of Ned, a broker suffering from depression and teetering on the edge of harming himself. Here is Ned's story as told to Mr. Thomas:

Ned loved the thrill of the hunt, the excitement of trading. He used to be a cold-calling machine. Smiling and dialing up to 400 prospects a day, he was a 32-year-old on a roll. In 1999, he raked in over $500,000 in commissions and rewarded himself by buying thousand-dollar paintings and artifacts during his lunch break. He had a luxury condo in Brooklyn and a beautiful young wife who enjoyed living the high life. Ned was a top-gun broker early on in his career.

But now, 9 out of 10 prospects hang up on him. And most of his clients have either deserted him or have sued him. What happened?

Things started to change when he began to expect rejection on every cold call and have thoughts like "These people don't want to hear from me," or, "I sound so stupid to the other advisors listening to my prospecting calls." His daily contact calls were cut roughly in half as his motivation waned. He became socially withdrawn and avoided company outings and potential networking venues. His wife was less affectionate at home lately and Ned arrived home from work feeling empty inside. He felt like a shell of a man.

He became short-tempered, emotionally distant, and hypercritical of his wife for her mistakes. Communication with her was impaired and he often retired to his den after work drinking glass after glass of expensive Scotch. His mind raced and he was convinced that "I am not a good provider anymore, I'm inadequate, and incompetent as a husband and as an advisor." For Ned, the bulls stopped stampeding.

He was on the run; in retreat mode. He learned an important lesson; all that glittered wasn't gold after all. The market turned on Ned in April 2000, just like it did for thousands of other advisors. He plunged all of his and his clients' money into ICG Communications, Global Crossing, and Healtheon (now WebMD)—all thundering tech stocks, profits going through the roof. When the bubble burst, stocks collapsed, he lost millions of dollars, and his life began crashing at breakneck speed.

Ned was in constant pain, his stomach was always in a knot, and as he sat at his desk in his coat and tie, he clutched his midsection and threw up in the garbage pail by his desk.

Recalls Ned, "You have to realize: This was not like Intel going from 40 down to 20. At least then, you still have the stock. My clients were on margin—their stocks went to zero and they still owed ten thousand dollars. You try telling a client whose stock has gone to zero that he still owes ten thousand bucks."

Currently, Ned's daily goal is to make at least 200 calls to small business owners, doctors, and lawyers around the city. And he tries to meet that goal because, as he says, "Except for my mortgage, I'm behind in everything," he said, his tone matter-of-fact in one of our counseling sessions. "I've liquidated every investment I've ever had; I've got $75,000 in credit card debt, and now I'm dipping into my 401(k). I've become a rags-to-riches-back-to-rags story. I started out renting movies in a shop on 42nd Street in my early twenties to make ends meet. I was always great at selling and I proved it all the way up the ladder at my new job as a broker. I fought tooth and nail for my rewards and then they were taken away. It's a slap in the face. It hurts that much more to have lived such a comfortable lifestyle and then retreat back to living like a recent college grad eating pizza." Self-defeating thoughts such as "I can't change this situation and this slump in my lifestyle won't improve anytime soon," streamed through his mind.

Back then, he says, he had nightmares every night. "I would get about three hours of sleep a night, and would wake up with eye twitches, neck twitches, and my skin would break out in a hot, itchy rash, that my doctor diagnosed as being eczema, a skin ailment exacerbated by stress." When morning would break, Ned was so depressed that, many times, he was tempted to just stay in bed. "I lay in bed thinking about how much I enjoyed the comfort of darkness in my room. I woke up next to my wife, yet I still felt alone and incompetent. When I made it into work, I had palpitations every day," he said. "But, I finally realized that I didn't hate myself; I hated my *life*."

Ned is no churn-and-burn boiler-room con looking to get rich quick. Back then, all his clients had his home number, and he fielded their late-night calls as they wept together over their wiped-out portfolios. He felt so guilty about one particular client who took a bath on one of his stocks that he still sends him a monthly check of $300 to help ease his financial burden. Said Ned, "I used to feel so guilty, like this client's loss was totally my fault. It made me nauseated to think about it. I even starting going to church!"

His wife is now in poor health and his expenses run about $15,000 a month. Since he's a transaction broker, every month he has to start over to earn his monthly income. "Crazy things go through your head," he said. "Like trying to hurt yourself and go on disability. How about suicide? At its worst, I entertained the thought of ending my life. I fantasized about jumping off the Verazzano Bridge, and how I would enjoy one last rush before experiencing complete silence and peace. But that's a quitter's way. It took me a long time to get where I am. Doing that would make me a real loser."

Ned is not a bad man; he is a broken man, suffering, and he needs to be fixed. Do you have a Ned in your office? How will you help him?

What Are the Consequences of Ned's Bearish Thinking?

Before you can help Ned, you need to understand the consequences of Bearish Thinking and what the best solutions are to help turn them into Bullish Thinking. (The next chapter deals with these challenges.)

But what is the first step in acknowledging that Ned is in crisis, and how do you approach him? If an advisor in your office appears to resemble Ned and he hasn't approached you for help, remember that it's because he is afraid of appearing weak, or he may not realize the extent of his pain and the damage it could be causing. This advisor needs someone to talk to, someone to trust. This is one reason it is crucial to have some sort of interpersonal relationship with your advisors and allow yourself to be approachable. In this case, you need to let your advisor know that you understand he is going through a difficult period. We have known advisors who have gone to branch managers and have told them, "Listen, I'm going through a divorce," or "I'm having trouble with my child," or simply, "I'm going through some personal problems at home." Some managers are willing to help; others can't be bothered. Which kind of manager are you?

These are things that you, as a manager, need to know about because offering your help is the compassionate thing to do, and because—as a responsible manager—if there is a direct correlation to this advisor's decreased performance, then that will at least be an explanation for his behavior and you help alleviate his anxiety so he won't be worried about losing his job—the problems are all on the table.

Let your advisors know that they shouldn't allow misconceptions about appearing weak prevent them from talking to you about their challenges. The biggest misconception on Wall Street is that an advisor can't show emotion to her branch manager or her colleagues without being looked upon as pathetic. If you teach (by example) and allow your advisors to use emotion and direct communication strategically, they will be respected for their honesty and for being brave enough to show you and others their vulnerability. As a result, they will discover that you want to support them and their business because they have shared something personal with you. If you explain to your advisors that you consider them to be on your team, and that their success depends, in part, on your continued support and guidance, they will feel good about themselves and feel validated and appreciated. They want to be part of the group, to belong. Deep down, everyone wants to feel this way.

The next chapter illustrates how Bullish Thinking strategies teach you to recognize the Bearish Thoughts that are holding back your advisors. We discuss the fascinating science behind the Bullish Thinking concept as well as the various strategies that can eliminate negative thinking before it becomes destructive to their emotional health, their job, and their personal life.

3

Linking Emotions and Feelings, Behavior, and Thinking

THE SCIENCE BEHIND BULLISH THINKING

Now that we have discussed the concept of Bullish Thinking and how it can help your advisors overcome bearish thoughts, feelings, and actions, we need to talk about the substance behind the concept. We believe it is crucial for you to know that Bullish Thinking strategies are based on scientific evidence and stem from your advisors' personal reality.

After we cover the science, a light bulb should come on and you will better understand the psychology of what is driving your advisors. You will then be able to truly embrace the powerful strategies available to you for intervening when your advisors' performance is being hampered by hidden feelings of helplessness, hopelessness, and worthlessness. A significant benefit of knowing the science is that it will help you quickly recognize and understand the underlying reasons why they feel this way. The strategies will help you deal with the anger outbursts, the entitlement, burnout, withdrawal, anxiety, alcohol and drug abuse, and various other acting-out behaviors. You will learn how to identify problem areas before they become out of control, as well as how to give (or get) your advisors help if they are currently in crisis.

In many respects, you may be the only person who can help them; the only person in their life who will extend a life support system that they so desperately need, but are afraid to ask for. Consulting to Wall Street and other financial leaders worldwide has afforded us the opportunity to meet visionary managers who were not afraid of intervening on their top producers' underlying problems. We work in closed-door meetings designed to identify solutions to help their employees become more aware of how their behaviors negatively affect their production and the workplace. These managers didn't stand by and let their future stars wither away and implode. They acted on a red flag and saved a few careers in the process. You can be that person. We will show you how.

The Science: Or, "How to Be a Mind Reader"

First, let's touch on two areas that you may have already considered in your work as a manager. In all probability, you know about the popular Myers-Briggs Type Indicator (MBTI), a personality inventory that helps make the theory of psychological types described by psychologist C.G. Jung understandable and useful in one's life. According to the Myers & Briggs Foundation, the basic theory is that ". . . much seemingly random variation in the behavior is actually quite orderly and consistent, being due to basic differences in the ways individuals prefer to use their perception and judgment." Myers-Briggs offers 16 personality types that can be summarized on four dimensions: Extroversion-Introversion; Thinking-Feeling; Judging-Perceiving; Sensing-Intuitive personalities. For example, if you are an extroverted, intuitive, thinking, judging type you would fit into their category EITJ type. These characteristics are quite stable. There is no *good* or *bad,* no *right* or *wrong* . . . instead, it encourages people to become more aware of themselves.

Managers have used this system to get a read on their advisors and vice versa. We also use a personality system to help you identify advisor mindsets and your own leadership style.

You also may have heard of Emotional Intelligence (EI), popularized by psychologist Daniel Goleman, Ph.D., in 1995 through his book, *Emotional Intelligence,* about the subject and its application to business. Goleman defines it as the capacity for recognizing our own feelings and those of others, for motivating ourselves, and for managing emotions well in ourselves and in our relationships.

EI focuses only on *understanding* the feelings an individual has. While we agree this is a great start, it falls short in our opinion because it doesn't help you *change* others or their *work environment.*

For example, high emotional quotient (EQ) managers know how to perceive and access their emotions and the emotions of their team. Having these skills is an important start; the key point is *how to manage* the staff after understanding their emotions. Where do you go from there? What do you tell your troubled advisors when you sense that they are struggling with something in their lives? You have all of this valuable knowledge, so now let's solve the problems! You want—and need—to take action, and we understand that.

Now, stay with us on this. We'll try to keep from bogging you down with psychobabble, but please bear with us because we will quickly get to our approach on how we link emotions/feelings, behavior, and thinking that is different from the usual suspects in this field.

Our concepts of Bullish Thinking are quite different. It is a practical, intervention-oriented approach that will *help you take the steps to solve your most challenging issues,* not just inform you. Our methods are simpler and lead to immediate action. If practiced, you and your advisors will change for the better, personally and professionally. And that's what you need. As a busy individual with enormous demands on your time and hard issues on your desk, what you don't need is any more theory. We will give you hands-on tools, but we must ask that you spend a little time digging deep with us about the approach first.

So, again, the real questions become, "HOW to manage after understanding the emotions? WHAT do you do when you recognize self-defeating or destructive behavior?" This is where Cognitive-Behavioral Therapy (CBT) enters the picture. Since very little research is available on what actually *works,* we created concepts for Wall Street that are rooted in CBT, which has undisputed evidence of success since the 1980s. Simply, CBT is a system of psychotherapy based on modifying everyday thoughts and behaviors, with the aim of influencing emotions in a positive way. CBT helps people perform at the highest levels of their job. It is outcomes-focused and based on sound scientific evidence.

Bullish Thinking, which was explained in the previous chapter, is, in fact, just our translation of CBT, using familiar language and terms specific to Wall Street that helps managers, advisors, and others in the financial services industry to understand what can be done to help. Our goal is to normalize these underlying problems so that you and your advisors can open up a more fluid form of communication. We want problems to be expressed and dealt with, rather than submerged out of fear of being humiliated.

The effectiveness of CBT and of Bullish Thinking can be demonstrated, and it is important to discuss the "scientific thinking and the evidence" behind it. If you will indulge us for a few minutes while we share the powerful psychological links between emotions/feelings, behavior, and thinking, you will leave with a greater understanding of yourself and your advisors. Then we'll head into the next chapter and focus on personality and leadership styles.

So, let's get started.

Are You a Good Poker Player?

Creating a sense of confidence and control is key to navigating your way through challenging situations. Just as in a strategic game of poker, chess, or any intellectual pursuit that demands a grasp of understanding human nature, a manager must learn the thought process of linking emotions, thinking, and behavior.

The first step is to *recognize* the powerful links between:

- *emotions* and *thinking*
- *thinking* and *behavior*
- *emotions* and *behavior*

Simply put, the process is to first observe your advisor's emotional state and behavior and *then* connect these observations to the advisor's underlying bullish and bearish thoughts. If you understand the connections, you will gain an improved sense of control over challenging situations. If you continue to have mastery experiences, you will see a significant leap in your self-confidence.

Before we illustrate how you can do this, let's make sure we all understand the difference in terminology. Feelings and emotions mean the same thing, right? Wrong. Feelings refer to a person's *experience,* and emotions refer to a state involving both *feelings and physiological reactions;* quite a difference. Many people get thrown off track by their powerful emotions when their body starts acting like it has a mind of its own. This experience is most obvious when the person is under pressure.

Feeling/Emotion and Thinking

Here's an example. Let's say a person may feel afraid or scared and we refer to his emotional state as *anxious.* Anxiety includes *both* the fear and the bodily reactions that go along with it. These bodily reactions to anxiety include increased heart rate and rate of breathing, sweating, tunnel vision, muscle tension, headaches, stomachaches, shaking, and lightheadedness. An astute manager, like a good poker player, can pick up on these overt emotional reactions and connect the observations to a feeling. In poker, they call these observations *tells.* "Brian (your advisor) is very anxious right now. He is at his desk with his head down. He is sweating and sighing. He is afraid of something."

Your job is to connect *emotions/feelings* to *thinking*.

The key is to connect this feeling (fear) and emotion (anxiety) to his thinking (what is going through his mind). His thinking includes catastrophic thoughts ("What if the boss finds out that I screwed up on that account?") and images ("He's going to start screaming at me in front of others in the branch").

If you, the manager, can connect these emotions and thinking, you can then make a prediction about your advisor's behavior. When people (and animals) are very anxious, their behavior is less predictable. They may act out of character and do some things that seem odd. For example, Brian just snapped at his assistant. He started screaming at her for no good reason. This is the *fight* response, a behavior associated with *both* anger states and anxiety states. Alternatively, you might observe Brian avoiding any meetings with you. ("What is going on with Brian? He just ducked around the corner when I was walking down the hall," or, "That's odd, Brian can't look me in the eye today; he keeps looking down and he is all flushed.")

Your ability to make these observations and connect them to *thinking* states is one of the key building blocks. If your advisor's behavior or emotional reactions are confusing to you, you can try to use an educated guess about his thinking.

But let's get a little deeper into emotion and its variations.

We psychologists know there are many forms of emotion. We will narrow our choices down to those that are the most familiar to all of us. For our purposes, we discuss the following feelings:

- Fear (afraid, worried)
- Anger (hostility, frustration, irritability, disgust)
- Sadness (disappointment, depressed, down, unhappy)
- Guilt (shame)
- Happiness (joyful, content)

Each feeling has a corresponding thought or image associated with it. This thought or image sometimes comes from a person's memory, and sometimes it just hits them. If one of your advisors seems troubled, you can ask him, "What was running through your mind?" or more simply, "What were you thinking just then?" If he is caught up in his feelings, he will most likely say, "Nothing!" And this is where you can use your educated guess. Once you get some practice, you will start to read minds just like professional therapists and poker players. We are exaggerating a bit. Psychologists, of course, can't really read minds either, but they can come up with some pretty good educated guesses, and so can you. It's okay to use your intuition.

Fear. If one of your advisors seems anxious and you think he may be afraid, then his thinking may have involved some type of threat. So, what could be threatening this individual? He may fear looking stupid or incompetent, losing control, being caught in a lie or a mistake, losing an important business relationship, money, or career opportunity. Here is the basic process:

- Once you catch the *feeling*, you can *start to intervene.*
- Example: "Hey, Brian, you don't appear to be yourself today. You look flushed. You seem worried. Is there something I can help you with?"
- Here is where it is vital that you *listen carefully.*
- Brian may tell you what is threatening him. "I'm just wondering about one of my accounts" is translated by you into, "He may be threatened with losing an account."
- *Speak carefully* and use a simple, directive statement like, "Tell me about it."

So, you can see that by linking emotions and feelings to thinking, you can get a little deeper into problem solving with Brian.

Important: Notice that you didn't offer reassurance to Brian: "Oh, don't worry. Everything will be fine." *That type of false reassurance doesn't provide the link.* It will be perceived by Brian as a minimization of his problem. Instead, remember you need to find out what is actually posing the *threat* to Brian.

Anger.   The other emotions have typical thinking patterns as well. For example, anger is associated with resentment. "It isn't fair. He had no right to do that. He's taking money out of my pocket!" or frustration, "I can't believe my manager just did that to me. Now, I won't make my bonus. I can't seem to get any support from him!"

Sadness.   Sad feelings are associated with loss; this person is suffering from the loss of something important to her. "My daughter failed her exam." "My A-list prospect said he wasn't interested." "I have been sinking further and further down on the leader board each month. I'm losing respect from everyone."

Guilt.   Guilt is associated with *both* loss and threat. It is a complex feeling and you may need to understand a little about this advisor's background. "My wife told me she was disappointed in me because I forgot to buy her an anniversary card," or "I am having an affair and my husband has no idea what is going on."

Happiness.   Happy feelings are, of course, associated with pleasure and contentment. They usually involve good or satisfying things happening to us: "I just opened a new account," or "My clients' portfolios have been up for three consecutive months now. I'm on a roll!" Sometimes, people feel happy when they are in fact, *relieved*. For example, one of your advisors thought he was going to be fired, but you only gave him a strong warning. He said he was "happy" but he was really relieved of his anxiety—the threat of being fired was reduced or eliminated. Happiness evokes pleasurable memories and images. ("I was just thinking about being up at the lake in my canoe.")

Thinking and Behavior

The next connection to make is when you notice a pattern of behavior in an advisor and you want to understand the feelings. The classic situation involves the manager receiving a gift from an advisor—what we call "bringing an apple to the teacher."

On the surface, it looks like an expression of caring and goodwill—and it may be just that, *but* you have to check out *the thinking or intention behind the behavior.* No, you don't have to suspect that every gift is a Trojan Horse, but ask yourself, "What is the thinking behind the action?" We know that seasoned pros like you already are good at picking up on smoke and mirrors, so this part should be rather easy for you.

Your job is to connect the *behavior* to *thinking*.

In most of these cases you need to understand motivation and behavior. Behavior either increases (that is, it occurs more frequently) or it decreases (it occurs less frequently). Psychologists know that there are two ways to increase a person's behavior and two ways to decrease a person's behavior. Each approach is associated with changes in the person's *thinking*.

If you want to increase a person's behavior, you can *reward* good behavior ("Here's your bonus.") or you can take away a negative ("Okay, now you don't have to attend the early morning detentions anymore."). If you want to decrease a person's behavior, you can *punish* the bad behavior (for example, by fining him) or you can take away a positive ("Your privileges are suspended for the day.").

For example, let's say for now you want to see an increase in the number of referral calls that an advisor is making. You can reward the person as the number of calls increase to a goal. "Okay, Jill, I want you to increase the number of calls you make to current clients asking them for referrals. For every 20 clients you call and you receive at least two referrals, I will pay you a $500 bonus." This is called positive reinforcement.

Or, you can put the heat on Jill and nag her (a negative) until she meets the goal. "Okay, Jill, I want you to increase the number of referral calls you make to clients. I will come to check on you every 10 minutes to see how you have progressed." This tactic is similar to what many of our mothers used to get us to complete our homework when we were in elementary school. This is called negative reinforcement. You are going to keep the pressure on until Jill performs.

Let's try to guess what Jill might be thinking when she makes the first 20 calls. She thinks, "I like the challenge and attention when the boss stands over me. It shows how much he cares that he would take his time, and he helps me achieve." She will increase her number of referral calls. Or, she may be thinking, "I can't stand the pressure. I'm sweating buckets already. I will never get the bonus money because I don't like to ask clients for referrals; I feel like I am begging. It isn't worth the embarrassment." Jill will not increase her number of referral calls.

You can see that by connecting Jill's *behavior* to her *thinking*, you will be able to understand how to help her increase her referral calls. As you will also see, the actions of the manager—even if both are intended to help Jill—can produce different results. Again, you must connect the *behavior* to the *thinking*.

The advisor's motivation is linked to her behavior and can, sometimes, complicate how people respond. The easiest system of motivation requires an understanding of needs. We all have basic needs (food, water, shelter, sleep), and we also have other, less obvious needs (privacy, power, monetary, achievement, affection, respect). If the person is fulfilled, meaning that her needs are satisfied, then she will be less inclined to perform certain behaviors, no matter what the rewards or punishments are. You may have to escalate the battle to get the person's attention. On the other hand, if he is deprived (for example, starved for food), he will respond with tremendous energy. For now, we won't muddy the waters, and will keep it simple. (In Chapter 4, when we speak of the different types of managers' and advisors' personalities and styles, we come back to a discussion of motivation.)

Emotions/Feelings and Behavior

This connection can be more challenging, because everything may be on the surface, like an iceberg; the real danger may lurk below the surface.

Your job is to connect the *behavior* to the *emotion/feeling*.

Susie was a hard-drinking party animal who had no trouble keeping up with the boys. At work, she was an outstanding producer; she consistently made her quotas and asked for more. You started to hear a few complaints about Susie's tendency to send seething late night e-mails to some of her co-workers. She would ream them out if she thought anyone was being critical of her. She would not tolerate even the smallest slight, such as the one when Fred, a colleague in the office next to hers, neglected to inform her that a catered lunch was being served in the conference room that afternoon.

How do you connect Susie's behavior to her thinking? You could write it off to, "That's just Susie." Or you could jump to a conclusion, "Must be that time of the month." But in both cases, you would be missing the opportunity to understand what was really going on.

Speak carefully. So you say to Susie, "I hear that you were angry with Fred. Can you tell me was it was that upset you?'

Now, *listen carefully* for her feeling. "He is such an inconsiderate ass. He has no clue to what is going on around here. And, by the way, I don't need you coming around me and prying into my business."

What is a manager to do? Do you quietly slink out of the office and leave her alone? Do you attack and say, "Don't you talk to me that way; I deserve some respect. I'm the boss, not you."

Or, do you connect her behavior with her feelings. "Susie, I can hear that you are angry and resent Fred and some of the others when they make mistakes. I want to understand what upsets you. What are you not getting from all of us here? I can see that you are upset, and I need to understand what you are reacting to so that I can work with you to find a solution. It seems like you are upset by the way others are behaving."

You have to constantly be aware of behavioral abnormalities in your office so that you can use some of these subtle tactics to get to the bottom of the problems before they negatively affect the entire office. Susie was not really angry at her colleague for neglecting to tell her about the lunch. She had recently missed an important benchmark that would have entitled her to a larger office after the new year began. Thus, she lashed out at everyone else rather than deal with her own feelings. No one was immune from her fury, not even her branch manager.

KATE EMPATHIZES WITH ED

Ed was a man of few words. He kept to himself and was loyal to his clients. Ed stayed on the periphery of the office, but he was a team player. He pulled his weight and, in general, the admin staff and other advisors who got to know him, liked him.

Ed had a daughter who suffered from a serious medical condition. As a result, he scheduled his personal time away from the office and worked on time lines that were different from most advisors. His branch manager, Kate, knew that Ed was under considerable personal pressure, but she was also under pressure by her many responsibilities of managing the second-largest high-producing office in the system. She needed maximum effort from all advisors during her push to make her office number one, gaining all of the benefits that that would offer her and her staff. Being number one would mean making some changes in the office: some hiring, some firing, and a few new technology additions. Kate had to take action. She had to lead. And she knew she had to deal with Ed on a personal level and not add too much to his plate at this time in his life.

Kate asked Ed to meet with her in the middle of his day. She was careful in the scheduling because she wanted to take whatever time was needed for their conversation. She prepared the package of expected changes to the system that she expected all staff to follow. She was prepared to observe Ed's mood and emotions and disciplined her thinking to *read his reactions* rather than try to control the meeting. This was a management challenge for her. Here is their dialogue:

Kate: Ed, thanks for the meeting. I want to discuss some changes that I am going to introduce to the office in the next few days. As you know, we've been attempting to make our office number one in the branch system, and I have some ideas and some new procedures that we need to follow. I wanted to meet with you beforehand so you would have an idea about what I am trying to achieve. Before getting into the business, though, I want to know how you are doing.

Ed: I've had better days.

Kate: How are you feeling?

Ed: I'm worried sick. I am stretched to my limit. I think I've been doing a good job for my clients, and my daughter has faced some difficult times, but is being very brave. The problem is me!

Kate: Seems like you feel exhausted. I can understand if that's the case, because you have faced some major stresses yourself.

Ed: Nothing like what my daughter has to deal with.

Kate: It must be so hard for her.

(Continued)

Ed: (stiffens his lower lip) Yes, it's hard. Our philosophy has always been to press ahead. Thanks for asking about how we are doing. What do I need to do here at work?

Kate: I need your opinion and support on terminating a few advisors who are not carrying their weight, and on whether or not our office should spend another million dollars on outside training and consulting coaches, as well as on the technology we need to follow through with the increased wealth management business we are doing.

Kate understood the importance of relating to Ed's personal feelings and thoughts. She knew that he had a sense of helplessness ("No matter what I do, I can't control certain painful events in my life"). She was aware that associated with this helplessness, most people feel fatigue and emotional strain. She assumed that Ed had similar feelings and thoughts and she was correct! Kate didn't read Ed's mind, but she made an educated guess using what she had learned in the Bullish Thinking seminar for managers.

EMOTIONS IMPAIRING A SUCCESSFUL BRANCH

Self-Report from Alison, a Thoughtful Manager in Our Practice

I am a manager of a small, successful office. We had a group of advisors who formed a very tight social group. We liked each other and socialized on a regular basis. We had a good mix of advisors. For fun, we played pickup baseball in the summer and worked out at a local gym (where we had a discounted fees arrangement). Our business was very successful because we were leaders in our community. Sadly, I experienced first-hand how emotions can spread and impair an excellent unit.

The first event was a conflict between Christopher and Charlie. It started simply. Christopher teased Charlie about his small-town ("hick") roots and joked that Charlie had to learn which fork to use when he started in our business. Charlie was normally very easygoing, but this comment hit a nerve (really an aspect of Charlie's background that embarrassed him). Charlie was furious. He complained that Christopher was ignorant and he didn't want anything to do with him. The chill in the office when the two advisors had to be in the same meeting was intense. It went on for two months. Sarah, one of our top assistants, approached me and asked me to please do something. She said, "Alison, we can't keep going on like this. I am dreading coming to work because I don't want to get caught up in their war. I'm tense and can't wait to go home." Jake, one of our top advisors, also approached me. "Alison, you have to get Christopher to apologize!" I was surprised with the intensity that Jake displayed. He seemed furious at me! I started to react and then realized that his anger was really anxiety. He was worried, worried that the conflict between two of his colleagues would hurt business.

I decided to take an action. I had raised three children and I wasn't about to let two advisors bring their school-yard fight into the office. I called Christopher and Charlie to a meeting. What a mistake. The meeting escalated in about three nanoseconds to a full-blown yelling match. It was incredible. I thought they were going to come to blows.

What was even more upsetting was the group of four uninvolved advisors who came into my office later that afternoon and confronted me with the fact that I had made the situation worse and they had all been thinking of starting another branch, leaving me with the warring advisors. *Leaving me!* I had done nothing to offend anyone. I was stunned. Thank goodness I attended a CBT (Bullish Thinking) seminar. Within two weeks, the emotions had calmed down and I am proud to say that I defused the situation.

(Continued)

How did Alison use Bullish Thinking to help resolve her advisors' conflicts? She learned an important lesson. As Mark Twain said, "You can't reason someone out of something they weren't reasoned into." She took the emotional temperature of the office and observed that it was hot. Advisors and staff were anxious and angry. Christopher and Charlie were in a cold war, but the other staff experienced the heat of their conflict.

Alison learned that taking action to resolve conflict has to start with an understanding of the conflict. Ordering adults to behave doesn't work. Instead, she went on a fact-finding mission. She asked the aggrieved party (Charlie) into her office in the early morning. Here's how their conversation ensued:

Alison: I want to understand your relationship with Christopher.

Charlie: He is such a ******. I have no time for him. He is an embarrassment.

Alison: I want to hear more about what he said (in reality, Alison was asking for what Charlie heard, but this was an easier approach). And I also want to hear about your reaction.

Charlie: There's not much to say. Chris is a ******.

Alison: Charlie, please. I want to hear more about what he said. And I also want to hear about your reaction.

Charlie: He called me a hick. He has no idea how hard I worked to get here. I am the only person in my family who went to college. He grew up with a silver spoon. He is such a ******.

Alison: So Christopher hurt your feelings. He insulted you. Was he trying to hurt you?

Charlie: Who knows? He is totally insensitive.

Alison: I need to work with Christopher so that he understands the impact of his comments. Do you think he was trying to hurt you?

Charlie:	Probably not, but *he did piss me off!* He made me look like an idiot in front of everyone. (Alison noted that Charlie translated his hurt feelings into anger—he felt embarrassed and assumed that Christopher wanted to humiliate him.)
Alison:	Let me discuss this situation with Christopher.

The bottom line is that your advisors probably will not seek you out to settle disputes in the office. Be proactive. Be calm and understanding. It worked for Alison.

4

Getting to Know Yourself and Your Advisors

INTRODUCING THE OCEAN SYSTEM OF PERSONALITIES

In the previous chapter you learned how to link emotions/feelings to behavior and thinking. We also clarified the difference between emotions and feelings: Feelings refer to a person's *experience*, and emotions refer to a state involving both *feelings and physiological reactions*. Your emotions are a function of your thinking (what you say to yourself and the pictures in your mind). If your thinking is bullish, you will experience primarily positive emotions. If your thinking is bearish, your emotions will be primarily negative. These emotion-thinking connections in turn, drive your behavior, especially when you are under stress. You also learned about the science behind this process, and how to learn more about how to manage your advisors using our techniques.

Now we are asking you to be brutally honest with yourself. First, take some time to be introspective (we know you have little time, but this exercise is about change). This next section is an important piece to understanding yourself, and then understanding your advisors. After this exercise, we will outline the five dimensions of personality and the four leadership styles. So, get ready to meet the bull!

Mirror, Mirror on the Wall

We know this is a leap of faith on our part, but we believe you truly want to make a difference in your own life and your advisors' lives as well as a difference in how smoothly your office operates. You are ready to make a change! During your introspection, it's okay to admit your flaws, fallibility, and biases. Look in the mirror, see the imperfection, and relax. Listen to your inner thoughts. They might sound something like this:

- I am comfortable with myself
- I am prepared to change
- I am willing to improve
- I will adapt to the changing environment and changing culture
- I will accept staff changes and management changes
- I recognize that the world changes just as the markets change—every day!
- I am open to feedback and suggestions
- I want to learn how to improve my coping strategies

You might want to try it again and see whether you discover anything else about yourself. Once you have learned to *listen* to your inner thoughts and images, you can connect your thinking to your feelings and your behavior, and back again. It's circular, and it's productive, too.

Fred secretly hoped that nothing in his life would change. He had just completed the most successful year of his life. Business was booming; his marriage to Annie was bliss; their two young kids were a joy to be around; he had purchased his dream vacation home. Everything in his life was as good as it gets! Fred had a problem, though—creeping into the back of his mind from a place that he didn't understand, was the thought, "It's all downhill from here." Now, where did that come from? He started to worry. He didn't know why. What if the market stumbled? What if the new issue flopped? What if his parents needed help? What if . . . even the inkling of a thought that something might happen to Annie or the kids sent a shudder through him.

Tension began to take hold of Fred. He felt it in the evening before bed. He started getting headaches and his stomach churned. Fred had a few drinks and his tension eased . . . but the next morning he awoke in a full-blown panic attack! He was sweating, breathing hard, felt dizzy, and couldn't focus. "This is ridiculous," he thought. He was furious with himself. But the symptoms wouldn't go away.

Fred turned on the TV at night and all he could hear were the negative stories. He picked up the newspaper and read an article about a troubled hedge fund. He seemed to be consumed with negative stories. What if his clients picked up on his negative vibes? Then, he would really be in trouble. He was paid to perform, to deliver. "This is ridiculous," he thought.

As you can see, Fred's thinking started a shift in his feelings and emotions (fear, dread, anger) and these gave way to anxiety and Bearish Thinking. Fred had to regain control; he had to get back on the bull! He decided to go and speak to his manager.

You can see from Fred's example that you may also have some hidden warning signs of distress. This introspective process and linking your emotions and feelings to behavior and thinking helps you identify signals of emotional distress, behavior acting out, and the silent predator of Bearish Thinking. As a manager, you hope that most of the Freds (and Marys) in your life will eventually seek your wise counsel. Others will be more reticent, so you may have to dig a little more to uncover their concerns. When a staff member approaches you, it will be a meeting of two people, each with his own personality. How you understand your own leadership style and use it to connect to the advisor's mindset is critical. You have to understand how you normally would react and how you may have to adapt, to learn, and be open to change. (First, go back and re-read the self statements about change in Chapter 2.)

Once you grasp how your personality fits with your staff's personality, you will begin to know how to interact with them for maximum benefit. In time, your read will be quick and you will know what to say and do when an employee is in meltdown.

You've Got Personality!

Personality refers to the enduring and consistent emotional, thought, and behavior patterns in a person across a wide range of situations, including ones of stress. Personality can be seen prospectively, when a person is confronted with novel situations, and can also be seen retrospectively, when a person recalls situations and reacts to unpredictable events.

There are many ways to describe personality and many ways to measure these constructs.

There are five basic dimensions in personality that have stood up to considerable research scrutiny and scientific review. In psychology circles, the dimensions are known as the "five-factor model of personality," or the "Big 5."* These dimensions are useful because not only will they will help you understand the personalities of your group, but they also will help categorize your leadership style *as well as* your advisors' mindsets. Mindsets refer to the way in which people approach the situations and events in their lives. They are powerful aspects of the self-fulfilling prophecy: The way that people interpret the situations in their lives and the lives of others influences their outcomes (see, for example, the central philosophy in Norman Vincent Peale's 1952 edition of *The Power of Positive Thinking*, and of the modern-day interpretation in *The Secret* by Rhonda Byrne).

The five dimensions in personality (**OCEAN**) are as follows:

- **O**penness to Experience—appreciation for *art, emotion, adventure, unusual ideas, imagination*, and *curiosity.*
- **C**onscientiousness—a tendency to show *self-discipline*, act *dutifully*, and aim for *achievement*; planned rather than spontaneous behavior.
- **E**xtraversion—energy, positive emotions, *action-oriented* and the tendency to seek *stimulation* and the company of others.
- **A**greeableness—a tendency to be *compassionate* and *cooperative* rather than *suspicious* and *antagonistic* toward others.
- **N**euroticism—a tendency to experience unpleasant emotions easily, such as *anger, anxiety, depression*, or *vulnerability*; sometimes called *emotional instability.*

Now, let's explore each dimension.

Openness to Experience

Openness to Experience is a dimension of personality that differentiates creative people from the conventional. Those who are open are intellectually curious, appreciative of music and art, and sensitive

---

*J.M. Digman, Personality structure: Emergence of the five-factor model, *Annual Review of Psychology*, 41 (1990): 417–440. R.B. Ewen, *Personality: A Topical Approach* (Mahwah, NJ: Erlbaum, 1998).

to beauty. They are more aware of their feelings than most. They prefer straightforwardness and are not comfortable with the complex or subtle. On the other hand, a person who is low in the openness dimension is less aware of his feelings; he wants the facts; he wants to get on with the journey; he doesn't care to smell the flowers; he just wants to get on with the job.

Conscientiousness

Conscientiousness includes such traits as self-discipline, achievement-oriented, and thinking before acting. It also concerns the way in which we control our impulses. While acting on our first impulse can be an effective response in some situations, people high on this dimension will not act impulsively. This personality dimension also includes the need-for-achievement factor. Conscientious individuals avoid trouble and achieve high levels of success through thoughtful planning and persistence, and are most often regarded by others as intelligent and reliable. On the negative side, they can be compulsive perfectionists and workaholics, sometimes perceived as stuffy and boring. Low conscientious people are ready for the action. They may act first and think later. They are free spirits who can get the party started, providing energy and a sense of excitement.

Extraversion

Extraversion (also known as ex*tro*version) is behavior that is directed toward the external environment, outside of one's self. Extroverts enjoy being with people, are full of energy, and often experience positive emotions. They tend to be enthusiastic, action-oriented individuals who are likely to join a crowd, be the life of the party, and look for opportunities for excitement. These individuals like to talk, laugh, and draw attention to themselves. People low on this dimension, the introverts, are quiet, unobtrusive folks who are intensely private. If an introvert seeks advice from others, it is likely to be about very serious matters.

Agreeableness

This personality dimension reflects an individual's level of cooperation and desire for social harmony. Getting along with others is very important to these individuals. They are considerate, friendly, generous, and helpful. Agreeable personality types also have an optimistic view of human nature. They believe people are basically honest, decent, and trustworthy. Agreeableness, though, is not useful in situations that call for tough or objective decision making. Low agreeableness types, the contrarians, can swim upstream; they may be pessimistic, but certainly won't buy a bill of goods. They have to be convinced of the value of any change! They are from Missouri, the "show-me" state.

Neuroticism

The most powerful personality predictor of behavior, emotional response, and thinking is known as *neuroticism* (sometimes called *emotional liability* or *emotional instability*, meaning that your emotions fluctuate in response to the situation), a construct introduced to us in the early 1950s by Professor Hans Eysenck, a psychologist most remembered for his work on intelligence and personality, and author of more than 50 books on the subject. This personality feature is associated with people who worry, who sweat the small stuff. These individuals *know* the details and are often focused on facts and details. They expect a lot of themselves, and may be very self-critical. They are also critical of others. People who are low on this dimension are easygoing and fly at 30,000 feet. They may miss the details and only start worrying when it may be too late. They are forgiving of others, and move on easily from defeat or loss.

Personality Meets a Challenge: The OCEAN System and the Big Five

Leadership demands introducing and managing change. The world changes and we have to adapt. As life's challenges can come out of the blue, a leader has to be prepared. Staff can break down, they make poor choices and bad decisions. They have complicated lives. Nothing goes smoothly for long. Adapting to the challenge and setting a course is key. As Jim Collins pointed out in his book, *Good to Great*, it helps to have the right people on the bus, but a leader has to work with—and develop—the staff who come to the office every day.

Now, once you understand the Big 5 dimensions of personality, consider how they blend together to create different types of advisors and different types of leaders. A *leadership style* refers to the way that a leader manages herself when challenging others to adapt and to execute a strategy in the face of uncertainty. The leadership style involves the ways leaders understand their staff and how they interact to get the best outcomes. We prefer to consider these styles when everyone is under enormous pressure or stress because at these times, one's true colors emerge. There is no faking it.

From our considerable experience, the dimensions of personality blend into four recognizable leadership styles. The personality dimensions (the Big 5 and OCEAN) combine together to produce leadership styles that are well known to all executive recruiters (even though they may use different systems to categorize leaders).

We like our descriptions of leadership style because they quickly help leaders identify themselves (in a general way), and combined with some knowledge of advisor mindsets, can help any leader get the best from the staff. If you understand your leadership style using our OCEAN system, then you will be able to predict when conflict will occur under stress conditions. Knowing how to manage advisors under stress and significant change (the madness of Wall Street) will greatly increase the productivity of your group of advisors.

The Four Management Leadership Styles

Now you've reviewed the five personality dimensions and can pick out how these characteristics combine to describe your personality. Rate yourself *(high-moderate-low)* on each of the five dimensions and then we can examine your *Leadership Style* (see Table 4.1). Each of the personality dimensions fit into the leadership styles as well as the advisor mindsets (which we cover for you later in this chapter).

Leaders are so often stretched for time that they have too little of it to examine their own style. They usually play the cards they are dealt, reacting and delivering the desired outcomes as agreed with their bosses for the week, month, quarter, or year. Again, introspection and honesty is crucial here. It is a serious evaluation of the potential problems, poor fit, and, in some cases, the frank resentment of some advisors. These powerful emotions have to be examined because under stress, they only get worse!

But just what is a manager leadership style?

A manager leadership style refers to the way in which managers lead others, how they interact, how they tell their staff what is expected of them, and how they motivate people to do what they want. Some leaders are kick-ass leaders, others lead by example, others set out clear objectives and oversee the details, and then there are the inspirational leaders, the ones who provide energy and

Table 4.1: Rate Your Leadership Style

(Read down and across)	Leadership Style	Leadership Style	Leadership Style	Leadership Style
	Double D (Disciplined Decision-Maker)	Reason & Tranquility (Calm & Collected)	The Igniter (Ideas and Action)	Details & Fear (Command & Control)
OCEAN Rating Medium-High-Low	M-H-M-M-M	M-H-M-H-L	H-M-H-M-M	L-H-M-L-H
PERSONALITY FACTORS				
OPENNESS TO EXPERIENCE	I like new things, but I also like my routine. Discipline in investing and advising means staff working hard to understand the numbers. I keep an open mind.	I am open to new experiences. I love to learn. I just don't put those new activities high up on my priority list.	Give me a new experience and it turns me on. I love learning about new ideas.	I would rather do what I like. I am a traditional person who likes the classics.
CONSCIENTIOUSNESS	I do my homework. I map out the goals for my group. I keep an eye on rule changes. I won't tolerate slackers.	I am conscientious and follow through on my commitments. I do what is expected; no one prepares better than I do.	I meet all expectations. I don't like the paperwork.... I do it, but it's not my main interest.	I have no compliance problems; I follow orders.

EXTRAVERSION	Balance—that's the key. I love a party but I'm not a partier. I want my staff to have fun *after* they have completed their work.	I like people. I care what happens to them, but I also need time for myself.	I'm big into team building. We socialize to get to know one another. I want them to get excited, to enjoy the action.	I work with my team. I get around to my staff and tell them what I expect. I'm not their friend, I'm their boss!
AGREEABLENESS	I like helping people to help themselves. I teach my staff how to do something themselves instead of me doing it for them.	Once I understand the game plan, I execute it. I'm always willing to listen.	I am a supporter of staff. I like them to have energy and passion for what they do.	I make up my own mind. I run my own show. I work hard to communicate my expectations to my staff.
NEUROTICISM/ EMOTIONAL INSTABILITY	I have my moments when things aren't going the way I want. I get frustrated when staff don't follow up on opportunities.	I rarely react emotionally. I am calm, cool, and collected under stress.	I am emotional at times. If under the stress to perform, I feel it.	I do not like surprises. I want everyone to drill down—they have to understand the facts and details of their accounts. They'd better be accountable. I will not stand for insubordination.

innovation. There are obvious variations in style, but we choose to focus on the four manager leadership styles listed here.

1. The Double D (Disciplined Decision-Maker)
2. Calm and Collected (Reason and Tranquility)
3. The Igniter (Ideas and Action)
4. Command and Control (Details and Fear)

We also have provided the *OCEAN Rating System,* which correlates with each manager leadership style. Try to determine which type of leader you are.

The OCEAN Rating System:

OCEAN = Openness, Conscientiousness, Extraversion, Agreeableness, Neuroticism

Each dimension is rated as either:

- HIGH—I am very much like the description
- MODERATE—I have some of these characteristics but others are the opposite
- LOW—I have few of the characteristics and see myself as the opposite of the description

1. The Double D/Disciplined Decision-Maker (DD)

OCEAN = M-H-M-M-M

The DD leadership style is characterized as a manager who likes to weigh alternatives before making a decision. This pattern of leadership reflects a true moderate type, balanced and stable in most interactions. Her most notable personality characteristic is her conscientiousness. She likes predictive models and data to inform her about the group's or team's functioning. She has no trouble asserting a business plan, but will check on how it is working with regular reporting and a review of the numbers.

The following self-reports are consistent with the DD leadership style:

O-Openness: "I like new things and ideas, but I also like my routine. Discipline in investing and management means getting the right information. You can be open to new things but have to stick to your plan for the long run." OCEAN Rating—MODERATE (M)

C-Conscientiousness: "I do my homework. I map out goals for my group. I use 360 degree feedback. I look at all of the alternatives before executing the plan. Like the Boy Scouts, I like my staff to be prepared. You can take that to the bank." OCEAN Rating—HIGH (H)

E-Extraversion: "I believe in balance here. I will attend a party or social event and I'll have a good time. But I don't like to overdo it. I like my staff to have fun *after* they have done their work. I follow the same discipline in my personal life." OCEAN Rating—MODERATE (M)

A-Agreeableness: "I enjoy helping people. My staff knows that I support them. I think that to help others you have to see that they are willing to do the work. If they don't do the work, then they will have to pay the price. I won't tolerate slacking off until we get the job done." OCEAN Rating—MODERATE (M)

N-Neuroticism: "I keep myself under pretty good emotional control, but there are times when the pressure is really on, that I start to sweat (feel anxious). I try to do my worrying at the office and let my preparation and planning get me through the hard times. If I find that staff aren't following the plan, I get pretty annoyed. Sometimes, they will see it, but often they don't." OCEAN Rating—MODERATE (M)

2. Calm and Collected (Reason and Tranquility)

OCEAN = M-H-M-H-L

The Calm and Collected leadership style leads by example. These individuals are essentially unflappable, managing significant change, unpredictability, and stress with reasoning and tranquility. The managers are well prepared for most contingencies in business and in their personal lives. They are knowledgeable about policies and procedures and get the job done by motivating staff to meet their high standards. Calm and Collected leaders succeed by getting the best from their staff. They do not overreact. Their biggest weakness is their tendency to stifle creativity and autonomy. They like advisors who follow the rules and do what they are told; that is, who do what the leader directs them to do. They will not tolerate dissidents. They would rather fire a naysayer than deal with him. They are loyal to the staff and advisors who are loyal to them.

The following self-reports are consistent with the Calm and Collected leadership style:

O-Openness: "I am committed to my system—my way of doing business. I can consider change and like discussing new ideas. On the other hand, I prefer simple, straightforward planning. Plan your work, work your plan—that's my philosophy." OCEAN Rating—MODERATE

C-Conscientiousness: "I believe that it is fundamental to follow policies and procedures. If management takes the time and sets policy, then advisors have to follow. We hit our goals, we hit our deadlines, and we are in compliance." OCEAN Rating—HIGH

E-Extraversion: "I am fairly low key. I have no trouble supporting advisors who need to socialize. I like to be around people who can play after they have met their goals and responsibilities. I am very family-oriented, so the most fun that I have is with them." OCEAN Rating—MODERATE

A-Agreeableness: "I believe in my advisors. I care for people—my staff are extensions of my family. I support senior management. I believe in following the strategy and implementing the tactics." OCEAN Rating—HIGH

N-Neuroticism: "I am pretty low key. I don't let my emotions get the better of me. I have strong beliefs and values. I keep myself under control in most, if not all, situations. I sleep well at night and start each day with a renewed zest." OCEAN Rating—LOW

3. The Igniter (Ideas and Action)

OCEAN = H-M-H-M-M

The Igniter leader promotes energy, involvement, and innovation. She likes to create the right environment for her staff to succeed. Igniters are encouraging and supportive of staff, but push hard for the outcomes they desire. Under difficult conditions, Igniters often find novel ways to motivate their staff. They keep their eyes on the ball, know the end game and key outcomes, and know how to get there. They are dependent on staff who will follow the details and support their vision.

The following self-reports are consistent with the Igniter leadership style:

O-Openness: "I appreciate innovation, out-of-the-box thinking. I love a challenge that involves new products and marketing savvy. I love to motivate staff by finding what they love and using it. I am open to innovative compensation and rewards for a job well done." OCEAN Rating—HIGH

C-Conscientiousness: "I'm not the best on details. I know enough to hire staff who will keep me on track. My assistant is fantastic at getting me organized. I hate bugging advisors about the regulations, but it comes with the territory. I have learned over the years. I'm better at this now." OCEAN Rating—MODERATE

E-Extraversion: "I am big on team-building. I think the group that plays together builds spirit and creates a winning atmosphere. I am always up for different, out-of-the-ordinary experiences. I know how to create energy and how to get my advisors excited about winning." OCEAN Rating—HIGH

A-Agreeableness: "I am supportive of my staff and advisors. I appreciate it when they have a passion for their work. I won't go overboard—I'm not a 'yes' manager. I don't mind questioning senior management if I think they are off track." OCEAN Rating—MODERATE

N-Neuroticism: "I try to get away from work. I know how to have fun and relax. My losses hit me hard. People like me and I like people. If I get into trouble or if I miss my numbers, I get anxious. I hate feeling that I'm underperforming. It will keep me up at night." OCEAN Rating—MODERATE

4. Command and Control (Details and Fear)

OCEAN = L-H-M-L-H

The Command and Control leader expects every advisor to follow orders, dotting all i's and crossing all t's in the process. They earned their authority and responsibility in the organization and expect others to earn their stripes. They are outstanding in the execution of strategy. They follow direction and relish the challenge of a smooth-running unit. These leaders do not like surprises. They will tear into you if you deserve it. They gain respect of staff as they are committed to the cause. They are willing to create opportunity for advisors. They can be trusted to cover the advisor's back if they are following the prescribed plan.

The following self-reports are consistent with the Command and Control leadership style:

O-Openness: "I don't really get too excited about the arts and all that soft-headed stuff. Consultants and those psychology types leave me cold. I like basic things in life. I want my world to be neat and orderly. I don't like a lot of clutter. I'm meat and potatoes, not sushi and whatever. Don't try to pigeon-hole me—I hate that." OCEAN Rating—LOW

C-Conscientiousness: "No one who works for me cuts corners. Don't expect me to tolerate slackers. If you want to have fun, get your job done. You can count on me to hit my targets. I am very disciplined in my work. Everyone can count on me." OCEAN Rating—HIGH

E-Extraversion: "If you can do the job, you are on the team. When you work for me, it becomes very clear that I like people who execute the plan. I hate people who make excuses or whine about change. I am pretty friendly with my staff. I can poke fun at myself. I surprise a lot of people who think that I can't have fun. The only thing I like is to plan my fun." OCEAN Rating—MODERATE

A-Agreeableness: "I make up my own mind. I run my own show and work to communicate effectively. I don't have to agree with anything that I don't think will help our group. I have no trouble telling senior management exactly what my group can achieve and what they can't achieve." OCEAN Rating—LOW

N-Neuroticism: "I do not like surprises. I want everyone to drill down—know the details of their accounts and to be accountable. I get very upset if people don't hit their goals. I blow up if people don't look after the details. I expect everyone, including myself, to perform, no matter what! If there is one thing that keeps me up at night, it's worrying about the execution of our careful plans." OCEAN Rating—HIGH

Pros and Cons of the Most Common Leadership Styles

Personality is fairly stable across different situations, but personality psychologist Professor Walter Mischel of Columbia University reminded the field that behavior is best predicted from an understanding of the person, the situation, and the interaction between person and situation. Therefore, behavior is not the result of some global personality trait, but by people's perceptions of themselves in a particular situation.

People are usually adaptive to roles and when a role changes, they do their best to fit in. For example, the role of parent comes naturally to most people, *but* it takes work. It isn't easy and we may need to learn from wise elders or other sources (including—gasp—psychologists), how to manage some challenging situations. The same applies to management. Many manager roles require some adjustment, but *how* you do your job as a manager is, in part, how your personality dimensions match up with the role.

One thing is certain in all aspects of life and in all roles: *Change is inevitable and adapting or rising to the challenges of change can make the difference between thriving, surviving, and dying.*

With these caveats in mind, the leadership styles each have pros and cons on certain stress situations. The Disciplined Decision-Maker style and the Calm and Collected style work best when change can be planned and managed over a reasonable time. In a crunch of time and under the pressure to adapt quickly, both the Command and Control and Igniter styles have an advantage. The Command and Control style is best when execution and precision are needed, while the Igniter leader does well with a blank slate of creativity combined with the imperative of time.

Each leadership style can adapt to most tough business situations, but for *all* styles to function at their best, the right mix must be in the room—that is, the right mix of *advisor mindsets* enabling you to follow through on the strategy and tactics of business plans.

What Are Some of the Cons?

At their worst, the Disciplined Decision-Maker can be a plodder, getting swamped by an array of conflicting information. Making a decision is often emotional (remember your first date or first house purchase?). The rational approach of the Disciplined Decision-Maker has trouble under highly emotional situations when his composure may start to falter.

Calm and Collected leaders do well under emotional pressure. They are mostly unflappable. They have some problems—at times significant—with time management. (They work long hours and may not see their family and friends enough to get respite.) They are prone to burnout because of their dedication. If you want to rally the troops, the Calm and Collected leader is going to do so quietly. If these managers work for bosses who misjudge their quiet style for weakness, look out. These leaders can be very intense behind closed doors. They stick to their values and principles and have to be convinced of the wisdom of new ideas or approaches.

Igniter leaders seem to have it all during times of change. On the outside, they are social and open to new thinking. They thrive on change and love the action. Under high stress, they have two areas of concern, one of which can be fatal under the wrong circumstances. This Igniter leader *may not do the detailed work necessary to finish the job.* He may be flying at 50,000 feet with no sense of how to implement the details of a strategy. He needs a second-in-command more than any other leadership style does. The second area of concern is that such leaders are more emotional than others perceive. They may be seen as cool under pressure but, in fact, they can run hot when things aren't going their way.

Command and Control leaders have one major con, or flaw: They do not tolerate naysayers (disbelievers, cowards). They expect that if they give an order or set a strategy, it will be followed. *They can snuff out creativity and spontaneity.* One of the worst things that these leaders may do in times of high stress is blast their advisors, hoping to shake them into action. This scorched-earth approach to stress management usually has the opposite effect, crippling some of the staff with anxiety and resentment.

How Each Style Is Perceived by Advisors

Shakespeare wrote in *Love's Labours Lost* circa 1588, "Beauty is bought by judgment of the eye," and later Margaret Wolf Hungerford wrote in *Molly Bawn* in 1878 that "Beauty is in the eye of the beholder." Leadership is like that. For the most part, your advisors will pay attention to your leadership style. They want to fit in and may even want to please you (bringing an apple to the teacher) to get your special attention.

Advisor Mindsets: The Missing Piece of the Management Puzzle

To understand what is driving your advisors, and to recognize their various mindsets, it's important to think of advisors as whole people, of course, and not as component parts. Understanding the deep complexities of individuals and how their attitudes and values can influence their day-to-day decision making allows you to reach out to that individual. An illness of a parent, an argument with a spouse, or the joy of their 10-year-old daughter passing into the next grade at school can have a significant influence on mood *and* their productivity in the office. Your advisors and staff have enough events in their lives and enough variation in their moods to leave you feeling helpless in the task of really knowing them. We understand that, and we deal with these events every day in our own practices.

Besides the fact, the issues on your desk needing your attention *right now* may be so overwhelming that taking an exercise break (or a bathroom break, for that matter) seems a monumental challenge. But your advisors will still vie for your attention. But remember, if they get enough back-off signals from you, they may avoid telling you about a run-in with one of their clients, for example, or about a potential legal problem that could hurt the office.

We all know life is unpredictable. It is not possible to control most of the events in your life, despite diligent attention to your family, your work, your health, and your world. The major purpose of this book, and the various systems, science, and solutions we are offering, is to help you *manage* these unexpected, unpredictable stressful events that come across your desk routinely. You cannot control these events and you certainly won't know when one is coming around the corner. That is the nature of life in the real pressure-cooker world in which you live and work.

Let's move on and begin our next chapter on Advisor Mindsets and apply the OCEAN personality dimensions to your advisors, using the same process we used to determine your own personality dimensions. This way, you will have a system to connect your personal management style with your advisors' mindsets so you can find the best way to manage these inevitable, unpredictable, stressful events.

CHAPTER 5

Advisor Mindset Categories

WHAT IS DRIVING THEIR BEHAVIOR?

The toughest challenge in stress management is understanding where the conflict between two people is coming from. It's even harder if you are one of the people. Once you see the hot spots, you can use your new Bullish Thinking skills. Understanding how to deal with Bearish Thinking is a powerful intervention between you and your advisors.

The Bullish Thinking system requires an understanding of:

1. Bullish and Bearish thinking and how to deal with the Bear. It is critical to understand the emotional responses of your staff to stress or bad news. This area of concern has been emphasized by the emotional intelligence (EI) literature. Bullish Thinking teaches you ways to intervene, and how to be a powerful agent of realistic optimism and focused attention.

2. The personality dimensions (Openness, Conscientiousness, Extraversion, Agreeableness, and Emotional Instability) make up the *Manager Leadership Styles* (described in Chapter 4) and the *advisor mindsets* (in this chapter). This understanding will point out the hot buttons and help you identify where the core conflict is likely to occur.

3. The stressful situations that occur every day! Many of the situations require your attention and can't be ignored. Bullish Thinking strategies require an initial time investment to master them,

but will make your task speed more efficient with significantly less need for damage control. We emphasize the reality of *change* in the financial services industry. This approach is designed for change management.

4. Change Management. This area requires skills and knowledge of how the different personalities on your team respond to change (and stress), how to deal with resistance and criticism, how to predict when conflict will occur, what the conflict will look like and what to do about it.

So, let's get started learning about the various types in your office.

There are five different types* of advisors you may be in daily contact with and each type has a distinctive mindset in the way they approach their life, their family, their job, and the problems they must solve to survive in stressful environments. A *mindset* refers to the way the advisors think about themselves and how they like to handle stress. Knowing their mindset *will help you help them* while keeping their job and goals in full view. We will describe these advisor mindsets in enough detail so that as you compile a list of your advisors, you will be able to characterize them.

Remember, these mindsets will be most evident while the advisor is under stress. While no one person is predictable all of the time, you will have enough information to make the best educated guess about your advisors' emotional reactions, behavior, and, most important, their thinking. Knowing how they think under stress is the ultimate key to managing them effectively.

As a reminder, each advisor's personality type gets a rating (High, Moderate, Low) on the five OCEAN dimensions (OCEAN = Openness, Conscientiousness, Extraversion, Agreeableness, Neuroticism). Note: Not everyone is a perfect fit, since personality can be as unique as snowflakes. Nonetheless, the mindsets are a good base on which to begin to understand your team.

---

*There are actually *six* advisor mindsets, but the sixth mindset ("I'll take what's mine *and* yours") is found in only 3 percent of advisors. You will not want advisors with this mindset on your team! This advisor mindset is so deadly that it requires part of a chapter (Chapter 12: You Are Not Alone) on its own. For now, stick with the five most common advisor mindsets you will manage as you build a successful team.

The Five Common Advisor Mindsets: Take Your Advisors on an OCEAN Cruise

Think of this exercise as taking your entire staff on an OCEAN cruise. You set sail with all the positive hopes of enjoying a smooth journey, but there are rough waters ahead. As the captain, you need to know how your staff will respond during a storm. Some will get seasick, some will be fearful and hide below deck, and others will go to action stations. Some advisors will want to take your job and will be your biggest critic. Still others will wait for your commands and execute them with precision and loyalty. In rough waters, as in all team inter-actions, you need a quick read on who is ready, willing, and able. It's crucial to know all of this *before* embarking upon the journey.

So, let's take a look now at the five common advisor mindsets and their OCEAN ratings (H=high, M=moderate, L=low). (See Table 5.1.) If you need to review the ratings and their meaning again, please review the previous chapter. Again, please note that there may be some characteristic overlap among the categories. For example, an individual may have traits that transcend more than one category, and in that case, look at the category with the trait predominance (or the closest to the behavior of the advisor you are attempting to cat-egorize). You are learning to read people and to predict their emo-tional response, their behavior, and their thinking. Also, if you are initially unsure in which category to place yourself, it can be helpful to think of how others in your office might perceive you.

1. The Decision-Maker/Problem-Solver

OCEAN = M-M-H-M-L

These advisors are calculated risk-takers. They focus solely on the bottom line. First and foremost, they care about results and measure most things they do by those results. If an advisor is not showing good numbers, then he probably won't be on your good side for long. These advisors will let you know when they are disappointed in you or the firm.

Obviously, this mindset describes individuals who are very deci-sive, competitive, and usually harbor a great deal of anger, which could become evident in bursts when the advisor is frustrated (and have the highest propensity to take it out on others, including you

Table 5.1: Common Advisor Mindsets

Advisor Mindsets	Decision-Maker/Problem-Solver	Catalyst	Voice of Reason	Contrarian	Perfectionist/Facts and Details
PERSONALITY FACTORS					
OPENNESS TO EXPERIENCE	M-M-H-M-L	H-L-H-M-M	M-H-L-H-L	H-M-L-L-H	M-H-M-L-H
	I like to go to events as part of a group. I'm cautious, but interested.	I go for it. I like to party and to socialize. I love new activities that are fun!	I like learning new things. I know what I like and what I don't.	I love new ideas, modern-fine art, and new financial products. I love a challenge.	I respect excellent technical analysis. I like work that can support its claims.
CONSCIENTIOUSNESS	I do my homework. If I do my job, I will be successful.	I get things done— eventually. Paperwork is not my strength. I like to be in the action. I like spontaneity.	You can trust me to do the work. I won't let you down.	I am disciplined but like procedures to make sense. I'm not a follower of the next trend.	I am very organized. I keep up my files. I plan to the work and work to the plan.

EXTRAVERSION	People have problems and they worry. I solve problems and ease anxiety.	I love people. I can motivate them. I'm an advisor who can help you achieve your goals.	I keep a low profile. I prefer to be alone or with a few close friends.	I watch others but stay behind the scenes. I'm quiet and secure.	I can take it or leave it. I like working with people who respect what I do.
AGREEABLENESS	My clients make mistakes. They aren't that knowledgeable. I help them with life planning.	I like people, but I trust only my close friends. Watch out for the quick-fix people. They can hurt you.	I really care for my clients. I like them. They trust me.	Most people simply don't know enough. I plan—they react. I'm not a yes person.	Most clients don't understand the trends and the fact base of investing.
NEUROTICISM/EMOTIONAL INSTABILITY	I rarely get upset. I keep my cool. I count on my own skills and coping.	I can worry about my files. I know that I miss details sometimes. If someone doesn't like me, it's upsetting.	My clients never see me sweat. I'm careful, so I'm not a big worrier. I take change in stride.	I can run hot—I get emotional. I don't run with the pack and can get frustrated with the herd mentality.	I worry—a lot. I leave nothing to chance. But I can't control everything, so I suffer more than I should.

and clients). They do not have patience and tend to make quick decisions—quicker than most—which adds to their success, especially if those quick decisions are good ones. These advisors require less information to make tough decisions. They have an extremely difficult time working with others who think slowly or act slowly. It drives them crazy. If co-workers get emotionally upset (no matter what the cause), the advisor with a problem-solving mindset may miss the cues entirely. They will have very little patience for whining and complaining. They are perceived as being arrogant by some and confident by others. This perception comes in part because the Decision-Maker/Problem-Solver mindset is so territorial. She protects her turf and challenges anyone whom she thinks may be encroaching upon it. Competition is the name of the game, and she plays to win.

So, take the Decision-Maker/Problem-Solver on an OCEAN cruise! Her rating is M-M-H-M-L, which means she has a Moderate level of Openness, a Moderate level of Conscientiousness, a High level of Extraversion, a Moderate level of Agreeableness, and a Low level of Neuroticism. Advisors with this mindset are very effective in the spotlight and, using a sports analogy, they want the ball. In rough waters, Decision-Maker/Problem-Solvers get right down to business. If you, as their leader, are hesitant or make poor decisions, the Decision-Maker/Problem-Solvers will jump right in.

2. The Catalyst

$$OCEAN = H\text{-}L\text{-}H\text{-}M\text{-}M$$

The Catalyst mindset creates energy in the office and among clients. These advisors are often effective change agents. They are open to new experiences (High O) because they are risk takers. They often demonstrate eccentric behaviors and interests and are capable of producing out-of-the-box solutions. Their preference for creative abstract thinking may cause problems for more conventional managers (and clients).

Their conscientiousness is low (Low C). They hate doing the detailed work and often look for others to do it. They require an outstanding assistant. Under pressure, they will respond and may be quite motivated when they have an opportunity to influence others (that is, if they see an opportunity, they will force themselves to do the detailed, regulatory work but they will hate it). Catalysts are high (H) on the extraversion dimension. They are viewed as dynamic, even magnetic, individuals who are friendly and socially driven. They seek stimulation in new activities.

Catalysts are moderately high (M) on the agreeableness dimension. While they are enthusiastic and optimistic about their own ideas, they often appear as superficial and political. A tendency toward being social butterflies, they quickly retreat if they perceive that others may challenge or disagree with them.

On the neuroticism dimension, Catalysts are moderately high (M). They may worry when they are not on familiar territory. They can be distracted and even anxious when they become bored with a routine task, or if an account remains stagnant. At that point, Catalysts may become very absorbed in their own work with little caring about what others are doing or thinking. Daydreaming about success and how to spend their next (or first) million may preoccupy their thoughts when they are not working, so challenges or deadlines can usually stimulate their ability to focus. Like Charlie Sheen's character Bud Fox in the movie, *Wall Street*, they can often fantasize about future success and forget to do the paperwork. When their neurotic tendencies start to dominate, most Catalysts look for a social outlet to relieve their stress (in other words, "Let's *party!!*").

On the OCEAN cruise in rough waters, the advisors with the Catalyst mindsets are going to move directly to their action station. They are going to get the job done. At the end of the day, they will open and close the bar. They will look to you as their leader for praise, encouragement, and support.

3. The Voice of Reason

OCEAN = M-H-L-H-L

These individuals are very reliable, very steady, and make thoughtful decisions. They don't get rattled easily (low N-Neuroticism). They will stick to the rules and rarely have compliance problems (high Conscientiousness; high Agreeableness). They are very slow to trust, which is fostered only after careful consideration of your character and behavior. You must prove over and again that you are trustworthy to win them over (low Extraversion—that is, introverted). The Voice of Reason advisor mindset asks questions. They want to know the lay of the land. They want to know what others think. They may use a pollster approach with their colleagues. Their clients consider them thoughtful and attentive.

Unfortunately, these advisors mask their emotions. They don't let you in to their emotions or allow you to see who they are (low N-Neuroticism). Others are sometimes intimidated by them, including their colleagues, because they will actually think the Voice of Reason advisor is uninterested in them. This is a huge problem for you, the manager, when it comes to managing social order in your branch, unless they are vocal about the way they behave: "This is the way I am, but just because I act this way it doesn't mean you shouldn't come over and talk to me about important issues. . . ." In fact, the advisors with this mindset are likely to follow advice, accept policy changes, and take a modest, thoughtful approach.

They make excellent advisors for your office. They will be relatively conservative with clients' money. After the tech bubble burst in 2000, Wall Street learned that conservative investment strategies were the best weapon against irrational exuberance. These advisors are not risk takers and they are not flashy. They work very much by the book; they know their business; they are respected. They just don't like mixing it up too much socially. It's not their thing. These are very controlled individuals who lead by example. They listen carefully to their clients' direction and follow through.

The Voice of Reason advisor mindset is an OCEAN = M-H-L-H-L. They are Moderate in Openness. They will go along for the ride, accepting new experiences and challenges but don't have a burning curiosity. Conscientiousness is High. You can count on them to do the job. Typically introverted and quiet, they will retreat to the background. On the OCEAN cruise in rough waters they could run the engine room and you can be most certain that they will follow orders. Tending to be agreeable to policies and procedures, you can almost always count on the Voice of Reason advisors. At their worst, under stress, they drop out and may be passive-aggressive (for example, "What do you think of Joe as a manager? Do you think he's doing a good job?"). Emotionality is Low. Under severe or prolonged stress, they are prone to psychosomatic problems. These problems include gastrointestinal symptoms (ulcers, irritable bowel), headaches, and skin conditions (eczema, hives).

4. The Contrarian

$$OCEAN = H-M-L-L-H$$

The Contrarian goes against trends and doesn't care about being tactful. He doesn't care what people think of him. This advisor may come across as arrogant and nonconformist. While others may see the Contrarian advisor as intellectually elitist, they do so at the risk of missing an incisive critical mind. He or she may be a complete renegade, and many are agnostic (they challenge most of the usual social institutions). They can display bizarre behavior at times (especially with their esoteric interests), following their own counsel and going against the grain.

The advisor with the Contrarian mindset can be counted on to give you the facts, and to know his research (quantitative and qualitative). If you are going to get into a substantive discussion, you had better bring your hard hat and your lunch. Contrarians are bright, persistent, and abrasive. They are the ultimate critics. The Contrarian is not a sociable person and may be very awkward in social settings. This person has basic social skills, but tends not to look outside of himself because he is just very much into his own world. Contrarians may not take the time to think about what others are feeling or thinking. It's not that they don't care; they are just not aware. This advisor is comfortable being a loner. "No one is going to tell me what to do. I'm doing my own thing, regardless of what anyone else is doing." Interestingly, they don't mind being in the spotlight as long as they have influence, control, and authority.

These individuals tend to dress in a quirky fashion (usually plain and comfortable), because they are themselves quirky in their actions. They may love art and have an office or home that is at the cutting edge of design, art, and architecture. They are eccentric in their investment styles as well. They have the potential of being extremely successful like Steve Jobs. The Contrarians are rare birds. When we speak at different seminars and take polls of mindset types, about 5 percent of the audience claims to be Contrarian.

Advisors with the Contrarian mindset are OCEAN = H-M-L-L-H. They are high in Openness, love research, data, books, new knowledge, modern art, and design. They are moderate in Conscientiousness. They do the job and follow through but get caught up in outside interests and passions. The vast majority of Contrarians tend to be introverted. They keep to a small group of friends and advisors. They tend not to reach out to people when they are in trouble, but can be loyal and faithful to leaders whom they respect or (more commonly) to a cause or organization they believe in. They are not agreeable (A is low), recognizing that most clients simply don't know how to manage their money in the most effective ways. ("I understand that it takes hours to manage your portfolio and most clients don't have the time and inclination. They don't mind paying for my diligence and responsible plan of investing.")

On the Neuroticism dimension, Contrarians are surprisingly High. They are very emotional people under their blunt, adversarial mindset. They have passion and commitment. They can be self-critical and brutally honest. If they fail, make mistakes, or are shown to be wrong, they may get depressed or retreat. In a storm, managers need Contrarians. They are the balancers, the critics, the analysts. They make terrific second-in-command types in tough times because they provide clear, unambiguous advice.

5. The Perfectionist/Facts and Details

OCEAN = M-H-M-L-H

The advisor who is a Perfectionist/Facts and Details kind of person can be one of the best compliance officers in your branch. They are reliable and systematic in behavior. They are tremendous behind-the-scenes advisors, but may lack the flexibility or risk appetite to be the front man on a business venture. Most do not make very good entrepreneurs. These advisors are generally the type who will remain at a large brokerage firm. They usually do not attempt to go independent even if it means making more money, having more control, and enjoying more freedom. They make great analysts, solid financial planners, but not necessarily great traders or solo wealth managers. They can be a tremendous asset to teams that already have a Catalyst or a Decision-Maker/Problem-Solver on board.

These advisors are orderly, neat, and quiet. They hold themselves to high standards. They will make sound research decisions, don't like risk, and are completely averse to decisions on the fly. Having a lot of internal anxiety and worry, they are driven by obsessional, ruminating thoughts. They need their environment and their life to be in order. They don't like surprises.

Some of the troublesome aspects of having a Perfectionist/ Facts and Details person as one of your advisors is that he doesn't think out of the box, is not as creative in his marketing methods, and may be uncomfortable asking for referrals. This advisor, who needs control in all aspects of work, tends to have trouble in our world and our markets that are filled with uncertainty. Ironically, he enters this uncertain business because he loves numbers. He has an excellent sense of the data and sophisticated analyses. Math and compliance regulations help him feel comfortable and safe, whereas selling and servicing volatile clients creates stress for this person. He works well on teams where his skills can be put to good use.

On the OCEAN cruise, in rough waters, the Perfectionist/Facts and Details advisor mindset has to be given a job and be left alone. These advisors do not like criticism and can't be motivated by fear because it tends to freeze them. They have an OCEAN profile of M-H-M-L-H. Their Openness to new experiences is Moderate (Low if unpredictability or high stress is involved). They tend toward the technical aspects of art and music, appreciating the execution of challenging designs, music, and art. Conscientiousness is High—a manager will only have to assign the task and occasionally check on progress, because this advisor type is prone to procrastination and avoidance. Most Perfectionist/Facts and Details advisors are Moderate on the Extraversion dimension. They can exhibit a take-it-or-leave-it attitude to social interaction. They avoid situations only when they may be embarrassed. They don't mind showing off skills (for example, playing music) in which they feel confident. Interestingly, their level of Agreeableness is Low. Perfectionists are show-me people; they recognize that most people simply do not understand probabilities, never mind regression analyses and predictive modeling. On the Neuroticism dimension, Perfectionist/ Facts and Details advisors are High. They worry and obsess about areas of life they can't predict or control. They are very tough on themselves for errors and mistakes. They need to learn ways to relieve stress. They agonize over decisions and suffer in bad times. They worry in good times.

As you can see, the characteristics in the categories are unique to each individual, although as we mentioned at the beginning of the descriptions, some characteristics overlap, so be mindful of that, but base your evaluations on the basis of trait predominance.

The Soup: Get the Right People on the Bus

The *soup* is the combination of different advisor mindsets working together so they can produce results. Your job is to understand these mindsets so when you and your advisors succumb to Bearish Thinking or you are faced with an unexpectedly stressful situation, *you will know what to do*. Keeping these mindsets in your back pocket will allow you to be proactive in implementing a quick solution to put out a fire in your office. You will do it efficiently with no need for damage control. It's the soup that makes managing diverse employees more enjoyable. You will know what the management outcomes are, produce results, sustain gains, and keep on rollin'. To refer to best-selling author, coach, and teacher, Jim Collins, once again, he says in his book *From Good to Great,* "The main point is not just about assembling the right team; it is to first get the right people on the bus (and the wrong people off the bus) before you figure out where to drive it."

Understanding different advisors and how they fit with the goals of the organization is key. You will be able to recognize more easily how some advisors are self-promoters who elicit conflict and ultimately serve as significant distractions to the team. These people have to get off the bus, but watch out . . . in the process of making changes, you are also vulnerable to attack.

Are You Ready for Monday Morning?

Now that you've studied the characteristics of the various mindsets and have made your own list matching your advisors to their mindsets, let's look at some typical scenarios that you encounter frequently on the job.

- You arrive at work and discover that one of your advisor's accounts has crashed. The client left you a voicemail saying that he has been ripped off and wants the firm to put the money back in his account immediately or he will sue for fiduciary negligence.
- You get a call from your regional manager telling you that there are big changes coming from the home office, and these changes will have a big impact on you.
- A top producer in your branch unexpectedly enters your office demanding a bigger office with additional administrative

support. He appears very hostile and threatens to join a competing firm if his requests are not met by the end of the month.

- One of your top producers drops in to your office, closes your door, and starts crying. He unloads details of the crisis in his home life. His 16-year-old daughter has started using drugs and is seeing is a 21-year-old college student.
- The compliance officer sends you an e-mail saying that the NASD regulator needs more information on your submission. You know from past experience that trouble is brewing.

You get the point. Who knows what is coming through the door, over the phone, and across the e-mail system on a daily basis? If you have a Command and Control leadership style, for example, which one of the situations would have bothered you the most? Think about these situations. Which one(s) would you cringe at, hate managing, or try to solve? How do they make you feel?

The point is, each manager involved in the hypothetical scenarios has his own way of coping, and each problem must be addressed . . . immediately! But before you can solve any problem, you must be prepared. How can you be prepared for the unknown? The best way is to truly know yourself. And know how you would react and behave in certain situations that call for diplomacy, empathy, discipline, advice, and, yes, solutions. Just as important, you absolutely *must* know your advisors' mindsets.

We'll show you why it's important in the following examples.

Case Study: How the Command and Control Manager Works with a Contrarian Advisor

Sally was a Command and Control, driving, tough-as-nails manager and leader. She took no prisoners when it came to the hard-nosed aspects of business. She ran with the big boys and her mentor was Henry Q, one of the most feared men on the Street. She could handle it all. No one questioned her authority. If Sally went off on you, you never forgot it.

Sally always wondered how Ralph—who was a Contrarian advisor—could handle the pressure. He certainly had heart (and guts). He could swim upstream against the tide, confident in his technical analysis. He followed through and made Sally's job easier. In fact, she rarely even spoke to him. Today, she had to let Ralph know about changes in compliance procedures that were coming from the head office. What can Sally expect in this meeting? Studying our analysis, she had better be prepared. Let's look at a few facts:

- Ralph is an outstanding producer
- He delivers consistent results
- He keeps to himself and reacts differently to new rules from the other advisors in the office

But on the other hand, Ralph also:

- Challenges authority with a cynical attitude
- Has no time for bureaucracy
- Does not like to be told what to do
- Hates meetings—especially ones involving changes that may threaten his practice

Ralph is a classic Contrarian. The last thing Sally wants or needs during a busy day of change is to meet with Ralph. So she puts the meeting off until Friday afternoon. So what happens? Sally has pushed several hot buttons. She is impatient and wants to get on with the job. First, she reacts to her own emotions (anxiety) and Ralph will sense this change. It will actually make him more uncomfortable because he *respects* (but doesn't *like*) Sally's leadership style. Second, by waiting to meet later in the day on a Friday, Sally gives Ralph an entire weekend to obsess and fume about the changes.

You get the idea. Sally's "normal" course of action would be to get the order out as soon as possible and to ensure that it was carried out. Ralph may grouse and complain (to his wife or friends) but he will comply. The *goal* is to minimize his emotional reaction, which could put him in a defensive mindset (we call this *passive-aggressive behavior*). Sally wants Ralph to *adapt* to change.

After learning about the Bullish Thinking approach, Sally realized that Ralph's Contrarian mindset means that he is open to new experiences (and can even embrace them) but he will not agree to change because, emotionally, he *worries* about how it will affect his work (and success). Using the Bullish Thinking system, Sally could see that Ralph will not run with the pack.

Sally's new tactic, then, is to approach Ralph first thing before most of the other advisors; she will give him a heads-up and outline the changes in a clear and commanding manner. Ralph may not like it, but, he truly understands that change is inevitable. He just needs time to digest it.

Sally suggests to Ralph that he devise a plan by Friday so that she knows he is complying. She listens to his concern that the new approach has several flaws and that some defy logic. She comments on his concern that the changes will potentially affect his production *before* he introduces the comment himself. As a result, by the end of the week, he leaves secure in the knowledge that he is okay. She can commend his efforts and thank him for his support.

Case Study: How a Decision-Maker Manager Works with a Catalyst Advisor

Typically, this is an interaction that works rather well as long as the Catalyst advisor is producing and meeting the bottom line. In other words, the Double D Decision-Maker (DD) manager, Tim, is focused only on results, not necessarily how the Catalyst advisor was able to meet the end goal. An advisor named John was a Catalyst advisor who ran a successful wealth management team. He was creative and energetic. He was a great networker who thought of out-of-the-box strategies for generating referrals and new accounts. He took some risks, but none that got him or the branch in trouble. His manager, the Double D Decision-Maker, appreciated his optimistic attitude and the results of his work. When they interacted, Tim set time boundaries for how long the interaction would go because John had a tendency to talk too long about his plans and to be too chummy. Tim knew that this was the quality that helped him cater to clients, but if he was consumed by his chatter, he would lose a great deal of time in his day.

Case Study: How the Igniter Manager Works with a Perfectionist/Facts and Details Advisor

This interaction works out fairly well although there can be a few bumps in the road for this relationship. Perfectionist/Facts and Details advisors are by-the-book employees who are compliance all-stars. This makes a branch manager very happy, and as a result, they spend less time worrying about these individuals in their branches. They become, in essence, invisible because they are not usually the squeaky wheel. Unfortunately, these advisors are not rewarded with the branch manager's time and effort despite the amount of stress they save them. Instead, they remain targets for criticism if they are not generating enough new business. Igniter managers move very quickly and expect quick returns on their involvement with employees. In many ways, the Perfectionist/Facts and Details advisor can be too analytical a thinker to get along personally with the Igniter manager. There is often mutual respect in this relationship, though, because the manager wishes that he had the discipline and focus to be as detail-oriented as this advisor.

Reverse Engineering

Reporting up the ladder is just as important as managing your advisors. So let's look at a stress situation, and attempt to match up your own mindset rating (not your leadership style . . . you also have your own mindset) with your supervisor's leadership rating. If you will take a few minutes to do this exercise, it will be of value when dealing with that person.

Let's say you have the Voice of Reason mindset (Moderate Openness, High Conscientiousness, Low Extraversion, High Agreeableness, Low Emotional Instability). Your boss has the Igniter leadership style (as listed in the four leadership categories) (High Openness, Moderate Conscientiousness, High Extraversion, Moderate Agreeableness, Moderate Emotional Instability). You can immediately see that the two of you are in direct opposition with each other on the OCEAN Extraversion scale (see underlined terms.) You are an M-H-L-H-L. Your boss is an H-M-H-M-M. You will conflict strongly on the Extraversion scale.

Your boss loves team-building events, retreats, social mixers, and golf. He is very much in tune with where the action is. You have always admired his ability to challenge you with new ideas. You are often at a loss for words in his presence. A major business planning session and recruitment retreat is scheduled and you have been dreading it—a full week of activities and schmoozing—ugh, just what you want to avoid. So, how can you keep up the pace with him, get through the event, and turn it into a positive experience and achieve the rewards that you need and deserve at the same time? Let's start with some Bullish Thinking!

The secret to effecting change and developing better relationships with another individual (like your boss) are, of course, better understanding, better communication (including careful listening), and taking the time to analyze personalities, styles, mindsets, and how and why people act and react the way they do. If you take a close look again at the leadership characteristics of your boss (the Igniter) and your own personality (the Voice of Reason—review the descriptions at the beginning of this chapter) you'll see clearly that the hot button is on the Extraversion dimension, where they are exactly the opposite on the OCEAN rating scale; that is, high versus low in direct alignment.

So what is your best move?

Say to yourself, "I need to communicate two important aspects of my own mindset (the Voice of Reason). First, I am there to support the implementation of his ideas, and I am also there to consider the pros and cons of each one. Every creative action type (Igniter) needs a balance person and I will take that role. Second, I will do it quietly, in the background. The boss's extraversion can connect with others. I will be totally clear that I will support him even though I will not attend all of the events (ask him to understand my intense dislike for group socializing by emphasizing that I will be the behind-the-scenes supporter)."

You can see how this potentially explosive situation can be extinguished and both you and your boss can benefit in the end. Knowing how your own mindset can complement your boss's leadership style and having the skill to communicate this insight will serve you well. The Reverse Engineering technique makes your life and your job less stressful, and being able to use it with your advisors and your boss makes it a double-header.

Mindsets, Leadership Styles, and Bullish Thinking

So, you've made it though this important chapter. We hope you were introspective and that you spent some time thinking about how to understand (and relate to) your advisors as well as your own boss or supervisor. There are so many management systems and approaches, it may be hard to imagine there is *one* integrated approach specifically designed for your business that connects significant emotional problems, stable dysfunctional personality characteristics, and self-defeating responses to stress and change. We believe the Bullish

Thinking hands-on strategies we outlined in this chapter will help you smoothly transition across these aspects of human behavior and thinking.

In our next chapter, we give you various strategies for communicating with your advisors, how to get them to open up to you, and how and whether you can predict their behaviors.

CHAPTER 6

How to Talk to Each Type of Advisor

TOP DO'S AND DON'TS

We hope that the previous chapter was helpful to you in understanding your advisors' mindsets, and how certain mindsets affect their behavior, their communication skills, and the achievement of their goals, among other things. Now that you've learned the various personality traits and reactions to stress associated with the advisor mindsets, we'll give you more case studies, various strategies for communicating with your advisors, ways to get them to open up to you, and techniques to predict their behaviors in certain situations (conflict, change).

Establishing Clear Lines of Communication

You communicate with your advisors every day—in the office, through e-mails, cell phones, PDAs, and so on. Your method and level of communication with them is critical for a smooth-running office. You also need these skills yourself to articulate clearly any and all important information to your boss, compliance department, national sales managers, and other executives at the home office.

No matter what your leadership or management style, the strategies in this book *will* improve your communication. You will learn to discuss the most stigmatizing issues with confidence. We want to help you build a team that welcomes—and sails through—the most challenging workloads, and the roughest corporate waters. Your team will have the ability to serve even the most difficult clients.

But, before we continue, we should define the word *communication*. The dictionary defines the word like this: "Communication allows people to exchange thoughts by one of several methods. There are auditory means, such as speaking or singing, and nonverbal, physical means, such as body language, sign language, touch, or eye contact." Since we have so many ways to get our messages across to people, we have the opportunity to repeat the same or similar messages in a variety of interesting ways, all of which can make communication more effective.

For example: If you want a challenge, try communicating with a group of delinquent, acting out (sex, drugs, booze) teenagers. (No, we are not trying to be cute here—these adolescents require serious psychological attention.) Opening the lines of communication with the toughest clients in the world—teenagers—can prepare you for approaching your own advisors, who will be much easier!! Using basic skills developed for communication with challenging teens, we will teach you how to apply these principles to your own communication with the toughest advisors and staff members in your office.

It doesn't really matter whether the format of the communication is verbal (face to face or telephonic), nonverbal (text message, e-mail, memo, body language), or code (hand signals and so forth), the key to all communication is *simplicity with wisdom expressed with goodwill*. Avoid procrastination and perfectionism at all costs; you must deal with the issue at hand directly and clearly. There is no time like the present!

Define the Problem or Situation

Successful coaches, teachers, and managers know that the best way to start any interaction with an individual is with an attitude of active listening and keen observations of behavior. You know your business goals. You know the numbers. You have considered the strengths and weaknesses of your staff in the performance evaluation process. Now we encourage you to *think further* about your advisors' mindsets and vulnerabilities. Most nonwork interactions with an advisor will begin with a good lead-in question that starts with an observation ("I noticed that you have been working very long hours. How is that affecting you?"). Now, *listen actively* and *carefully*.

Active listening means that you can capture the words and the music; that is, you understand what the advisor says and you can also hear the emotional tone in the voice. (For example, "I'm worried about the next economic downturn" may also include "I hope I can afford my kids' summer camp.") Your advisor will respond with some clues about his feelings or emotions, thinking, and behavior. Quietly reflect on the response until he gives you a clear signal, one that you understand. ("Your approach makes sense to me. If the market takes a downturn, you have to know how to respond to your clients. You might also consider . . .") Do not give a general reassurance or, for that matter, any reassurance prematurely (for example, "Things will be fine."), because your advisor may conclude that you just don't get it.

Ways to Get Your Advisor to Open Up

Most people value their privacy and don't want to expose their feelings. Your *attitude* toward their problems is important. No matter what your leadership style, showing an interest in the lives of your advisors is a good starting point to getting them to open up to you. Showing an interest does not mean having idle conversations about the weather, sports, or the latest news story (although any communication is a start). Ask about their lives, their families, and what "impassions" them outside of work. If you sense that your advisor is having difficulty, keep your hunches to yourself (like Colombo, the TV detective) until you have a reasonable understanding of the problem or situation that your advisor is facing. Remember the teenagers— most often you have only one chance to get it right.

Start with an observation that describes behavior ("You have missed the last three social functions. Is there an activity that you would be more interested in?"). Avoid premature speculation ("Don't you want to be part of the team?"); then you are ready to listen. Through active listening, you will be able to summarize what your advisor said in a few short words. One skill is to pick up on the *feeling or experience* of the advisor as he deals with the situation or issue or challenge. ("I understand how you might feel anxious about managing this account.") Again, your job is to observe and listen.

Here is an example of an interaction between an advisor, Larry, and his manager, Dan:

Larry approached his manager, Dan, and asked for a meeting. Dan, a Calm and Collected leader, (OCEAN = M-H-M-H-L) has worked with Larry for three years, but they rarely exchanged more than friendly banter. Larry's advisor mindset (the Perfectionist: OCEAN = M-H-M-L-H) blended reasonably well with Dan's leadership style, with the exception of two striking differences:

1. Dan was agreeable to most changes; Larry hated change.
2. Dan rarely worried about life's challenges; Larry on the other hand, worried a lot.

Immediately, Dan realized that he must rein himself in, avoid giving Larry a *general* assurance and, instead, listen very actively and carefully to his concerns. Dan knew that having considered the different styles of coping and the advisor mindsets, there was no right way. It was more productive to understand where Larry was coming from and to support his usual approaches to problems.

Larry, in a very matter-of-fact way, told Dan that he and his wife were getting a divorce. Larry's wife said he was rigid, controlling, and "pleasureless." All he wanted to do was work or immerse himself in his hobbies. According to her, Larry "wasn't interested in a family" and she wanted to move on despite the fact that they had three school-age children. Larry wanted Dan to know that he was going to work even harder, as he had nothing but time on his hands.

What is Dan's best response to Larry's concerns? How can he support his advisor while, at the same time, address the inevitable, depressed emotions that Larry was or would be experiencing?

Dan decided to pick up on Larry's anticipated challenge with change. He acknowledged Larry's request for more challenging work assignments. He also emphasized that Larry would likely be in shock given the news and that he (Dan) wanted to help Larry. Dan was not surprised when Larry blew off any suggestion that he needed help. He didn't want any pity. Dan suggested that Larry's strength was his tremendous attention to detail and that if he had any worries about the future, Dan would be there for him. Larry asked Dan again to give him more work! Dan, knowing that by overworking, Larry was coping with his emotional pain, agreed to check back on several issues and a new assignment so that he could support Larry. Dan knew that in this time of shock he simply needed to stay near Larry and listen. They kept in touch and Larry offered updates. Dan was able to introduce the idea of getting some support from a counselor that he knew.

Interestingly, 10 days later Larry asked Dan if he could call the counselor. Dan, already prepared, had identified the best counselor who was able to help. The rest of their time was spent discussing business. Dan commented on Larry's achievements on the recent projects. Larry admitted that if he wasn't thinking about business, he was lost. Dan understood that his shock had turned into grief and sadness.

Get Out Your Crystal Ball: The Five Advisor Mindsets under Stress, and How to Predict Their Reactions and Help Them

Managers who have a mix of advisor mindsets in their group will want to start with an acceptance of their own style. For illustration purposes, review and identify your leadership style again as described in Chapter 5, and do the same for the description of the advisor mindsets. Remember, when a person is stressed, you often see that individual at their worst. On the other hand, the advisor who learns under stress to cope effectively builds a resilience that will last a lifetime. This is where you can help.

The following includes additional details about the various advisor mindsets and the stresses they may experience, along with some problem-solving techniques that you can use immediately. These examples have to be mixed with your leadership style information to get the best predictability.

1. The Decision-Maker/Problem-Solver under Stress

$$\text{OCEAN} = \text{M-M-H-M-L}$$

Decision-Maker/Problem-Solvers under pressure want the facts. They want to gather as much information as they can about the issue at hand. They like to have a specific goal to achieve. They need a connection to other people and may seek your advice directly and come back again asking for more advice. They can be very demanding of support staff, snarling instructions and jumping down their throats. At their worst, Decision-Maker/Problem-Solvers tend to feel entitled and be arrogant, blaming others for their mistakes and complaining about the lack of information to make informed decisions. They can be intimidating, but fundamentally want others to agree with them. In return, they will be cooperative and helpful.

The general principles (again, no matter what your leadership style) to help Decision-Maker/Problem-Solver advisors include:

1. Ask them what information they are seeking, but hold them accountable for their behavior.
2. Set reasonable limits and do not back down on your expectation of their professional behavior at all times.
3. Engage in goal-setting, but listen to the alternatives they present.
4. Watch that your advisor doesn't jump to conclusions.
5. Arrange for drop-in time to provide updates and feedback (aka emotional support). *Important:* Problem-solvers do not like a lot of emotional support. They are, in this way, very much like Perfectionist/Facts and Details advisors. They hate being pitied for their problems. "I don't need your crying towel." They just need to sense that you care about the outcomes they are trying to achieve.
6. Remember to press for areas of agreement; where you can agree with their efforts and strategy. In return, the Decision-Maker/Problem-Solver will want to help you.

2. The Catalyst under Stress

OCEAN = H-M-H-M-M

Catalysts under stress cannot tolerate sitting still and waiting. They are impatient and highly distractable. They wear their hearts on their sleeves and make no bones about what they need and want to achieve. Catalysts can be charming and friendly with staff, hoping that staff will rally around them with needed support.

At their worst, they may fail to deliver, having spent their energy on worrying and on gathering political support for their case. If rebuffed or criticized, they may be resentful, hurt, and lost. They are sensitive to rejection and prefer to be the rejector rather than the rejectee. They love it when the staff rally around, but if they don't, the Catalyst may sulk.

Here are a few general principles to support Catalyst advisors:

1. Build on their trusting nature, giving advice that emphasizes your preparation for their responses. Know that they will most likely take your advice and act on it.

2. If something goes wrong, be prepared to dig the Catalyst out of her cave. You will need to be firm and supportive to get her back on the horse.
3. Do a regular review of strategy and actual attempts at coping. This may be helpful, since she is prone to gloss over important details.
4. Give her reassurance combined with a goal (for example, "I'm sure that you will be able to come up with an innovative way to approach this issue"). We call this type of thinking Means-End problem solving. For example, you might say, "I don't know how we are going to get there, but I know how this story has to end." Then, introduce the desired goal or outcome. Goal-setting is often a powerful leadership tool with Catalysts. Their main coping approach involves staying calm and steady.
5. Watch for catastrophic failure predictions ("The sky is falling! The sky is falling!"). The reassurance is good as long as they are challenged to think of their own possible solutions to the problems and issues—that is the real key.

3. The Voice of Reason under Stress

OCEAN = M-H-L-H-L

Under stress, this advisor type may surprise you if you are not prepared. They are often seen as unflappable, keeping their cool and slowly, methodically, going over possible scenarios. The major risk for these individuals is a lack of assertion because, despite protests to the contrary, they hate confrontation and spend more time trying to smooth relationships than they do to solving problems. They are lovers, not fighters, so if they work in the background with another advisor or staff member who can provide the voice, they are remarkably astute, logical, and thoughtful.

At their worst, they are conventional, looking for answers from others and trying to reduce conflict. As negotiators, the Voice of Reason advisors are excellent listeners who can reflect the opinions of others. They may hate being the decision maker, deferring to others and observing. You will rarely know what they are really thinking or feeling. There is rarely any obvious passion in their response to stressful situations. Another shock for managers is that when Voice of Reason advisors blow up, they often go on a rampage. Think of them as a volcano. You see this solid rock: You don't see the molten lava. The level of anger and hostility toward others may be a big surprise. The main clue is whether the Voice of Reason advisor holds a grudge. If he discusses past hurts and losses in a matter-of-fact way ("I don't get mad; I get even"), you can expect at some point to see the volcano erupt. On the other hand, this eruption may never happen (the dormant volcano) and your team will be happy that it doesn't.

Here are a few general principles to support Voice of Reason advisors:

1. Knowing that they fundamentally hate confrontation, you want to be clear that you depend on these advisors in hard times (when many others are losing their focus and their cool). Tell them that you need them. They will demonstrate their high level of Agreeableness and you will be able to count on them.
2. Be very clear about the strategic or damage control strategy. Get input from the Voice of Reason advisor early on in the process. Confide in them when appropriate.
3. Give these advisors a key responsibility in a crisis. Do not get them in over their heads. Instead give them a well-defined task and trust them to deliver. Remember that you are using their high level of Conscientiousness and building from it.
4. Use praise when possible. The Voice of Reason advisor will not react openly, but he will hear you. Praise for excellent service and achievement creates loyalty.

4. The Contrarian under Stress

$$OCEAN = H\text{-}M\text{-}L\text{-}L\text{-}H$$

Because this advisor mindset may be quite arrogant and feels a sense of entitlement, they shrink further into their own world when under stress. He doesn't want anyone analyzing him or giving him advice because he doesn't want anyone telling him what to do. You have to be absolutely clear about what you want the Contrarian to do. Spell out the goals and targets in detail and expect that you will get an argument or, at the very least, a blunt, no-nonsense response. Do not expect the Contrarian advisor to support you, but he will do the job.

His level of Emotional Instability (OCEAN-N) is high, and as a result, this advisor may surprise you by freezing under the toughest conditions. Sometimes they simply don't show up for work.

At their worst, they exude confidence and come across as supremely confident, only to falter under pressure. If, on the other hand, they know their numbers, know the job, and have adequate staff support, these advisors can produce! They can hold their position if they believe. Here are a few general principles to support Contrarian advisors:

1. Capitalize on the Contrarians' openness to new experiences. They love a challenge and can handle criticism with ease. Just be equally open to getting back what you give. Reflect on their criticism. It may be very useful to you.
2. Do not try to bully them; getting up their nose about an issue will incite an attack.
3. Accept the fact that they are able to see the big picture. Avoid discussions of policy or procedure minutiae unless it is essential.
4. Work the numbers. (After all, the goal is to produce positive outcomes!)

5. The Perfectionist/Facts and Details Advisor under Stress

$$OCEAN = M\text{-}H\text{-}M\text{-}L\text{-}H$$

This advisor feels comfortable in his own safe environment, which he has created for himself, and if anything gets out of order, or if he feels he is not in control, he is in big trouble. An individual with a lot of internal anxiety, put into a stressful situation, will almost never ask for help. The Perfectionist/Facts and Details advisor may get caught up in "the tyranny of the shoulds" blaming himself for past errors in judgment. ("I should have sold when I saw the first sign of weakness; I should have questioned that analyst's report. If only I had taken more time on that account.") As emotional instability (constantly undergoing change, or about to change) is high, you can expect the Perfectionist/Facts and Details advisor to worry. You may see the stress of the situation on her face. Alternatively, she may deny there is a problem. The Perfectionist/Facts and Details person will not accept advice easily. She will question most everything (Why? Why? Why?). She is prone to discounting any positive actions (her pattern of worrying keeps her focused on the threat). She may even discount or discredit your efforts.

Here are a few general principles to support Perfectionist/Facts and Details advisors:

1. Build on their strengths. There is less value trying to shore up their weaknesses. They will go slow, so be methodical and analytical. They will catch mistakes that others make and it will cause them to lose confidence unless you keep reminding them of the big-picture goal.

2. Help these advisors with assertion. They have to learn that as the pace of a crisis increases, they are prone to flash anger. They tend to react to the anger or hostility of others and throw gasoline on the fire.

3. Let Perfectionist/Facts and Details advisors go off into a corner and work. Do not thrust them into the limelight. They will be very prone to avoidance and psychosomatic illnesses (headaches, irritable bowel symptoms, rash) if pressured. If you are clear about the goal, these advisors will earn a high degree of trust. Express your confidence that they are covering your back. Make sure to point out successes and positives. These advisors love to hear that they did a good job.

When Problem Solving Doesn't Work

After you have exhausted all of the rational and practical solutions offered in this book, you can really pat yourself on the back and know that you tried your best. The quotation, "You can lead a horse to water, but you can't make it drink" best sums up a scenario whereby you have really tried to show your advisors the correct path to success and they continue to behave in a self-destructive manner. It is a very tough decision for any manager, but one that needs to come down to one, simple determining factor: Is this advisor's behavior negatively affecting anyone else in your branch that contributes to your bottom line?

We know that you will overlook quirky or obnoxious behavior from some of your most elite advisors, but it is advisable that you tell them to look elsewhere once their behavior becomes abhorrent to other teams, individuals in the office, or the reputation of the firm as a whole. Once you've made your decision, you are then in control and have the upper hand. Sit them down, and give them some tough love. Tell them that they have forced your hand and that you would really like to come up with an alternate solution if they can conjure one up. Most advisors who feel they are above your management need to eventually hear that you can sacrifice their productivity for the sake of the office and that you will not allow their behavior to continue. But don't say it if you don't believe it. If this doesn't work, tell them it was nice doing business together and wish them good luck.

I Have This Teenager I'd Like You to Meet

At the beginning of this chapter we promised that you would be able to manage some of the most challenging advisors (angry, disenfranchised teenagers). In working with this group you cannot be their buddies, coaxing and prodding them to do what you want. Instead, you have to take a neutral stance, set very clear behavioral goals (expectations, guidelines), listen actively, and figure out their style of coping (OCEAN system). Of course, each person is unique, but once in a group, (or for that matter when they are excluded from a group), their areas of conflict and vulnerability become clear. For example, consider the following teenagers, use the best-guess OCEAN system and determine whether we have helped you understand the types of conflict and vulnerability in each character.

1. A straight-A student, always trying to achieve and do the right thing, who develops a severe eating disorder.
2. An action-oriented, popular person who loves a party, but who has missed handing in critical homework assignments.
3. A moody, withdrawn, cynical rebel who cracks up the class by arguing with the teacher.
4. A friendly team player who seems to get along with everyone and never causes trouble. He has just blown up in a rage and turned over a desk when being teased by another student.
5. A student leader who is overcommitted with activities and who enjoys having responsibilities. She has just quit everything and is waiting in the principal's office to speak to him.

Do you recognize any of these mindsets? We hope so! If you have a sense of being able to handle these difficult teen scenarios, you are on your way to helping your advisors.

Emotion Commotion

THE MOODS, VULNERABILITIES, AND EMOTIONAL STATES OF YOUR ADVISORS

When all is said and done, productivity is the name of the game. Managers have a primary and fiduciary duty to the firm. They need to provide a work environment that fosters the highest levels of productivity and professionalism. Managers are truly the unsung heroes on Wall Street. Today's compliance environment is more intense than ever. Good branch managers anticipate problems, diligently follow up on those that may arise, and surpass any FINRA or SEC audits. They deserve recognition for doing a great job. They must be able to spot a potential problem client, keeping their advisors out of legal hassles, and are expected to terminate problem advisors before any damage is done. Litigation and compliance issues have forced managers to become more like a watchdog and police officer along with their roles as mentor and motivator.

Recruiting is one of the top priorities for branch managers at virtually every firm in the industry. Simply put, the branch manager is expected to grow her firm according to the productivity plan, and is pitted against other managers in competition for the top branch. Finding, hiring, and retaining the top producers in and of itself can be a full-time job. The competition for top advisors is highly competitive. Independent recruiters and broker-dealer competitors solicit your top people constantly, and you have to know what it is they are offering when they try to lure them away. Industry recruiters say,

"Your best assets walk out every evening, and you're taking a leap of faith that they'll show up the next morning." Other managers hear whispers that an advisor is researching other firms, and that is when they give them the extra attention they wanted all along. Usually it is too little, too late.

Managers must be incredibly adept at multitasking. From helping a new advisor who is starting his own practice, to keeping a rein on the million-dollar advisor who displays a larger-than-life ego, a manager must move quickly among the ever-changing scenarios. Working with the operations manager on branch and regulatory issues is a major time consumer, especially with the strict regulations that require understanding and compliance. Helping a seasoned advisor whose production has reached a plateau, and offering advice to a handful of advisors assembling a wealth management team is all in a day's work, too.

The manager must coach in goal setting, in business planning, practice management and marketing, and in time management issues, among other things. Staying on top of the firm's continuing education mandates from the Financial Industry Regulatory Authority (FINRA) on a yearly basis is another aspect of the job. Paperwork, red tape, e-mails, phone calls, dinner meetings, sales meetings, budget meetings, it goes on and on. Sometimes, managers at the larger firms must face the fact that they might be relocated to another branch, just when their own branch was beginning to run smoothly. A blessing in disguise for these unsung heroes is that the trend in the business is toward nonproducing managers.

The Bottom Line: The Numbers

The challenge of organizational management is to create the environment where advisors can produce maximum returns no matter what happens in the markets, in the world, in the office, and in their personal lives! There are no excuses. There is only one outcome: productivity at the highest levels while maintaining ethical behavior in the office! Wall Street and the financial services community across North America, Europe, and Asia know the challenges of the business. No one really thinks that the competitive environment is getting easier. And as the industry grows, the stress levels will likely keep pace. That's because despite a number of factors that should contribute to booming growth for advisors—defined benefit pensions are dying out, baby boomers are retiring, Generation X is more financially savvy and reaching its peak earnings years—it's getting harder and harder to succeed in the business. Some recruiters say that fact is borne out by the brokerage industry's 10 percent to 20 percent success rates for training programs. For the newer advisors, the initial expectations of the job aren't being met; the financial reward versus the stress isn't matching up. This work is for the strong—people who can get tough—people who can survive hits and losses, get back up, and go to work. This is a job for an individual who can get up each morning and is ready for anything to pop up at a moment's notice.

Consulting firms such as McKinsey & Company, Boston Consulting Group, Gallup Consulting, and Tiburon Strategic Advisors, have become extremely skilled in developing strategies to help companies achieve a competitive advantage combined with the ideal work environment. Top books like *Hardball* by George Stalk, Rob Lachenauer, and John Butman describe what makes great strategy that is implemented by tough competitors and leaders. Others, such as *Winning* by Jack Welch, and *Management Challenges for the 21st Century* by Peter Drucker are but a few books that have helped companies compete to win. Smart firms measure their outcomes and processes with a precision that seems to improve year over year. Wall Street has embraced statistics, trend analysis, and so on. Managers have the data to hit their productivity goals. There is very little ambiguity about what is expected. Everyone is under as much scrutiny as the New York Yankees third baseman whose stats are in the paper and online every day.

We have worked in extremely competitive environments for many years. We have clients who learn how to win, how to survive, and how to remain productive despite some of the toughest challenges known to humans. Human emotions must be understood in *all* stressful and challenging conditions. Your advisors must learn to keep their heads despite what is going on in their own worlds. Read the classic poem, "If" by Rudyard Kipling (with apologies to our female readers; the gender bias is written into the poem).

IF

If you can keep your head when all about you
Are losing theirs and blaming it on you,
If you can trust yourself when all men doubt you
But make allowance for their doubting too,

If you can wait and not be tired by waiting,
Or being lied about, don't deal in lies,
Or being hated, don't give way to hating,
And yet don't look too good, nor talk too wise:

If you can dream—and not make dreams your master,
If you can think—and not make thoughts your aim;
If you can meet with Triumph and Disaster
And treat those two impostors just the same;
If you can bear to hear the truth you've spoken
Twisted by knaves to make a trap for fools,
Or watch the things you gave your life to, broken,
And stoop and build 'em up with worn-out tools:

If you can make one heap of all your winnings
And risk it all on one turn of pitch-and-toss,
And lose, and start again at your beginnings
And never breath a word about your loss;
If you can force your heart and nerve and sinew
To serve your turn long after they are gone,
And so hold on when there is nothing in you
Except the Will which says to them: "Hold on!"

If you can talk with crowds and keep your virtue,
Or walk with kings—nor lose the common touch,
If neither foes nor loving friends can hurt you;
If all men count with you, but none too much,
If you can fill the unforgiving minute
With sixty seconds' worth of distance run,
Yours is the Earth and everything that's in it,
And—which is more—you'll be a Man, my son!
                    —Rudyard Kipling (1910)

Mr. Kipling was indeed wise and judicious. But he failed to tell us *how* to trust, *how* to keep our head, and *how* to meet with triumph and disaster. So just how do you manage the emotions? How do you maintain a working environment capable of producing the numbers that you need? How do you achieve the discipline required to produce every day, every week, every month, day in and day out?

Manuel Buchwald, Ph.D., a renowned geneticist (he helped discover the gene for cystic fibrosis, a serious disease of childhood), described his job as manager of some of the world's greatest scientists as creating a "healthy aquarium/pond" for the "fish"/scientists as an environment in which they could thrive and grow. His thoughts are profound, simple to understand, and apply to all situations. The environment in which a person works is important, and that includes advisors!

So, how will you manage your work environment so advisors hit their numbers, meet quotas, and generally feel motivated to take their business to a higher level? You must learn how to manage the *emotion commotion* of the staff.

What's All the Commotion? Knowing How to Approach Emotion

In our earlier chapters on advisor mindsets, you learned how your advisors think, behave, and respond to certain scenarios with colleagues and clients. We outlined various techniques to help you effectively communicate with them which, in turn, enables you to establish better relationships and enjoy increased productivity. Once you understand how to communicate with your advisors and know what the keys are to motivate and influence them, it is time to turn your attention to their emotional reactions. Along with the personality and advisor mindsets that will help you predict their emotional vulnerabilities, you need to know how to respond when your advisors lose it.

One of the great strengths of the Bullish Thinking system and its base in cognitive-behavioral therapy is the approach to emotion, which will help you strategically as you deal with your advisors' emotional challenges or emotional states. But first, let's list some of the moods or emotional states that we recognize, and that are defined in psychological tests such as the *Profile of Mood States* (POMS) developed by McNair, Lorr, and Droppleman in 1971.

This test measures six dimensions of affect, or mood, including:

1. Tension-Anxiety
2. Depression-Dejection
3. Anger-Hostility
4. Vigor-Activity
5. Fatigue-Inertia
6. Confusion-Bewilderment

When advisors start to break down, the most obvious signs are emotional, and you will see a few of the apparent signs such as the mood dimensions listed here. You notice that an advisor doesn't look right; he is not his normal self. When you ask this advisor a question such as, "How are you feeling?" you must listen actively for the response. Normally, in everyday life, we hear this question, or a variation thereof, several times a day. Look into his eyes. If your advisor hesitates or looks uncomfortable, you will be alerted that something is off. Try a comment such as "You don't seem to be your usual self." Or "You seem to be anxious or sad." If your advisor expresses some concern, sit down and be prepared to listen.

At this point, you need to address the negative emotions that you hear in advisors and staff. To begin, let's focus on a common potentially toxic emotional state that can affect your branch environment and the bottom line: Anger.

Anger and anxiety are infectious. Unless channeled and used for motivation of the best kind, anger (in particular) can be destructive. You will see the impact of unchanneled anger on productivity and its effect on the office environment. Unbridled anger means that the emotion spews out of the advisor without a specific goal or target. If you have little power or control, you hide. If you have some power or control, you challenge. Anger may be expressed as blaming, looking for the weak links, or fall guys, and will produce a wide range of distressed behavior in colleagues. Most advisors and support staff have incredible emotional radars for anger. It is the most primitive of our emotions and, combined with fear and/or anxiety, is directly connected to human survival. Anger is also the most destructive emotion. Prolonged unabated anger is a killer!

The intensity of anger can be measured along a continuum ranging from competitive to mild irritation to frustration to fury and rage (see Figure 7.1). These states of emotion are accompanied by both physiological and biological changes. It can also be caused by both external and internal events, for example, a client taking his money away from your branch (which is external), or if you are having a serious problem with an advisor who is challenging you (which is an internal event). Often, those who turn anger inward display it to others using passive-aggressive tactics such as being unnecessarily critical, cynical, or hostile to co-workers, clients, or significant others You will see these symptoms in your advisors and in yourself.

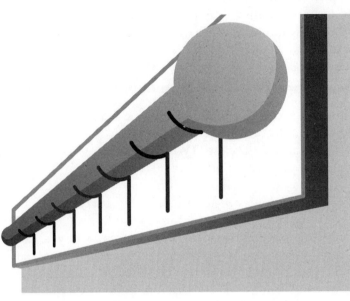

RAGE & FURY

FRUSTRATION

MILD IRRITATION

COMPETITIVE

Figure 7.1   Continuum of Anger

95

We would like to show you how to enrich your life and your advisors' lives with skills on how to reduce both the painful emotions and physiological arousal that anger causes. You can't get rid of, or sidestep, the events or people that enrage you, nor can you change them, but you can learn to manage your perceptions, and consequently your reactions to them.

Understand the Core Conflicts

Change is a reality of life. Changes precipitate opportunities and crises. The amazing thing about emotion is that in a group, emotional reactions can cloud reality. (Why am I feeling so upset?) Sometimes, when everyone in the office is stirred up, the agitator is off in her office oblivious to the commotion that she created. You must use a process that allows you to visualize the situation at hand, to judge the emotions surrounding it, and to use Bullish Thinking strategies to solve the problems. During this process, you will call upon your OCEAN leadership style to navigate your way through successfully.

Start with a behavioral description of the situation that is upsetting or concerning you. The situation is best described as a narrative, much like you are watching a video of the event and putting what you see into words. For example:

> *Situation Number 1:* Kerrie burst into your office saying that she was fed up with Gary's behavior. He was rude and over the top in his criticism of the junior staff. Gary was a perfectionist and details meant everything to him. His rule was "Don't expect, inspect," so he was often checking work looking for mistakes. Staff were often nervous working with Gary. Kerrie complained that she was always under pressure from him and she was furious with him. She exclaimed, "I can't take it anymore!"

> *Situation Number 2:* You had asked Hakim to complete his paperwork in time for an important review of office procedures. Hakim has a Catalyst advisor mindset and tended to put the detailed work off until he had to do it. You knew he had to have a fire under him, so you decided to ride him hard until he produced the documents. Much to your surprise, Hakim was storming around the office complaining to everyone. He thought that you were unfair and unreasonable.

Even more surprising, several staff approached you and asked you to cut Hakim some slack as the mood of the office was on a real low.

Situation Number 3: You came out of your office to hear two advisors screaming at each other. Apparently, Jake started cold calling some of Andy's prospects. They both insisted that they had no idea that the other guy was working the same list. The big problem was that Jake's prime prospect complained to him that Andy was badmouthing Jake's service record.

Situation Number 4: Tracie, a successful female advisor, hosted an office get-together and was upset that you didn't attend. You had some other important business to take care of, but you sent flowers to her for the event. She complained that you never missed "one of the guys' events." She was embarrassed in front of her important clients. She was waiting in your reception area when you returned from lunch. You could see she was upset.

In all four situations, you get a picture in your mind of the event. The next step is to judge the emotion (obviously each of these situations deal with various levels of anger). Recall that some anger is based in resentment, some in frustration, and some in both. Once you have described the situations in behavioral terms, check to make sure that you can complete this simple sentence:

In Tracie's situation, for example, it hurts or helps the productivity of my group in the following ways:

1. There will be gossip around the office that the manager doesn't support the advisors.
2. There will be an increase in Tracie's apathy around her own business and team.
3. Tracie's production will drop and will cost the branch money.
4. Tracie will start looking for other opportunities outside the firm.

You can see how the completion of the sentence connects the situation to the reality of the office—your advisors were hired to produce and you were hired to manage the advisors. These producers are your fish and you have to manage the pond!

Bullish Thinking Resolves Core Stressors and Negative Thoughts

Now you are ready to put the Bullish Thinking system to work on the problem. First, you need to get as close as you can to the *core conflict*, the nut of the problem. The core conflict and stress situations typically give rise to base emotions. If your advisors and office staff are mostly worried or anxious, then there is something threatening them. If the emotions are primarily anger (hostile, irritable) then you know they are either frustrated (blocked from important goals) or resentful (reacting to a perceived injustice). Sadness is closely linked with loss or anticipated loss. Guilt is associated with breaking the rules or ignoring the basic needs of others.

Start with the emotional temperature of your office. What is the pervasive feeling in your branch? When some people get nervous, it spreads like wildfire through the office. When there has been a loss or a sudden, unexpected defeat, the heavy sadness can pervade the walls. Anger is an extremely powerful emotion in the office, as we mentioned earlier. Just like in the schoolyard, a fight creates commotion, anger gives rise to adrenaline in all observers (that's what is so exciting about football and other sports involving aggression: You are emotionally involved). You see it in the herd, or pack, mentality, which isn't that far back in our collective history. Those who are fighting are enjoying the limelight as well as the adulation from the crowd. But when the office fighting is over, the adrenaline is spent, the fighters are exhausted (or elated or relieved), leaving many to wonder (including the fighters) whether it was really worth it. Was the original problem or challenge or situation resolved?

So, after you take the emotional temperature of the office, you then remind yourself of your personal leadership style. If you are a Command and Control Leader or a Disciplined Decision-Maker (Double-D), watch that you don't blast off in anger, throwing gasoline on the flames. Remember, fire breeds more fire. Communication is always the key, but *before* proposing any solutions you first have to *listen*. Hold off on general reassurances like "It will all be fine," "It'll be okay," or "This problem will pass," because these general statements may block your ability to decipher what is going on.

If you're a Calm and Collected or an Igniter leader, watch that you don't gloss over the emotional reactions in staff. Don't deny or avoid their reality by escaping behind your desk and closed door.

The energy that you pick up may not be positive energy. You may see how self-defeating the affected advisors are. They may be emoting and not addressing their issues. It may be that your advisors' uncontrolled emotions are affecting the bottom line because they are consumed by their feelings, and they, in turn, avoid their clients. Every staff member cannot manage his emotions like you do. You need to reflect on the advisor's feeling ("I understand that you are upset and that I may have hurt you. What would help you? What will help this situation so that we can improve your business experience and bottom line?")

How Bearish Thoughts Affect Performance

The initial indicator of an office in conflict typically is emotional, but you can also look under the sheets for associated Bearish Thoughts and personality traits that cause problems. The doomsday predictions are trouble for most groups that are trying to achieve and hit their targets every day. For team behavior, the self-fulfilling prophecy is very much in play. Watch for the bearish *can't* thoughts and the catastrophic predictions from team members. "I can't take this misery or drought much longer." "I can't do it." "There is no way we are going to double our production; it's impossible!" In each case, a genuine challenge, using the Bullish Thinking techniques, is required.

This is what your advisor should be thinking: "Would another advisor achieve this goal? What would that person need to do? What are the necessary steps to achieve the goal? If I really don't know, I should ask my mentor or manager. Define what steps that I can't achieve and define what skills I need to achieve it. Watch that my expression of failure isn't an emotional reaction to a difficult challenge. Break the tasks and skills down and start on the first step. If I can't take it—what is the *it* I am referring to? Is it the job? The pressure, or stress? The boss? Do I need a break to regain my confidence or energy?" These are great ways for your advisors to use Bullish Thinking to break down the problem, and potentially turn it around.

Watch for Bearish Thinking advisors who label others or scapegoat them. This behavior or habit develops in public school (or earlier, in some dysfunctional families that blame outsiders for their misfortune) and may be a lifelong habit. "He just doesn't have it." "She is such a #$#@$&." "They are total losers." In situation 1, manager Gary was brutal on office staff that missed the details. He would call them out and let everyone know how incompetent they were. He hated mistakes but he came across as hating his staff. He had to change how he offered *constructive* feedback.

Another pattern of Bearish Thinking concerns the constraints of the system. The bearish thoughts usually involve *whys* and *shoulds.* These questions can consume a manager's time and, generally, are nonproductive. "Why do we have to fill out duplicate new account forms?" "Why can't we send marketing material to our clients?" or "We should be able to drop our small accounts if we want to." Head office policies are particularly ripe for criticism and complaint. This was Hakim's major issue. An advisor complaining about the bureaucracy in the office is likely to find support from colleagues. No one likes work that detracts from their productivity, even though it may be important to a smooth-functioning office. The saying "misery loves company" applies to this scenario and can lead to increased work apathy if a manager doesn't reward his advisors for doing the grunt work with praise and recognition.

Finally, check out the personality conflicts that are common in larger groups (and certainly occur in small groups). Often in smaller groups, conflicts can become more intense because the personality differences are magnified. Some advisor mindsets are like oil and water. For example, the Decision-Maker/Problem-Solver (M-M-H-M-L) has two strong dimensions (High Extraversion and Low Neuroticism) that can create fireworks with the Contrarian (H-M-L-L-H: Check out the Low Extraversion and High Neuroticism). They may start with the obvious disagreement about investing strategy, but it soon extends into lifestyle and preferences. Another conflicting duo of advisor mindsets are the Voice of Reason (M-H-L-H-L) and the Perfectionist/Facts and Details advisors (M-H-M-L-H). While they are a good match on high Conscientiousness—C—they differ on Agreeableness and Neuroticism (H-L versus L-H). This pattern can produce some explosive fireworks under group stress.

Combining this information will give you a good analytic base to predict where conflict may arise, other than from strictly business reasons. It will also help you to hear the emotions and Bearish Thinking in advisors and the group. At worst, you (the manager) call a meeting hoping to introduce a change and unknowingly plunge right into alligator-infested waters.

Carolyn was an experienced Igniter leader. She had two fabulous office assistants. She liked the action and was able to relate to almost everyone in her office. The Contrarian, Perfectionist/Facts and Details, Voice of Reason, and Decision-Maker/Problem-Solver advisors liked her energy and appreciated her willingness to deal with the head office. She trusted her staff and advisors implicitly. They liked her and she trusted them. That was the deal; and the office ran well. By the way, the Catalyst advisors liked the fact that Carolyn entertained their clients with one of the most generous expense accounts in the business. Carolyn's leadership style was ideal for the good times. She was confident and developed innovative sales models. She used her consultants wisely, bringing in compliance and other regulatory types to shore up the areas where she, admittedly, had little interest.

Carolyn didn't expect the bombshell that hit her one sunny morning in July. The office was slow and she was getting ready to go on vacation. It started with some catching up with her new boss at the head office. Jack was a sophisticated and highly intelligent man who had been appointed to the position of national sales manager a few months ago. She had heard him speak on a couple of occasions and knew that behind the charm was a disciplined and strategic mind. Jack expected everyone to produce. He was not happy with Carolyn's numbers for the branch and believed that her office was underperforming. This had never been a problem for Carolyn in the past. *Ever!* She always met her numbers and her offices ran smoothly. She was so positive all the time that she never thought there was room for improvement in her leadership style ("Underperforming! I can't believe it."). The very thought took her breath away. She believed that she was getting the maximum out of her advisors. Her office was running like clockwork. She was going on vacation! She could feel the anger boil inside her. "Underperforming!"

We got involved with Carolyn in late August. She had just gone through "the worst summer" of her life. Jack was unrelenting. She could not get through to him. He demanded that she produce better numbers. He would not budge from his analysis. Carolyn made many mistakes that summer because she felt like she was performing under a microscope. She was currently managing with a chink in her armor. It was a leadership crisis of the greatest importance . . . to her career and to her staff, not to mention her family. Here's what happened in less than 10 weeks.

Carolyn spoke with her office consultant and came up with a workable, if not excellent, business strategy. She needed more production from the advisors. She is going to crack the whip. She knew that she had to act quickly, so she called a full-staff meeting. She tried to be matter-of-fact in her delivery, but her hurt, disappointment, and resentment were easy to see. At the end of her presentation, the message was obvious. *This action was unfair!* The advisors initially rallied around and Carolyn received considerable support. She was well-liked and respected. She had given years of quality service to the organization.

The wheels started to fall off when Carolyn tried to squeeze more productivity from her staff. They started to resent her intrusions. The advisor mindsets under stress of challenge wanted an innovative solution. They knew how to discipline themselves; hell, they were more disciplined than Carolyn ever was. She should cut back on her expenses and promoting. She was such a social butterfly in the eyes of many of her top producers. It was time for a change and Carolyn had to go! She had shown her weaknesses to the staff and thus, they started to take her less seriously around the office.

Where was Carolyn going wrong? Nothing seemed to be working. She was more depressed and irritable than she could ever remember. Her friends noticed the change in her attitude. She was a *bear* to be with and to live with. She decided to meet with one of us (Dr. Brian F. Shaw). After two weeks of intensive work, we were able to get Carolyn back on track. She had a lot of work to do. She listened to her own counsel, started working effectively with her top producers, and decided that they were going to hit the numbers. They would produce. She would *lead.*

How did she do it?

She decided to sit down with each advisor or team over the course of the next two months and discuss their business strategies. She would require them to reevaluate their current business plans and then revise them to match current market changes that had occurred since the original plan had been drawn up. Carolyn knew that she needed to take action in a very overt and definable way. She needed to use an intervention that would ramp up the performance of her advisors. By having her advisors drill down into their business plans and making them accountable for keeping them fresh and practical, she knew that would equate to improved business performance. During each meeting, she would discuss benchmarks for performance and then designed a strategy that tied discretionary funding for value added services for their clients if they met certain performance criteria. Finally, she was holding her advisors to task and making them earn their extra financial luxuries. She had incentivized her office and she realized that she needed to follow up with each employee to ascertain whether they completed their new business plans. Follow-up was always a problem with her, but now she put it in her schedule with the help of her assistant. She made the change.

The Quiet Spirit-Killer

The most destructive challenge in the workplace is the one that most people will not see. Known as passive-aggressive behavior, staff passively resist change and cover themselves well enough so that they have easy deniability. ("No, that wasn't me but I can see why you are upset, Carolyn." *Smile*, while thinking, "She is such an idiot.") Passive-aggressive behaviors are often difficult to detect because the person is often so nice to your face. They go behind your back or fail to produce on key items but have well-conceived abilities to blame others or a weakness in the system. "I didn't know. No one ever told me. I was just doing what I was told. I want to help you, but no one has ever shown me how to do that."

A manager has to work hard to pinpoint and confront passive-aggressive behavior. You have to be on top of the issues and hold the person accountable for the negative outcomes despite their excuses. You have to interact with a calm, firm style that says, "Don't even think it, much less try it." Call advisors and staff on their complaints. If you hear about one complaint, assume there have been 20 that you didn't hear about.

In all teams that require a high level of performance, unchanneled anger (both frustration and resentment) is one of the prime explanations for failure. You hear it all the time. "Our team was in conflict. Some advisors were constantly grumbling about their role. There was so much jealousy and resentment on the team that everyone had to watch his back. No one could produce because the whole team was dysfunctional." If an advisor expresses frustration or resentment, you have to address those emotions directly and with a clear reminder of the rules and what is expected. You have to follow up!

Interestingly, if advisors share a dominant goal, they may like (or at least respect) being challenged and seeing their bosses' fury.

Passion is often motivating. On the other hand, all of the staff hate being blamed for mistakes and past poor decisions. They like to be challenged with the boss's explicit belief in them—"You can do better," "We can achieve," "I know you can do it!" Point out their mistakes with clear feedback about how to improve.

If you, as the leader or boss, have a blowup, expect advisors and staff to react in many different ways. Punishment usually produces inconsistent behavior unless the person receiving it knows how to correct his or her mistakes. We were working with two well-known athletic coaches who were legendary for their blowups. One obtained outstanding results from the team and, in general, the respect of the players. The other was despised, and even though he was coaching, did not win unless the team was extremely talented. What was the difference? The first coach was an outstanding teacher who gave concrete and specific behavioral feedback to players. He knew what he wanted and if he blew up, players knew what they were doing wrong. The second coach *expected* each player to perform, but unless they had exceptional skills, they couldn't do it. As a result, the players' attempts to please him led to inconsistent behavior and a tendency to choke under the pressure (a kinder and more accurate description was that the coach's anger created high levels of anxiety that impaired performance).

One of the wonders of behavioral leadership is the frequent observation that advisors cannot identify their feelings. Under stress, they may avoid key work assignments; they may walk around scowling, have headaches, stomachaches, backaches, and call in sick. When asked how they are feeling, most will answer, "Fine." They may admit under questioning that they are stressed or upset, but this will take some probing.

Using the H.A.R.D. – E Technique with Your Advisors During a Sit-Down

It is essential to address problems efficiently and directly, no matter what your leadership style. If your top producers are unhappy, *listen*. Start with a review of the advisor mindsets. Identify your advisor's mindset and schedule a sit-down meeting with her, either in your office or at a local restaurant. The key is for you to be honest, direct, and aware of the emotions involved in the interaction with the advisor. Without being sensitive to your own emotions as well as those of your advisor, your key message or points may be missed, or worse, a conflict can be made worse and blow up in your office. Then, try the H.A.R.D. – E Technique.

Since, we understand how difficult it is for advisors to express emotions, we created the H.A.R.D. – E acronym to help you (and your advisors) script out assertive responses on cue. The term, at its core, means "hard-to-use emotion." The H stands for Honest, A for Appropriate, R for Respect, D for Direct and, of course, the E stands for Emotion: H.A.R.D. – E. The basic premise of the technique teaches you that when you react to something or somebody, you instinctively do so based on emotion and past learning, without prethought, like a football player in the heat of a game. If you use the H.A.R.D. – E technique, you will begin with identifying the appropriate time and place to have an assertive discussion about a topic that has been on your mind. Then you begin the process as follows: Each letter of this acronym represents a specific element or ingredient of this strategy. Once you make sure you have all of the letters scripted out, you will learn which order to put them in when making your assertive statement.

The letter "H" means be "honest" about your feelings with your advisor, and honest with how you are being made to feel by them.

The letter "A" is for "appropriate," meaning whether you must choose an appropriate time and place for meeting with your advisor.

The letter "R" is your assertive statement lead-in—"Respect." Respect for the feelings of the advisor you are going to talk to and for your relationship with them. This is the most important element in the H.A.R.D. – E (in close second to the "E," which is the emotion). When you make any statement using the H.A.R.D. – E, you always want to lead off with Respect. This approach disarms your adversary and diffuses conflictual or aggressive styles. Try giving respect to the person you either need or want something from so they can hear you loud and clear. This approach works because you begin the conversation with something positive about the person, or about your relationship with them. It allows you to empathize how they might feel in that situation or why they behaved or reacted the way they did earlier.

The "D" in H.A.R.D. – E stands for "Direct." Talk directly with firm conviction to the person you are speaking to, and if you are meeting in person make eye contact. Explain exactly what behavior is contributing to the way you feel and react, and what behaviors you would like to see changed in the future in order to improve the situation and the relationship. State clearly what steps need to be taken by the other individual to help alleviate your concerns or make you feel like you have received what you wanted or deserved. Describe behavior change and be specific and Direct.

The "E" remains an element of the acronym just to serve as a reminder that the core of this intervention revolves around Emotion. Too often, it is easy to forget what your goal is during this type of interaction which is to display empathy for their emotions and for them to get a real sense of how you are feeling.

Then, you must summarize your statement by articulating how you can work collaboratively on the current situation.

So, the first step is to defuse a potential conflict you may be having with one of your advisors. You can identify this if you notice overt and abrupt behavioral changes or performance standstills with the advisor or her team. Then it is time for you to jump into action and set up a meeting at the earliest convenience in an appropriate setting like your office or the local steakhouse that she enjoys.

The goal of this sit-down is to let your struggling advisor know that she is on your watch list and that you want that individual to turn to you for solutions rather than impulsively act on emotions, which may be perpetuated by irrational thoughts or perceptions of the work environment. This gives you, as the manager, a chance to hear what is going on in your advisor's head and see how she reacts to your involvement. It is important to make this a collaborative effort so the advisor doesn't continue to feel powerless and helpless to break out of her emotional rut on her own.

Emotional Discipline: The Glue That Holds It all Together

It seems logical that the most emotionally disciplined advisors will make for the most well-rounded advisors. As Gordon Gekko from the movie *Wall Street* said, "The first lesson in business is don't get emotional about stock. It clouds your judgment." This seems to be true for the best traders and advisors, because doing a good job for each type of job requires that a person remain objective and focused on his investment or trading discipline, regardless of what bad or stressful events may occur. To handle clients who are emotional or overwhelmed by market gyrations, an advisor must be emotionally sound and self-aware to help them make prudent investment decisions during the most critical of times, especially during an abrupt market downturn. It is important to be rational and proactive about which clients need some hand-holding during rough weeks or months so they can be given the best client-centered services.

Having emotional discipline will help an advisor shrug off temporary setbacks and remain productive during times of uncertainty. Thus, they can come to be considered rocks of stability by their clients, which will translate into referrals and increased assets under management. After the loss of a big account, for example, an emotionally disciplined advisor will shrug it off, make the next call to a prospect, and schedule a meeting for the following week without missing a beat. He will remain hungry and unrelenting despite a major setback in his business. This will prevent a huge slump and apathy, thus converting into more meetings and opportunities to make up the deficit without noticing the financial hit that was just incurred.

Emotionally disciplined advisors and managers can enjoy the fruits of their labor better than everyone else. On Wall Street, there is a tremendous amount of competition to make money, but it is at the expense of everyone's mental health and quality of life. Emotionally disciplined executives can have their cake and eat it, too. They understand how to compartmentalize and memorialize setbacks and leave them at work. They can leave work and enjoy the other aspects of their lives; that is, family, friends, and recreations that make them happy. Life isn't all about work, and the happiest advisors have found a way to diversify their emotional investment into a variety of aspects of their life. These individuals tend to have better working relationships because they are more sensitive to how others are feeling. Consequently, people will trust them more and want to be around a more positive individual. We once worked with a client who was not liked by his colleagues because he always became "miserable and a downer" in the office when the markets were down for the day. This individual didn't practice Bullish Thinking and was a victim of the markets. People and colleagues stay away from those who bring them down and gravitate toward those who remain positive and optimistic on a more regular basis.

This is a similar scenario for client acquisition in that clients will be more attracted to an optimistic and positive attitude in an advisor than someone who looks and sounds beaten up by the job. Bullish Thinking can be infectious with clients because if the advisor believes in his products and in himself, people will have a need or desire to do business with that person rather than with a competing advisor who might not be bringing his emotional A game to the table on a given day. Advisors must be stable enough to block out all the negative events that they have experienced and let each new contact be like a clean slate.

How much time and productive energy is lost as a result of Bearish Thinking and emotion commotion? You will be the best judge of your branch or group. We understand from our research and the workplace in general that many hundreds of person-hours are lost each week because of anxiety or procrastination or avoidance, depression, discouragement, or helplessness, and anger or resentment or frustration. In-your-face conflicts and passive-aggressive behavior add to the problem.

People waste a tremendous amount of time ignoring problems and conflicts on Wall Street and usually wait until it becomes a full-blown crisis. As soon as firms decide to make assertiveness training and emotional regulation seminars a part of advisor training, then we can make some progress at reducing the costs associated with all of this emotion commotion. Fewer teams will implode and fewer lawsuits will be filed if the passive-aggressive behavior is reduced through coaching and training seminars. It is important for everyone to feel like his expectations are being met at work and that he is not just an asset gatherer. This will increase firm loyalty if these problems are addressed.

CHAPTER 8

Therapy for Your Advisors

IT'S ALL IN THE FAMILY

The impact of divorce, marital, or other relationship crises has the potential to seriously affect an advisor's productivity at work, and her overall emotional stability.

We have been helping advisors for many years and understand the types of communication problems in their relationships, inside and outside the office. In this chapter, we share the experiences we've had with advisors who battled family crises, and how we helped them. The exercises and case studies illustrate how you can communicate with an advisor going through a personal crisis, and how to help, if appropriate.

There's No Place Like Home? Our Findings

All relationships are two-way streets and we rarely assume that one partner contributes more than 50 percent to his communication problems. Always remember that it takes two to tango in any relationship and when there is a conflict it takes at least one party in the dyad to recognize it and change the pace of the dance. What is notable is that open and honest communication is fundamental to a healthy relationship.

We observed the following types of communication difficulties in the homes of advisors:

- *Family and friends.* Conflicts about time, money, lifestyle, and self-comparisons to others who are better off than you are.
- *Child-raising.* Conflicts about time, discipline, activities, perceived lack of support, lack of recognition for the work involved.
- *Work.* Conflicts about time, preoccupation with job, bringing work home, time to decompress and relax after work, remaining emotionally available.
- *Where to live.* Conflicts about location, type and cost of home, commute time to work, arguments about private schools and quality of school districts.
- *Sex and intimacy.* Conflicts about frequency, preferences, performance, and communication. Feeling appreciated and having the energy to be present both physically and emotionally, mental preoccupation, and work anxiety contribution to sexual dysfunction, side effects of medication used to treat depression or mood disorders leading to lack of interest.
- *Money.* Conflicts about spending, saving, luxuries, investing, priorities, and bank and credit charges, shopping, cars, second homes, vacation locations, and private schools for children.
- *Drug and alcohol abuse and dependence.* When things become unmanageable at work and at home, many advisors self-medicate their anxiety or worries with alcohol, marijuana, and opiates to relax. This leads to an emotional numbing and an indifference to his significant other.
- *Toothpaste.* When things are going really bad, conflict over simple daily living issues, like how to squeeze the toothpaste, may become an issue.

Since your advisors are heavily committed to their careers, we see the issue of balance in their lives continuing to create problems. Many advisors fear being away from their clients and the markets. As a result, they don't get away from the office enough and their family life suffers. The greatest impact is when their children are young and they miss out on all the experiences that may never come around again.

As you study the advisors in your office, you may observe a generational difference with Generation Y* (those advisors born and raised in the 1970s and 1980s), for whom work is less important than family life. Individuals born and raised in the late 1970s and early 1980s—the height of the self-esteem movement in parenting—Gen Y (sometimes called the MTV Generation) is an extraordinarily confident group, and its members have entered the workforce with high expectations for both themselves and their employers. Unlike previous generations, for Gen Y, work-life balance isn't just something to strive for, it's a given. In a Universum survey of 37,000 recent college grads, 59 percent pegged balancing their personal and professional lives as their top career goal.†

Many advisors (regardless of how old they are), nevertheless, struggle with time management, setting priorities, and keeping the balance that they want and need. What manifests in their homes will eventually emerge at work. When there are problems at home, you will notice the usual symptoms and signs (tired, irritable, sad, missing work or key assignments) along with overworking (not wanting to go home), increased partying, and so forth.

The Solution

We use a strategy called Lifestyle Portfolio Management because we feel that advisors should invest their emotional energy into a more diversified group of activities in their work and personal lives. If one area is receiving less attention and focus, it will suffer as a result. It is important to recognize when your advisors are investing more time than usual in their personal life compared to their professional life (or vice versa), because that is usually an indication that they are not dealing with some stressful aspect of their life.

---

*The term *Generation Y* first appeared in an August 1993 AdAge editorial to describe those children born between 1984 and 1994. The scope of the term has changed greatly since then, to include, in many cases, anyone born as early as 1976 and late as 2001. There is still no precise definition of years. "Generation Y," by Ellen Neuborne in New York, with Kathleen Kerwin, Feb. 15, 1999, *BusinessWeek* cover story.

†businessweek.com, "Welcome to the Gen Y Workplace," May 4, 2005; businessweek .com, "Work/Home Balance? It's Called Life," February 13, 2007; Universum helps companies recruit and retain top students worldwide.

When advisors struggle to discuss their feelings with a spouse or significant other in an honest and direct fashion, they tend to avoid conflicts at any expense. They stay at work longer and take the long route home just to maintain their space and composure before taking a chance at offending or stirring up a conflict at home. The last thing an advisor wants is to go to bed angry and then face a new day of work fraught with uncertainty and stress. Sometimes, a coach, a therapist, a branch manager, or the spouse or significant other has to take the hard line and point out that the advisor seems to be living an off-balance lifestyle. It is very easy for advisors to rationalize new work assignments as an excuse not to address a pressing concern at home, just simply because it is the easier way out. Talk carefully to your advisors and encourage them to communicate with their spouses and straighten out their home life challenges before they face the daily battles that await them each day at work. Communicating assertively, not aggressively, will assure that they will progress at home and will have a quicker return to normalcy.

What Happens at Home, Stays at Home?

Before examining the impact of relationship stress on productivity, let's look at relationship authority John M. Gottman's research in his books, *Why Marriages Succeed or Fail*, and *The Relationship Cure*. Gottman, a Ph.D. and director of the Gottman Institute, researches what factors predict successful and unsuccessful marriages. While researchers are always careful not to generalize their results, we believe that it is safe to take these lessons and apply them to all types of intimate relationships. Gottman describes a communication pattern that is very destructive for a relationship. With intimacy, there is a depth of understanding how to hurt the other person. (You always hurt the ones you love.) The troubling communication pattern begins with a criticism. No couple is perfect and while some couples will say that they never argue, few will say that they never experience any criticism. One member of the couple usually has the confidence, courage, or willingness to confront the partner with a criticism. These criticisms often fit into a complaint that needs aren't being met, that she isn't getting to do what she wants, or that his feelings are hurt.

If the criticized partner responds with defensiveness—that is, that person denies there is a problem or she accuses the critical partner as being the cause of the difficulty—then the relationship is in trouble.

The next response is crucial. If the critical partner responds with contempt, attacking his partner with deep, cutting comments targeted at her vulnerability or insecurity, then the crisis deepens. The final response in this relationship-destroying exchange involves the criticized partner stonewalling; that is, closing out the conversation—as unpleasant as it is—by refusing further comment.

Here is the process in brief:

1. Partner confronts the other with criticism
2. Criticized partner responds defensively
3. Critical partner responds with contempt
4. Criticized partner stonewalls, refusing further comment

Now, let's take a look at a case study that shows a married couple in confrontation and how better communication will help solve their problems. This will help you better understand why some of your advisors may be affected by challenges at home, and why they react as they do at work.

Case Study: Destructive Communication

Susan was married to Mark and they had been happy for the first five years of their 10-year marriage. They were devoted parents to their two young children and Susan was well-accepted by Mark's two older children from his first marriage. Susan complained to Mark that he was more and more distant from her and that as a result, sex was no longer enjoyable (criticism). Mark exploded in anger, blaming Susan for her habit of criticizing him for everything that he did (defensive response). He loved her *but* he hated feeling judged by her. Susan did a slow burn and then delivered a major blow to Mark. She calmly stated that Mark knew he had sexual performance problems and that his first wife had made similar complaints (contempt). When Mark heard that comment, he thought he was going to explode and he decided (wisely in this case) that he would leave and tune Susan out (stonewalling).

This destructive communication pattern warrants a careful review to understand how to stop it and what to do about it. In marriage or couples counseling sessions, as always, the first step is to help the couple describe behavior and feelings. This skill is fundamental to all important relationship communication; for example, advisor to manager, advisor to advisor; and so forth. To help the couple, psychologists typically ask clients to complete the following: "When you say or do X, I feel Y." This description of feelings has no blame attached, but identifies a perceived cause-effect relationship. For example, "When you tease me in front of your friends, I feel embarrassed." "When you laughed at me at the school meeting, I felt angry."

In addition to describing behavior and feelings, the other important skill is active listening. Listen to your loved one. Accept criticism and listen! It's part of the Bullish Thinking process.

Susan was concern about her marriage. Mark was building his business and Susan was consumed with child care and managing the household. Mark did very little at home and he was tired from the 14 to 15 hours he spent at the office every day. The couple didn't seem to have any time for each other. Susan honestly wanted to improve her relationship and she wanted Mark to know how much she was hurting. They had a good base to work from, but had neglected their relationship.

We counseled Mark in this regard. He asked for advice after a serious argument with Susan. We replayed the argument when Susan attended the second session.

Susan: *Criticism.* Mark is a very good provider and a wonderful father. I love him. But Mark never spends any time with me. He is at work, out with the guys, visiting his older kids, going to events with our kids—no time for me. Then, late at night, he approaches me for sex and wonders why I don't respond.

Mark: *Defensiveness.* Susan is always complaining. She has no idea how hard I work. I am pulled in so many directions. I have responsibilities, but all she does is complain about how I'm never around . . . and then when I try to get close to her and make love she rejects me. (Notice that Mark doesn't address Susan's complaint.)

Susan: *Contempt.* Mark thinks he is such a great lover, but the reality is that he suffers from premature ejaculation. He spends no time making love. He would rather watch pornography. He isn't attentive and he thinks because he works hard that everyone has to worship him. I can't stand the way he treats me.

Mark: *Stonewall.* Okay, that's it. I'm outta' here. I don't need this hassle. I'm under tremendous pressure from work. I tried. She is impossible! (He walks out; she rolls her eyes and sighs.)

This interaction in therapy reflects the communication problem. Over the next few sessions, Mark used the Bullish Thinking approach. He started to listen. He reflected the feelings that Susan presented and clarified her complaint. *He learned to listen.* So let's look at a rewind of the communication with a Bullish Thinking communication solution:

Susan: *Criticism.* Mark is a very good provider and a wonderful father. I love him. But Mark never spends any time with me. He is at work, out with the guys, visiting his older kids, going to events with our kids—no time for me. Then, late at night, he approaches me for sex and wonders why I don't respond.

Mark: *New Communication.* When you don't want to make love, I feel hurt. What can I do to make things better? *(Listen.)* I am under a lot of pressure at work. I want to be close to you.

Susan: To me, being close means talking and spending time together. When you try to have sex late at night, I feel angry. I want to be close, but you can't put me at the bottom of your priority list.

You can see that the communication is improving. The problems remain, but now we have a chance to help. They are communicating!

Significant Stressors in an Advisor's Personal Life

Battling the market, the daily stresses of maintaining a client-centric practice and other challenges in the office can disrupt the harmony in an advisor's private life. A few of the leading stressors that can wreak absolute havoc for these professionals are divorce, infidelity or adultery, domestic violence, and other family conflicts, such as children, blended families, and extended families.

Divorce

Marital conflict for both men and women is a significant source of stress. The disruption of a previously loving relationship is often unexpected and typically, like a tumor, grows unnoticed over time until it is noticed. Divorce is an expensive, time-consuming, and emotionally traumatic process that can steal an advisor's attention and productivity. Practically, going through a divorce consumes time. There are housing, travel and child care issues, conflicting expectations and arguments, and the hiring of lawyers and accountants (and in some cases, therapists). Time is lost outside the office and when at their desk, advisors may be irritable, distractable, and emotional. Women are typically more affected than men, but everyone hurts. Child access and custody battles increase the ante.

The good news is that, as a society, there are some stabilizing factors in the divorce rate. In a May 12, 2007 *Boston Globe* article, "Marrying Smarter, Later Leading to Decline in U.S. Divorce Rate," by Elizabeth Lopatto, divorce statistics are discussed:

> The U.S. divorce rate has dropped to its lowest since 1970, as people wed later in life, live together without marrying, and secure prenuptial agreements, particularly among the affluent. The rate, which measures the number of divorces against the total population, peaked at 5.3 per 1,000 people in 1981 and settled at 3.6 in the 12 months prior to September 2006, the most recent data available, according to a May 4 report by U.S. health officials.
>
> The marriage rate also dropped to 7.3 in 2005 from 7.6 the year earlier and 7.7 in 2004, the report said. People are taking longer to decide who they'll marry and more are considering financial security, whether to have children, and which religion to belong to before tying the knot, according to lawyers who specialize in matrimonial law and sociologists.

Divorce is a serious and stressful life event, but there are other serious marital and other relationship issues to be considered.

Infidelity or Adultery

> "You have Wall Street, which is a sexual culture of its own—these bankers work 80 hours a week, and there's the thinking that you are entitled to life pleasures, and one of them is women. On Wall Street, people have these bragging affairs with strippers. I also interviewed a corporate lawyer and a paralegal, and they described how the partners cheated and that sets the tone for what was allowed in the firm."—*Lust in Translation: The Rules*

of Infidelity from Tokyo to Tennessee, Pamela Druckerman, former foreign correspondent for the *Wall Street Journal*

A major threat to your advisors' emotional stability and productivity is a serious relationship outside marriage gone awry. The conflict involved in this type of relationship consumes the advisor and saps them of all of their creativity and emotional stability at work. Advisors' infidelity statistics aren't known, but we can safely assume that they fit the national standard.

At one time, it was more common to hear complaints from women that their husband committed the adulterous affair, but we have recently noted a higher rate of infidelity on the part of the wives in relationships than in years past. In most of these scenarios, the adultery occurred during a first marriage and the couple was in their late twenties and early thirties at the time. There was often a change-of-living context; that is, moving from a cosmopolitan city area to the suburbs, as well as some significant life transition, like becoming parents for the first time. These sudden changes, without proper communication patterns, can be perilous to most relationships if not addressed immediately. Resentment and anger over the new roles in the relationship are often at the root of the trouble as well as mourning over the loss of being free and unchained.

The best route is for an advisor to talk openly and explain to their spouse that their (the advisor's) needs are not being met. Sharing with a spouse that the marriage is a team effort and both partners need to support each other is the reason for having a "sit-down." If this seems too stressful and anxiety provoking, you might recommend couples counseling for your advisor, which will be facilitated by an objective third party. Your advisor should give his or her spouse the opportunity to air some of their own concerns, too, about what may have prompted them to be less affectionate. The individual should take some initiative in sparking some romance again. Motion creates emotion—so suggest your advisor take charge of the situation, and do what is necessary to "find" the love and respect they once had with each other.

Domestic Violence

This area of concern is part of our reality. The risk for female advisors is higher than for the males. There is a serious collateral concern if your male advisor is the perpetrator. Here are some startling statistics from the Family Violence Prevention Fund reported in 2007:

- While women are less likely than men to be victims of violent crimes overall, women are five to eight times more likely than men to be victimized by an intimate partner.
- In 2001, intimate partner violence made up 20 percent of violent crime against women. The same year, intimate partners committed 3 percent of all violent crime against men.
- As many as 324,000 women each year experience intimate partner violence during their pregnancy.
- Women of all races are about equally vulnerable to violence by an intimate partner.
- Male violence against women does much more damage than female violence against men; women are much more likely to be injured than men.

According to Assessment Intervention Resources (AIR) president Dan Cronin, if your advisor is involved with an incident of family violence, there is a reasonably high probability that alcohol or drugs are involved. The effect on emotional stability and productivity is obvious. The advisor's world is turned upside down. Typically, these situations have been percolating for weeks or months. They come to a head in one ill-advised moment. Legal authorities eventually get involved and complicate work matters as the court's decisions define their life and time.*

Family Conflict

Advisors may be responsible for extended or blended families. There is increasing evidence that the demands on the Gen Y advisors, like their baby boomer parents, are also going to experience the sandwich effect of caring for adult parents and young children. Baby boomers were responsible for the financial well-being of their elderly parents while the Gen Y advisors are going to be hit with extended life decisions and medical caregiving for their parents. Multicultural family

---

*Dan Cronin, *Alcohol and Drug Abuse Care Management*, A.I.R., Pasadena, CA, airalternatives.com.

issues create a further challenge, particularly when parents are far away in another country.

There are no easy answers when it comes to communicating with an advisor or staff member who is going through a divorce or who is experiencing family conflict or violence. The following section is the best advice we can offer.

Helping Your Advisors Work through Crises

When advisors go through a personal crisis of this nature they may confide in teammates or their branch manager. This is not an easy conversation, but it is often necessary, as they will not be able to avoid impending meetings with lawyers and therapists to get through it all. The key as a manager is to understand the reality of the event to them, reassuring them that many advisors have gone through this type of situation and rebounded successfully. It is important to reflect their feelings and let them vent to you about what they went through, without judging them. They need you to tell them that their business means a lot to the firm and that they should feel no shame or regret about taking care of what needs to be done to remediate their problems at home. You can recommend therapy or lawyers to help them, as this is a time when solutions are most often welcomed.

You will know if your advice is welcomed by their reaction to you. They often just want to get things off their chest and get the reassurance that they will have your support if there is a slippage in their performance. It is normal and appropriate for their focus to slip initially, but if the anger and sadness is channeled properly through therapy or coaching, they can turn a crisis into a tremendous boost for their business.

How to Channel a Crisis into Productivity for Your Advisor

As psychologists, we have helped clients who have been victims of serious personal problems. Such problems include the loss of a family member, health concerns, financial challenges, adultery, and so forth. Everyone needs a chance to grieve and take the time to heal from these difficult issues.

Often, even before grieving, an advisor goes through a stage of denial. Eventually he will, however, progress into a stage of sadness and grief. After that, this sadness may even develop into strong anger and rage. The basis of the treatment is to allow the advisor to feel safe with any emotion as they go through this difficult time. He often feels swindled and blindsided by this event, and the therapist's job is to offer quick and immediate solutions to empower the advisor. Seeking out the best counselors, therapists, lawyers, and mediators will be an important first step.

In the example of adultery, the advisor will want to explore whether or not the marriage is worth salvaging. It is always important to teach that, despite the affair, both parties contributed in some way to the broken marriage. Once again, impaired communication patterns are to blame for both parties, and usually lead to one spouse cheating on the other. It is important to bring this point out in case they decide to save the marriage, or at least to be more aware the next time they tie the knot.

Sadly, financial losses may be incurred as the advisor deals with these serious personal problems. As a result, the advisor may return to work in a highly motivated state trying to channel his emotions back into productivity. He may dedicate a lot of energy to restarting his practice. He may have more time on his hands and this often gets converted into extra meetings with clients, more marketing, increased attendance at networking events. This dedication should lead to increased referrals and more assets under management, thereby turning the negative, and personally upsetting, situation into a positive business outcome for the advisor.

How to Motivate Your Advisors

HELP THEM CAPTURE MORE ASSETS
AND PRODUCE AT HIGHER LEVELS

Motivating your advisors to produce at higher levels is one of the most difficult challenges you have as a branch manager. Not only is it a directive from the firm, but your advisors *want* to capture more assets, boost their production level, and make a higher income. Most advisors—rookie and veteran alike—are motivated by an office environment in which the manager demands peak performance and expects high-level productivity, while supplying the leadership that is needed. Managers set the tone for the environment, and strong, successful managers create strong, successful branch offices.

The key to successful motivation may lie in the power of expectations. Your expectations (as a manager) of your advisors and their expectations of themselves are key factors in how well those in your branch will perform. A self-fulfilling prophecy may play a role in successful motivation. It was described by J. Sterling Livingston in the *Harvard Business Review.** "The way managers treat their subordinates is subtly influenced by what they expect of them," Livingston said in his article on the subject. Many believe it is the mechanism

---

*"Pygmalion in Management," by J. Sterling Livingston, published by Harvard Business Review (July 7, 2007); harvardbusinessonline.com; "Pygmalion in Management," by J. Sterling Livingston, January 2003, 1988, 1969.

whereby advisors (and others in a competitive sales environment) excel in response to the manager's subliminal message that they are expected to produce at high levels and *succeed*. Livingston also said in the article, "If managers' expectations are high, productivity is likely to be excellent. If their expectations are low, productivity is likely to be poor. It is as though there were a law that causes subordinates' [advisors'] performance to rise or fall to meet managers' expectations."

We can summarize this self-fulfilling prophecy by illustrating:

- Every manager has expectations of the advisors in his branch
- Managers communicate these expectations consciously or unconsciously
- Advisors, consciously or unconsciously, read these expectations from the manager
- Advisors perform in ways that are consistent with the expectations they have picked up from the manager

With Bullish Thinking, expectations play a key role, as they are tied to both emotion (positive or negative) and to effort. The delicate balance is for the manager to set realistic, achievable goals that stretch the performance of the advisors. The skilled manager provides feedback in the style of the one-minute manager.* Brief, direct feedback that either praises or punishes the advisors' efforts (example). You also want to listen and observe signs that advisors are having trouble with your expectations. One of the possibilities is that you are trying to motivate them through aggression and demands as opposed to assertion.

Assertive or Demanding?

Motivating and leading your producers can be a *delicate* challenge. It's important to know the difference between being assertive and being demanding in your approach. Good producers can be insecure and still be overachievers. Most advisors are self-critical and competitive in nature and rarely need to be scolded or reminded if they are slumping. Some advisors may become motivated by the sheer competitive nature of your branch's leaderboard displayed at the

---

*A model of situational leadership, for example, *The One Minute Manager*, by Kenneth Blanchard, Ph.D., Spencer Johnson, M.D., New York: Berkley Trade, 1983.

monthly sales meeting. Others may resent it and obsess over it until their productivity falters. Those who care about what others think of their performance will be motivated by the use of self-comparisons to other producers or teams. An internally driven and focused advisor, on the other hand, will become more anxious and angered if asked to participate in this type of meeting. All advisors will have slow periods when they experience discouragement. This is when the skilled branch manager must jump in and nurture the producer back to strength. Your advisors can feel the difference if you are being demanding rather than being assertive. The difference is in the tone of your voice when you are speaking to someone. A demand also uses real or implied threats, which you don't want to act on. It demoralizes a person and angers them.

Determine instead what aspects of the job motivates her and use it as an incentive; for example, "If you get two referrals this week, I'll try to get you more funds to host your seminar. I'm trying to help your business. I want to be on your team and work collaboratively with you to bring you to the next level of your business and I can only do that if you are helping me by doing X, Y, and Z." No threats. "If you don't get at least two referrals in this week, I'll have to cut back your seminar funds." You can see the difference between being demanding compared to being helpful and assertive.

You can also use the H.A.R.D. – E technique (see Chapter 7) for assertiveness: "Bob, you are a valued advisor in this company; I really like managing you. *But,* I feel powerless to help you at this point because you're not making enough referral calls, you're not attending the morning meetings, and it's making it very difficult for me to help you out. *And,* I would appreciate it if you would start making your referral calls to your high net worth clients at least three times a week so that we can take your business to another level." (The italicized words emphasize an important part of the process.)

It bears repeating: Whatever you do, no matter how angry or exasperated you get, do not make threats. They just don't work. You will not get genuine productivity out of that person. You might get a little spike in improved performance but, in the long run, they may continue to create problems for you and their colleagues. On the other hand, if an advisor is the type of person who responds only to threats, he is probably creating a lot of havoc with his administrative team and other colleagues or accounts anyway, so this is something you need to deal with, sooner rather than later.

Motivating for Higher Production Levels: Don't Be a Cheerleader. It's Just a Quick Fix.

One issue, as we see it, is that we aren't witnessing the traditional motivational meetings and strategies used at the firms as much as they did in the past. Some managers seem to motivate by simply creating competition among their advisors. They seem to have lost the skill of motivating with words and action. A manager has to assess the individual advisor in what motivates that person. Sometimes, advisors don't even attend the cheerleading type of meetings because it actually hinders their productivity because they try to be *too* competitive. If they get too worked up, it can create anxiety. The higher-level advisors don't want the cheerleading and won't be interested in the meeting.

We do see branch managers who conduct sales meetings with their brokers and advisors to discuss business-building and practice management strategies that they all can use. It's a great way to get everyone sharing their ideas and their successful techniques. For example, they'll talk about referral business, about how to host a client appreciation night, or they may talk about the types of professional organizations they need to join for continuing education and designations, or how to get elected to sit on the board of a charitable foundation and so on. Community involvement is essential for most advisors.

The current trend is for a branch to bring in an industry coach or trainer to work with a group of advisors for a period of time. The trainer then takes on individuals for private and custom coaching. The coach is a motivator, but is also the skilled educator and teaches advisors strategies to grow their business and build their production. These programs cover everything from general sales, prospecting, and marketing techniques to the more specific target areas of wealth management, building strategic alliances, growing a referral business, time management, business plans, reaching the affluent, capturing assets through philanthropic planning, and so much more. Some coaches even have programs uniquely designed for the branch manager, such as those offered by the Oechsli Institute, and industry organizations like the Securities Industry and Financial Markets Association (SIFMA).

There Is No Cookie-Cutter Approach

You must be careful not to use a one-size-fits-all model for what motivates one advisor or another. If an advisor's performance is down consistently, it's crucial to get to the root of the barrier to performance.

We hope you don't believe that the supposedly magic words of "Get on the phone and start asking for referrals" are going to improve the situation. If that advisor feels safer just managing the current accounts he has accrued over the last 15 years and he's anxious about trying out new strategies or asking his affluent clients for referrals, well, he's not going to do it because you tell him to do it. He will only do it when he overcomes his anxiety and says to himself, "It's time to change."

You need to have a serious conversation with that advisor to determine his strengths and weaknesses, including how they come across to others; where their problem areas are with clients and what their behavioral tendencies are that equate to poor performance. There is no cookie-cutter approach to motivating your advisors.

Performance profiling can certainly help you and your advisors. You will be able to determine why certain individuals are not performing up to par or the reasons they are struggling. Signs of anxiety or burnout, for example, would be more readily apparent during a performance profile of an advisor. The profiling will uncover an individual's strengths and weaknesses as well as what her key motivators are, what's the best way to communicate with her, what her ideal work environment would be, and what the keys to managing her are for overcoming her limitations. It would also point to behavioral tendencies that need to be worked on over time. Performance profiling will give you a blueprint of each advisor, helping you to better understand what that person needs to be motivated.

Some advisors are motivated by incentives. Some individuals are motivated by benchmarking, by competition. Some individuals are motivated by being offered time off, or a larger office, a full-time assistant, upgraded technology, and so on. Many advisors (and people in general, of course) are motivated by recognition. You must use every opportunity to show that you appreciate the work of your advisors. Easier said than done, it takes a dedication and commitment to each advisor. Find every opportunity to appreciate good work. Here are a few basic ways to show your appreciation:

- Recognize that person publicly at meetings or casually in the office
- Offer opportunities to learn, improve skills, and knowledge through extra coaching
- Create a forum for sharing her success with others and discussing best practices

- Organize a special lunch or dinner for that advisor and colleagues or family
- Feature that advisor in a branch or a firm-wide newsletter
- Send a personal letter to that advisor's family showing how proud and satisfied you and the firm are of her accomplishments
- Have a nice recognition certificate made to hang in her office

Confidence-Building Strategies for Your Advisors

So, you have a high-producing, fee-based advisor with approximately $80 million under management, but he has reached a plateau. You wouldn't think of saying, "Hey Bob, you need to get off the dime; I've given you a list of qualified high net worth investors and you haven't prospected anyone yet." Whatever the reason, be it anxiety or the dread of making cold calls, if the advisor does not have the confidence or the willingness, it won't happen. Some advisors say they will do more prospecting as soon as their new marketing material comes back from the printer. Any excuse in the book. In some cases, this is true, but when an advisor stops making money for his clients during a market downturn, the phones do stop ringing.

We have found that, many times, it is simply a matter of not having the correct dialogue with which to open the referral conversation. Regardless, all advisors (large and small) need to feel confident in client situations. That's where you can help with confidence-building strategies.

Some of your larger producers who have been around the block a few times should be talking to their long-time and best clients about their (the clients') future on at least a quarterly basis as clients' financial needs can fluctuate because of lifestyle or career changes. These meetings are great opportunities to reflect over the long relationships they have had with them and to discuss the portfolio growth over the years. Even if an advisor is in a brief slump with the investment performance of their clients' portfolios, he can talk about the home runs that he and the money managers have made. Suggest to your advisor that he also talk to these clients about how important his longstanding relationship with them has been. At this point, the advisor can ask them if they know of anyone else who might benefit from his expertise (stock selection, wealth management, philanthropic planning, and so on) because his business is expanding and he is focusing on the higher net worth clientele now.

Some of your newer advisors, of course, may tend to jump the gun on asking clients for referrals too early in the relationship. Remind them that the first rule of thumb is that you can't ask for a referral until you have shown your clients some positive returns on their investments or some value-added service that was meaningful to them. If your less experienced advisor asks too soon, he may appear to be greedy and not focused solely on the client.

Motivation: Get It Straight from the Horse's Mouth!

We like the idea of the manager talking to the advisor about the subject of motivation either immediately upon hiring or during the interview process. You can find out how that individual prefers to be handled, what she responds to, the best form of communication, what inspires her, how she reacts to coaching, and so forth. It's a great managerial tool to ask questions such as where she sees herself in 5 to 10 years and how she plans to get there, which in turn creates a planning perspective for your advisor during this time of questioning and interviewing. It may even be good to assign her the task of redoing or updating her current business plan or initiatives. Why not just ask the advisor directly, "What motivates you to succeed?" You may be surprised at some of the answers you will receive, and it will help you immensely as you begin your relationship with that advisor. Some will be motivated by the almighty dollar, others by power and materialistic items, and still others by the freedom from supervision or detail work, or more support and job stability.

Here is a list of additional questions you can use, and just add your own to it:

- How do you prefer to be communicated with?
- What are some things that agitate you or make you less productive?
- What are some ways that people talk to you that will make you more agitated or frustrated?
- How would you prefer others to provide you with constructive feedback?
- When you are burnt out, how do you think you appear to others?
- How might others describe you if you are anxious, tired, or overwhelmed?

- What is your value to your team?
- What is your value to this branch?
- What behavioral tendencies would you like to improve on as an advisor?
- What sales skills could you refine to make yourself more flexible and productive?
- What drives you to succeed?

Dealing with Sensitive Topics

Dealing with sensitive topics with your advisors can be difficult and may feel at times like it is not an appropriate role for a branch manager. It may feel like you are stepping into the role of a psychologist when you have to address tough issues like substance abuse, criminal activity, depression, burnout, divorce, adultery, acting out behaviors in the office, and sexual harassment. When dealing with these issues, always have a closed-door meeting or meet at a local restaurant. The key is to have the meeting where the advisor feels safe and knows that no one else will be around to hear or see him.

We worked with an advisor who was going through a brutal divorce and his business was suffering. His branch manager and the entire firm knew about the horrible details of this matter, but no one mentioned it to the advisor at all. The advisor's emotions became unstable after the divorce was initiated and his production halted. His personality had changed and he was not getting along with his colleagues. The branch manager knew that he had to step in, but needed to do so delicately because of the advisor's recent problem with anger and mood instability. He decided to take the advisor out for dinner to check in with him about the divorce. He talked about the business and asked the advisor how he could be of help to bring back his A game. The end result was that the branch manager suggested counseling as a way for the advisor to get through his grief, anger, and shame, and turn it into positive action for his clients.

Using Emotion as a Strategy to Encourage Struggling Advisors

A manager can, at times, be very effective at motivating the advisors who are struggling when he can appeal to them on a human and emotional level. Try to identify with the advisor and how she may feel about a downturn in her performance. Show respect for your relationship with that individual. It is important for you to convey that you understand her value to the firm and you have high expectations for her business and won't settle for less than her achieving the distinction of being one of the top 10 in your branch. A pep talk that includes some powerful statements like "I'm behind you all the way until you are back on top of your game," can also be confidence-inspiring. Just letting your advisor know that you've seen these droughts before and that you know how talented she really is can give her a boost. Letting her know that you appreciate what she has contributed to the branch's bottom line over the years and that you know what she is capable of from a performance standpoint will also help her rebound.

10

Harnessing Your Team of Advisors

STRUCTURING, PROFILING, AND MANAGING

Today, the demands on managers to provide timely communication, and on firms to have the latest technology and analytic systems, are extreme. Advisor teams must consistently perform at high levels. There is little downtime, although the industry recognizes the need for advisor sabbaticals and vacations and breaks to help keep motivation high.

But keeping every member of a team motivated can be difficult, since they are always in a state of flux. Nothing stays the same. Consider the mergers and acquisitions in our industry over the past decade alone. For example, a recent surprise was the acquisition of A.G. Edwards (founded in 1887 by General Albert Gallatin Edwards) by Wachovia Securities in May of 2007. They previously had purchased the majority of Prudential's brokerage arm, which consisted of the old Bache and Co., and renamed Prudential Bache. UBS purchased Paine Webber, Dean Witter merged with Morgan Stanley, Citigroup/Citibank gobbled up Salomon, Smith Barney, EF Hutton, and Shearson. We could go on, but with the increased competitive pressure, it seems clear that the industry is driving toward more consolidation with banks and insurance companies, and more team-based activities within the firms themselves. It's difficult to win and even tougher to remain consistent.

Another factor in the industry is the significant amount of advisor attrition and mobility. According to the latest information as of this writing from SIFMA (Securities Industry & Financial Markets

Association, formerly the Securities Industry Association [SIA]), about 40 percent of the new brokers and financial advisors leave the business in the first year. CBM Group, a financial services industry consulting firm estimated that approximately 85 percent of brokers and advisors quit within four years! Advisors working in the traditional retail brokerage environment are breaking away and making their move to independence, while some are leaving the industry altogether because of increased industry regulation, compliance, and liability. In sports, teams and players used to be stable year in and year out. Teams changed slowly until free agency emerged in 1975, which allowed player movement in a more open and competitive market. Competition increased and the pressure on management escalated balancing budgets with skilled players. The utility players became more important and a team was only as good as its weakest link. We can compare financial advisor teams to sports teams in that its members are also competitive and the individuals all have their unique strengths that contribute to the success of the team, but if one member is not functioning at his peak, that deficiency can affect the entire team.

So, for branch managers, there is a steady pressure to motivate and inspire combined with surges of *intense* pressure to perform. They are the glue that hold the organization together; a critical linchpin between the home office, the regional and national sales executives, and their advisors and teams in the branch. Talk about *intense!* The teams, in particular, look to their leaders for guidance and support, and react to the surges in pressure that is heaped upon their managers; sometimes positively, sometimes negatively. It all depends on how you (as manager) handle your own stress and what strategies you use to provide leadership as well as solve communication problems among team members.

How to Help Your Advisors Structure Their Team

The teams today are far removed from the teams of yesterday (circa 1970s–1980s). Teams back then were composed primarily of *inside-outside* members. For example, one team member would be the cold caller or prospector bringing in the accounts or assets, and the second team member would be the one to handle the transactions and service the accounts. Rarely were there more than two members on a team, with the exception of the early 1980s when the fee-based business was in its infancy and three or more pioneers would form a team to gather assets, manage the money using the consulting process, service the clients, and develop marketing and PR activities like client appreciation nights and golf outings for their top-tier clients, including small institutions.

But the basic team back then was fraught with challenges. The structure was very informal; many times, the team broke up because of disagreements about growing the team, production splits, or what kind of clients to take on. Also, most had no prior written agreements going into the team (no prenup, so to speak), so the breakup was painful, and sometimes ugly. Branch managers knew very little about how to actually referee the team, or about the individual advisor mindsets, but did their best to motivate and just keep them in compliance. These days, with the focus on acquiring more high net worth clients and emerging affluent investors, as well as marketing to foundations and endowments, the way most high-level advisors are reaching and maintaining success with these groups is by forming wealth management teams. These teams consist of formal or informal alliances with CPAs, estate planning attorneys, business consultants, insurance professionals, and others who can help with overall wealth preservation and distribution for clients. Some advisors are forming specialized teams that focus on legacy planning, or philanthropic planning, or simply business succession (for advisors who service small business owners). So, teams have become quite a bit more sophisticated, and branch managers have quite a responsibility with overseeing these skilled and experienced professionals.

Because this kind of team may consist of five or more members, it is crucial to understand the mindsets of each member so that the team functions well and all members understand the strengths and weaknesses of each. Keep in mind that we are not implying that smaller teams no longer exist, those that may consist of a veteran broker or advisor, junior partner or rookie, and a registered assistant, and so forth, because they *do* exist, and most flourish today with the help of technology and the growing number of coaches and trainers available. This is where you can step in. You can even help your advisors pull together their team, recommending various mindsets and skill sets that would integrate well on a team level. We call it *advisor profiling*. We recommend you review Chapters 4 and 5 for a refresher on the OCEAN system and advisor mindsets, if it would be helpful to you.

Using the OCEAN System to Profile Your Advisors as Part of a Team

The OCEAN system serves managers by helping them create a team profile. Each member of the team is classified by her mindset and related coping strategy when she faces the intense day-in, day-out pressure of the industry. The system works by pinpointing personality sources of conflict and may be used for the positive development of teams, whereby one or two members can help one another shore up their vulnerability.

While it is not your job to create the teams per se, you can be instrumental in helping your advisors organize one. Keep the following in mind, and communicate it to the advisors interested in developing their own team: It is, in general, useful to combine job skills, mindsets, and Bullish Thinking skills to create a team that is professional, has a mix of experience, and if the group is small, has a complementary mindset.

1. The Decision-Maker/Problem-Solver (OCEAN = M-M-H-M-L)
2. The Catalyst (OCEAN = H-L-H-M-M)
3. The Voice of Reason (OCEAN = M-H-L-H-L)
4. The Contrarian (OCEAN = H-M-L-L-H)
5. The Perfectionist/Facts and Details (OCEAN = M-H-M-L-H)

As no categorization system is perfect, you may have other mindsets in your group, but these types, too, are easily defined with the OCEAN system. The purpose of these thumbnail advisor mindset reviews is to recognize where the conflict among advisors will play out. Aside from the real business issues, personalities will come into play. Using the Bullish Thinking techniques such as H.A.R.D. – E, and Channeled Anger (reviewed in Chapter 7) will also help in stressful times.

Interestingly, as we outlined earlier, the Catalysts and Decision-Maker/Problem-Solvers usually get along. Their profiles merge with no major personality conflicts. On the other hand, Catalysts conflict with Voice of Reason advisors on the Conscientiousness and Extraversion dimensions, with Perfectionist/Facts and Details advisors on Conscientiousness, and with Contrarians on Extraversion. Other advisor mindsets conflict as well. Simply compare the two mindsets and look for the H-L, L-H (high-low, low-high) pairings.

So when you help build a team, you should explain to your advisors why it is advantageous to have a variety of advisor mindsets working together. Advisors need to understand their differences and, in rough times, work on adapting to the tasks at hand. In tough times, it is very helpful to have Contrarians and Catalysts on board, as the Contrarians will be cashing in while the Catalysts will provide the energy for the group to recover.

When you have an opportunity to help build a team of advisors in your branch, start with an analysis of job skills (naturally), which are their areas of expertise, and then evaluate their Bullish Thinking skills. Next, consider the advisor mindsets before trouble emerges so that you will know how advisors will react to market downturns and upturns or other client challenges. Try to recognize the mindsets as you hire and fire advisors, too. You will hire and fire on the basis of many factors: most will be based on their professional skills and their dedication to the job. Mindsets are a secondary consideration after the team is up and running. This consideration of mindsets focuses on how certain advisors will get along and work together.

We developed the OCEAN system and the related descriptions of the advisor mindsets for advisors, and to help you create a team profile. The more advisors you have, the more cumbersome any system is in predicting reactions. For illustration, we start with a case study that involves a small team.

Case Study

Peter was given the challenge of his career when he was asked to open a small branch office for a major retail brokerage house. He had always been interested in a leadership position and had a classic Igniter leadership style. The Igniter (Ideas and Action, OCEAN = H-M-H-M-M) leader promotes energy, involvement, and innovation. Igniters like to create the right environment for their staff to succeed. They are encouraging and supportive of staff, but push hard for the outcomes they desire. Under difficult conditions, Igniters often find novel ways to motivate their staff. They keep their eyes on the ball, know the end-game and key outcomes, and know how to get there. They depend on staff who will follow the details and support their vision.

Peter needed to hire five advisors and three registered advisor assistants. He started the interview process and immediately recognized that he was drawn to Catalyst mindset advisors (which are similar in style to the Igniter leader). "I liked their energy. I wanted my office to buzz." Predicting successful advisors, especially young ones, is a challenge. Only 15 percent of advisors, according to industry statistics, will survive the first four years in the business. Peter started to feel anxiety about his choices. "All of sudden, I realized that I had to pick well. Our branch was small and we were investing so much in the advisors' training." Peter called us to discuss how other managers hired advisors for their branches. He was very serious and wanted to get it right.

Peter was excellent in analysis of the standard predictors of success in the field. He used a standard advisor profiling system to assess who might be the best candidates. Some predictors of being a success were based on some of the following: have an MBA before getting hired, be a CPA, have estate planning experience, the ability to make quick decisions without laboring over too many data points, experience within a family business, three to five years of sales experience, tenacity, social adeptness, competitiveness energy, analytical skills, and discipline. He wanted to make the best choices possible. Peter then considered the mix. Knowing that, as a Igniter leader, he sometimes overlooked the underlying value of other advisor mindsets, he decided to interview those with various mindsets. Lloyd was a Voice of Reason advisor who had nearly eight years experience. He wanted to leave his independent practice and join a small retail office where he would have more interaction with other advisors. He didn't think too much of Peter's style at first ("I don't really go for the rah-rah guys") but was surprised when Peter demonstrated a clear understanding of his strengths and weaknesses. Lloyd was amazed when Peter spoke of his own tendency to gloss over details and to go for the high-energy advisors. He was even more surprised when Peter contrasted Lloyd's quiet, introverted style as complementing his loud, extraverted approach. Peter seemed to really understand and value the differences in their approach. Peter spoke about how they could support each other if they were part of the same team. Lloyd didn't trust easily and wasn't about to be talked into buying a bill of goods by Peter, but he was impressed. Peter knew him. How, he wondered?

Peter used the OCEAN system and understood where Lloyd was coming from. He knew that he could count on Lloyd to be meticulous in his records, but also picked up on Lloyd's weakness. Lloyd's cautious "trust me" approach with his clients conflicted with the investors who wanted to get to know their advisor better through personal and social events. Peter hired Lloyd and asked Lloyd to assist him in reviewing the resumes of the new young advisors, and that he would appreciate his feedback. They worked together to develop a solid group of individuals with a mix of advisor mindsets. Peter knew how to manage each advisor and learned how to help his advisors adapt to their new environment.

How to Use Profiling Strategies to Solve Team Communication Problems

Advisor mindset profiling is usually an interesting exercise for branch managers and their advisors. As a leader, you know that communication during times of change and crisis is critical. You need to carefully consider the best way to communicate with your advisors. For example, let's assume that you are going to meet with five of your high-producing advisors. Everyone is stressed over the new push the home office is generating about capturing more high net worth clients. The high net worth market is being saturated, some of the advisors say. Several suggest focusing on the new emerging affluent market, which is being neglected. But the manager would need to justify the marketing efforts to this smaller capitalized group of prospects and why he isn't rallying behind the home office request for more of the significant assets.

Three of the advisors are Decision-Makers/Problem-Solvers (OCEAN = M-M-H-M-L), one is a Contrarian (OCEAN = H-M-L-L-H), and one is a Perfectionist/Facts and Details (OCEAN = M-H-M-L-H). The Decision-Maker/Problem-Solver advisor mindset is a team stabilizer. Emotionally, they usually don't react but, instead, look for ways to solve the problem. They are extraverted and use social interactions to throw ideas around—they love the bullpen, which is an exercise in creativity and problem solving where advisors generate as many creative alternatives as possible. This exercise is a freewheeling idea exchange. Both the Contrarian advisor and the Perfectionist/Facts and Details advisor are emotionally reactive. Under stress, you can see the strain on their faces and they *hate* (yes, hate) meetings and social events where everyone seeks to gain an upper hand over the others with deceptive or misleading stories. The meeting starts with a cynical comment from the Contrarian. The Perfectionist/Facts and Details advisor brought in a pile of data and research on the emerging affluent markets to help the discussion. So, this is how an inexperienced manager would observe the following scenario:

Harry, the Contrarian, grumbles quietly about why you called the meeting. He is impressed with Larry's data and research and starts speaking to him about one of the analyses. Maggie, Toby, and Izzy, the Decision-Maker/Problem-Solvers, want you to describe the issues. They ignore the data and Harry and Larry. As you try to direct the meeting, the Decision-Maker/Problem-Solvers get impatient. They comment that if all the advisors approached problems like they did, the office would be much more successful.

Using the OCEAN system, you have anticipated these potential conflicts at the team meeting. You know that the Decision-Maker/Problem-Solvers are impatient to solve the problem and that they will conflict with the Contrarian and be impatient with the Perfectionist/Facts and Details advisor(s). As the majority, they could talk all day while the Contrarian and Perfectionist/Facts and Details advisor, with their usual quiet, introverted approach, listen and *steam*.

You decide to set the goal of the meeting and insist that everyone review and give their opinion of the studies and the statistics, and how they came to their conclusion of whether they should go after the high net worth markets. This task forces them to cooperate. The Contrarian presents a different interpretation of the data, but agrees that Larry's pre-meeting hard work was valuable. Remember, you must manage this meeting with a strong command of the agenda. Keep the group on task and make sure that you go around and solicit each opinion (this approach means that all advisors have to participate). Remember that Problem-Solvers may show irritability, impatience, and decisiveness. They "don't get ulcers; they give ulcers" so whenever you observe this characteristic, *you take the blame* so that the other two advisors don't react emotionally. The Contrarian, if challenged, will be abrasive (any fight is a good fight; they have little tolerance when others don't understand their points) and the Perfectionist will get anxious (they like to please and are prone to self-criticism).

In summary, the goal is productive communication. You have to lead by taking control of the agenda and problem solving, involving everyone, and when you see the sensitivities showing, you take the hit and responsibility. Focus the meeting on the facts and make the team work together to provide *solutions, not* restated problems.

The OCEAN system can be very useful in meeting preparation. It will help you anticipate where things will go off the rails, and how to stay on track.

Combining Moods, Mindsets, and Skills: Managing a Team in Crisis

Each attempt to improve productivity and motivate advisors has a risk-reward contingency. The rewards are translated to the bottom line and improved advisor and staff morale. What motivates advisors? Obviously, there is a strong developmental aspect as rookie advisors and 20-year veterans have a generation gap and different motivations beyond *producing!* The common motivation is to produce, to succeed. Many advisors are afraid to fail! A higher order motivation (and one that is often missed in the workplace) is to have a happy, healthy life. How do you provide an environment to succeed? Success has to be defined by the bottom line, but there are other markers. What about attempting to reduce the attrition rate of your new advisors by helping them with their marketing strategies, so that 25 or 30 percent of them achieve the quotas (e.g., $10 million under management in year one and $50 million in year four)?

For every action, there is an equal and opposite reaction. Consider the many attempts over the years to help sales staff increase their energy and focus. Classics like *Think and Grow Rich,* by Napoleon Hill; *The World's Greatest Salesman,* by Og Mandino; *The Strangest Secret,* by Earl Nightingale; *The Power of Positive Thinking,* by Norman Vincent Peale; and the well-read industry books like *Top Gun Sales,* by Steve Kimball, and *How to Attract and Retain the Affluent Client,* by Stephen Gresham all help to motivate. Some embrace the ideas and some don't. Think about any new sales or marketing system or approach, including our Bullish Thinking, and it is highly probable that some of your advisors will react negatively, for example, "This approach is so stupid; just let me do my job; we don't need all of that mumbo jumbo." Would you like to predict which advisors will be negative to changes or to new ideas? If you want one of your naysayer advisors to read this section, she will learn how to state her concerns in a way that you and her colleagues can *hear* the concerns.

Let's say you are introducing a new approach to your advisors. You are going to recommend that several advisors from one team merge with the other to form one large wealth management team, and expect to get the top producers (team leaders) to act with synergy. As an aside, think of the task that managers and coaches have when they take all-star players and combine them into an Olympic team to "go for the gold!" They want to take these highly skilled and talented players who are stars on their own team and mold them into a new team concept, a team that can win on the world stage. You require various levels of analysis, including whether they can stick to a game plan when unexpected changes occur. You have to be brutally honest in your evaluation of skills ("Check your reputation at the door. What have you done lately?"). "What is your attitude about the team and about succeeding? Will you accept a role? Will you pull your weight or expect others to carry your bags?"

Let's say a crisis strikes your team of advisors. A competitor firm is raiding your branch office of top producers, offering them hefty bonuses to leave. One producer accepted the offer. While the others are remaining loyal, they resent that a fair number of accounts are transferring over as well, and are wondering why the manager did nothing to prevent it. They should try to understand that you, their manager, are fair, forceful, and fearless when dealing with the issue. You have to express confidence that, while not perfect, you will make decisions and discipline anyone on the team, when needed. Start by taking the temperature in the room. ("When giving a speech, know your audience.") When managing a crisis, know the mood of your constituents. Stressful events typically result in moods of anger (resentment and frustration), anxiety (fear, worry), and on occasion, guilt (self-criticism, if only . . .). What is the prevailing mood of the group? Use your Bullish Thinking skills to identify the moods and underlying thinking (hopeless, helpless, threatened). Listen and learn. You don't want to offer a premature reassurance; listen instead to what the advisors are saying. Are they grumbling and resentful? Are they frustrated with their lack of control or their perception of a lack of control on your part?

Most stressors or reasons for failure in the industry can be attributed to difficult challenges given the intensely competitive market for clients, raiding and recruiting of top producers, mergers and buyouts of brokerage firms by banks, insurance companies, market fluctuations, and macroeconomic factors such as interest rates, inflation, and so on. There are internal factors, including the advisors' knowledge of new products and their ability to sell to their clients' needs. More troubling reasons for failure involve poor focus and effort of the team. You want to know what your advisors are saying to explain their poor productivity. Listen. Once you understand the mood of the group and how they are explaining their successes and failures, you are on to the next step.

"There Is a Major Crisis and I Need Help"

Don was an outstanding Decision-Maker/Problem-Solver advisor (OCEAN = M-M-H-H-L). A 25-year veteran, he built a million-dollar book and was known by all of his colleagues as a solid performer. Most people in the office were impressed by Don's forceful, strong-willed, independent streak. He was truly a self-starter. He enjoyed building his referral business through creative marketing techniques, and he was always willing to help rookies with their approach or their confidence. He enjoyed being part of a dedicated team and contributed to the client-centric practice.

Melanie was a young and highly ambitious advisor. She was full of life and fit the Catalyst type of advisor (H-M-H-M-M). Melanie was very excited to be in the group. She really liked the branch manager, Harold, whom she viewed as a kindly, intelligent, and wise manager. Melanie started producing and capturing assets of young entrepreneurs into her book through contacts that she made through the social scene of Upper Manhattan. Melanie actually lived modestly on the Lower East Side.

Harold, an experienced leader with more than 15 years in the business, managed the office with his usual competent Calm and Collected leadership style (OCEAN = M-H-M-H-L). He preferred to manage the day-to-day activities of the office by walking around. He truly was a compassionate and cooperative person. He cared for his staff and wanted them all to succeed. He was an excellent mentor and coach.

Harold learned through a discreet office assistant that Melanie and Don were having an affair. Both were married, Don for more than 15 years and Melanie for more than five years. The problem was that the relationship was clearly hurting the office environment. Don was always critical of others and he could be mean-spirited at times. But lately, he was impatient and intimidating to staff. Everyone had noticed and Harold realized that he may have been the last to realize that he had an emotional bombshell in his office waiting to explode.

In retrospect, Harold realized that Melanie had stopped seeking advice from him. At first, she was always hanging around his office near the end of the day looking for tips and encouragement. Don was always prickly when things weren't going his way. Some of the staff viewed Don as arrogant, but no one doubted his skills and achievements. Don often smoothed over his blaming and criticizing others with a sincere apology (and flowers or cigars).

Melanie and Harold had a meeting first thing the next morning. She was clearly upset and was worried that her productivity might suffer unless she received more support from staff. Harold liked Melanie, but started to see aspects of her personality that irritated him. She was always looking to socialize (her High Openness) and he wondered if she was completing her paperwork (her Moderate Conscientiousness versus Harold's High score). She used her charms by flirting and he realized that she might be trying to manipulate him. He disliked her questioning of him about his allocation of staff time. (Harold's High Agreeableness score reflects his preference for others to agree with him). She hinted that she needed more help, but he insisted that she hadn't earned it. She needed to spend more time on her own paperwork! (That's Harold's pet peeve with Melanie.)

As the meeting progressed, Melanie's normal composure started to show some cracks. She was teary and "couldn't understand why Harold had turned on me." Harold was determined (jaw firmly set) that Melanie had to look after her own business. No one else could do it for her.

Put Yourself in Harold's Shoes

If you are in Harold's shoes, you can use the OCEAN system to decipher the minor irritants. Under stress, Melanie is exhibiting some of the most vulnerable aspects of her personality. (She is more emotionally labile than Don or Harold.) Harold could hear it in her thinking (good thing that he had taken that course on active listening!). He is also stressed because his smooth-running office is tense (High Conscientiousness, High Agreeableness). He believed that hard work was the answer, but Melanie kept complaining and asking for more support. The OCEAN system predicts that Don and Melanie are totally aligned on the Extraversion dimension while Harold is Moderate. Both Don and Harold are Agreeable; they always got along *when they agreed*. In this conflict, they are used to being unemotional under stress, but Don views Harold as withholding support from Melanie, while Harold believes that Melanie has to earn the support that she receives. Melanie isn't about to be agreeable when she isn't getting what she wants so she can light a fire under Don.

The meeting ended and Harold felt relieved. He had weathered the emotional storm. Now, if everyone just got back to work, things would slowly get back to normal. Harold didn't see the raging steamroller bearing down on him. After lunch, Don stormed into Harold's office, slammed the door, and started yelling at his friend. Why can't Melanie get more support? She was doing her job; the business depended on sales, not paperwork. If Melanie was going to be chained to her desk, how was she going to make the contacts she needed to grow her business?

This is a classic conflict between a Highly Extraverted Advisor and a High Conscientious Manager. This is the only conflict in their personality structures. And what was Harold doing to support people? He was making a pile of money, living off the hard-working efforts of advisors like himself (and Melanie). Don rarely seemed to get upset. He was usually a rock. And Harold listened. He couldn't understand why Don was so upset. It was so unlike him.

As a reader, what are your thoughts at this point about this scenario?

Harold's Bullish Thinking Coaching Session: Help Is on the Way

Harold decided he needed a coaching session, he wanted to learn Bullish Thinking strategies, and used the system to review his observations:

1. Bullish and Bearish thinking and how to deal the Bear
2. The personality dimensions (OCEAN = Openness, Conscientiousness, Extraversion, Agreeableness, Emotional Instability) that make up his *leadership style* and the *advisor mindsets* of Don and Melanie
3. The Stress Situation that couldn't be ignored

Harold was, as expected, very conscientious in his homework. He had listened carefully and didn't try to solve the problem without understanding it. He was very puzzled about what to do. But, his coach challenged him on his report that he ". . . *didn't try to solve the problem without understanding it.*" The coach pointed out that Harold hadn't really tried to understand where Don and Melanie were coming from. He tried to impose his solution ("be more conscientious") on Melanie. In fact, he had fallen into a trap with Melanie by imposing his style of coping (work harder; get your paperwork done!) on Melanie. Harold acknowledged this error and realized that he had potentially closed a door on his communication with her. Nevertheless, what was going on with both advisors? Harold was quite sure that they were having an affair, but he wanted to stay out of their private business. On the other hand, this tension had invaded the entire office. Some staff expected Harold to discipline Don for his shoddy treatment of them and Harold knew that Don's demanding, impatient, and critical behavior had to be toned down. But Don was such a good producer!

Bullish Thinking Solutions

Harold had to address Don's anger. He knew that it was unlike Don to be so angry. He used the Bullish Thinking system to question himself. Anger almost always develops when the advisor is frustrated (blocked from a desired goal) or resentful (sensing a perceived injustice). Harold decided to listen to Don very carefully.

Don started the meeting by saying that he was disappointed in Harold. He thought that his friend would understand that Melanie's requests were reasonable. Harold didn't take the bait. He told Don that he needed to understand what was at the base of Don's anger. He persisted by listening to Don rationalize about business. He then asked Don the following question: "Don, I still don't understand what would lead you to be so involved in my decision making. I work hard to see how my decisions affect the running of the office. What has changed in the last few months? I need to know what's driving your frustration with me and the resentment that you seem to be feeling." He waited. Don sat frozen. As if sensing that Harold already knew, Don acknowledged his relationship with Melanie. Harold accepted the admission and without focusing on it, asked Don to help calm the office and get back to work. Don seemed relieved. There was no fight left.

Harold had used his Bullish Thinking management skills to defuse the anger and refocus the discussion on what he expected for the business. This was a successful solution to a potentially explosive situation.

11

The Psychology of the Superstar

MANAGING EGOS AND ATTITUDES WHILE PRESERVING THE BOTTOM LINE

H ow do you manage your superstars? Make a list of the advisors on whom you depend for the branch to be successful. Consider these individuals and pay attention to their attitude and behavior; *their private, behind-closed-doors* attitude and behavior. What actions have you taken to make life easier for your top producers? Have you been tempted to cross the line, feeling intimidated by their aggressive or demanding approach to business? Do you have a concern about how to manage these big producers?

While most top producers are solid citizens who earn (and deserve) the rewards of the business, some develop an attitude of superiority. The combination of attitude and behavior is apparent to all; the vulnerability of the character is much less obvious. Recall the TV show *Boston Legal* character Denny Crane (brilliantly acted by William Shatner). Denny breaks most, if not all, of the rules and gets away with murder. Most of his partners fear him and others cover for him. The audience gets inside his head and sees his vulnerability.

In the psychology literature, the people with narcissism are those with a serious personality flaw or insecurity that results in a lack of empathy, grandiose fantasies, excessive need for approval, rage, social isolation, and depression. Dr. Robert Millman referred to the attitude and behavior of some professional athletes as a result of acquired narcissism. His central idea was that the system, particularly the star system, by its very nature teaches the young, impressionable athlete to develop an attitude of superiority.

Fame, money, and the personal power of celebrity dramatically change how some stars perceive others. In a few words, they lose sight of the people and see human objects not unlike the furniture. The most surprising characteristic is the rage. These individuals are constantly on guard and may blow up with very little provocation. Their reaction, callous and explosive, catches others off guard, particularly those people in their employ or entourage (when they realize that they, too, are part of the furniture). As a manager, you want to anticipate some of these reactions and, most definitely, you want to know how to act if the star erupts. As you know, the entire office is watching and judging how you respond.

But first, how do you deal with their grandiosity and their arrogance in the office? How do you work with those advisors whose successes have led them to conclude that company policies and compliance rules don't apply to them?

It's a fine line that you, as a manager, must walk with the superstar. You can't let one individual take advantage of everyone and everything at the firm, but on the other hand, you must be careful not to disenfranchise a skilled advisor who is adding a significant amount to your branch's bottom line. You've probably had considerable experience with superstars who insist on writing their own ticket in the office and making life for you a sometimes less-than-easy chore. We understand your dilemma and attempt in this chapter to offer some solutions.

Managing the Superstar Advisor

There are thousands of high achievers working on Wall Street, of course, and not all of them are prima donnas; most all of them, however, require and expect special treatment.

So, it's important to understand what does and does not motivate them, as well as how to work with them on a daily basis. Getting inside the heads of your superachievers is done by first understanding their psychology. You already know that their mindset is goal-oriented and achievement-based. Their motivation is clear. They want to produce the best results possible for their clients and themselves, elevating themselves to the stratosphere of advising that only a few achieve. As one superstar stated, "Doc, I always think of my worth to the client. I make it personal. I can get the job done; help them get to their life's financial goals. I deserve every cent that I earn." What manager would debate with this confidence? Problems occur when things don't work the way you (or they) expect.

It is very hard for a manager to see the vulnerability of a person who acts as though he is the best ("Never failed; never will"). It's even curious that managers may encourage their advisors to be the best, only to suffer from their behavior when they believe their own personal public relations spin.

You might tend to get upset or angry at their displays of superiority, but it's best to first understand, then communicate and work *with* their behaviors and attitudes (because you will never change them) for the benefit of everyone in the office. When it comes time to communicate with them about their behaviors, you must be specific. You could say things like:

> "I've watched you shoot from the hip in our weekly sales meetings. You hurt people's feelings and make enemies, but don't seem to notice."

> "It appears to me that you have trouble accepting criticism. When I asked you about your referral campaign last week, you got up and left the room."

> "It seems as if you enjoy insulting your colleagues, but you don't know how bad that makes people feel."

> "Your assistant quit because you yelled at her too often."

> "I left six messages on your voicemail while I was at a regional meeting and you never got back to me."

Expect that the superstar advisor may get defensive, denying that there is any problem and resenting your intrusion. It is your responsibility not to react with contempt, or cynical or condescending comments. Instead, simply repeat the observation. Pretend that you have a video camera strapped to your shoulder and describe what is on the tape. Example:

You: "I saw you yelling at your assistant to get off her butt and get you a coffee."

Advisor: "I wasn't yelling. She was instant-messaging with her friend."

You:	"You said to your assistant, "Get off your butt and get me a coffee."
Advisor:	"Aw, don't give me that political correctness crap."
You:	"I want you to treat all of our staff in a respectful way."

The first thing you must acknowledge is that you cannot dominate or control this type of individual because such a superior attitude usually trumps everything—anything that you might do, suggest, or demand will result in a defensive reaction. When an advisor achieves, she develops a personal view of what it takes to be successful. Communication with clients and a precise insight about how to blend various products into a solid portfolio usually results in long-term success for most advisors. What distinguishes superstars in the industry is that they are always looking for marketplace opportunities; it almost becomes like a radar system for them and it's in force 24 hours a day. They are always looking for resources to help them develop their business in the most effective ways. Superstars usually produce gross annual production in excess of $1 million, and it can come in the form of commissions or fees. Fee-based superstars will boast of assets under management starting at $200 million and upward. The megaproducers, though they are much smaller in number, may hold $1 billion in assets.

As a manager dealing with superstars, you will want to check out two different attitudes and behaviors. In the first case, we describe a well-adjusted and stable superstar. In the second example, we describe the more dangerous type.

The Everyday Superstar

The stable and secure superstars understand the business as well as you do. They appreciate your job and how you function to provide the necessary support. They are truly grateful for your efforts and the efforts of the staff. They are able to see the big picture, know their role, and remain aware of the relatively fleeting nature of their success and their career. In this regard, they also recognize how the pioneers of the industry created a legacy from which they are the beneficiary. Again, they are grateful knowing their place in the firm's history.

The stable and secure superstars are usually ahead of the public relations aspects of the business. *They do what is right even when no one is watching.* They stand up for any injustice in the system as a matter of principle.

Finally, on a personal basis, they go back to their roots (the old neighborhood and school friends) and they prefer fitting in ("I appreciate the simple aspects of life") rather than standing out ("Look at what a success I am"). They will extend help to others in need despite their personal time constraints (again, often when no one is watching).

The Vulnerable Superstar

Some highly successful advisors are driven to achieve, and their achievements will mask significant personal vulnerabilities. For now, consider the following aspects of vulnerable superstar advisors. These individuals typically hide key aspects of their background. There are gaps in relationships. They may be vague about where they came from, whom their important relationships are with, and what their feelings are. They present themselves as invincible, acting a role, or like a chameleon trying to blend into the background.

In bad times, their tendency is to blame others. They may even look for *your* head to roll. Their expectations move away from reality, particularly with requests for "cover-ups and damage control." In fact, they may need public relations staff to be on call to handle their "errors in judgment or action." In a crisis, they are smooth, blaming the client, blaming the staff, pointing arrows at everyone but themselves in an assertive or even aggressive style. Most social courtesies are ignored. They may walk right by a subordinate who offers greetings.

They may have an entourage and encourage and support them despite their own bad judgments and behavior. The function of the entourage is to support the vulnerable superstar, who doesn't want to be alone. These superstars love recognition and may look for special treatment no matter what the activity (the front-of-the-line attitude).

In summary, the following list of behaviors and attitudes are worthy of note:

1. Your time is not important. These superstars can always run late with the excuse that their life is so busy.
2. Commitments are optional. They may say "yes" with no concern about not showing up.

3. They expect special favors, and if the favors are not *special* (that is, if others get the same thing), they will be put off.
4. They need a damage control strategy. The question is *when* the damage control is needed, not *if.*
5. They have enormous resentment when thwarted.
6. Others handle the so-called dirty work with their close intimate relationships. Assistants are asked to do outrageous favors, such as telling an intimate that a relationship is over.
7. If recognized or honored, they may make nasty comments about the honoring group if they are not treated in a way that meets their expectation (for example, "Yeah, all they gave me was a stupid plaque and a cheap watch.").
8. They stay far away from other superstars on a day-to-day basis unless there is a business reason to be together.

How to Distinguish Snakes from Peacocks?

There are two primary vulnerable superstar advisors. The more dangerous is the psychopathic advisor and the less dangerous is the narcissistic advisor. We have our tongues firmly planted in our cheeks when we use anthropomorphic characterizations of real people. With apologies to the snakes, these individuals have been labeled "snakes in suits" by Professor Robert Hare, the world's leading authority on the dangerous minds of psychopaths in the business world.* You will occasionally come across this personality type in your office, so you need to be fully prepared to understand the behaviors and emotions of all individuals in your office, even the psychopaths in suits.

Now, we are not saying that a high percentage of the superstars in our industry are disturbed personalities like psychopaths or narcissistic characters. The advisors with these characteristics are attracted to environments where they can work independently with little supervision and have the potential to make considerable amounts of money. Approximately 3 percent of the industry harbors the dark side of these advisors, but even this small percentage is enough to get your attention. According to Professor Robert Hare, "Wherever you find money, prestige, and power, you will find them." (More in Chapter 12.)

---

*Paul Babiak and Robert D. Hare, *Snakes in Suits: When Psychopaths Go to Work* (New York: HarperCollins, 2006).

They are truly dangerous to clients, to the organization, and to *you!* They lack care and empathy for others, although with time (and sadly, with therapy), they learn to fake it. They are motivated to be the best and they don't mind paying the fees to the organization that gives them the credibility they need. Snakes usually charm managers and are very successful running up the ladder. They treat others poorly because, bluntly, they don't care. Watch for the following:

- Little or no concern for the feelings of others and a complete disregard for any sense of social obligation
- Dominance and control
- Egocentric, and lack insight of any sense of responsibility or consequence
- Callous, manipulative, and incapable or uninterested in forming lasting relationships
- Only act unless they determine it can be beneficial to them
- Poor impulse control and a low tolerance for frustration and aggression
- Their manipulative skills are valued for providing audacious leadership

Peacocks, on the other hand, may fit any of our classic advisor types (for example, Problem-Solver, Catalyst, Facts and Details, and so forth). They can be distinguished by their displays (hence, the peacock reference). These individuals have a powerful persona. They are dressed for success and know how to connect when they are making the sale. They present themselves to their clients in highly effective, competent ways. And they produce. Their clients are happy to make referrals. ("You should use Gary Austin. He's the best.") As a manager, you will have few complaints about their core business functions, acquiring new clients, and serving their needs. What you will observe is that "everything revolves around Gary." He is totally goal oriented and has very little care for anyone who doesn't do his bidding. Gary is a narcissistic character, and it is only in hard times that you will see the snarl and underlying rage.

Get in the way of his goals and the self-serving attitude may overwhelm you. ("You don't understand my business. It's my right to do business my way. Don't tell me how to run my practice.") The two most unpleasant areas of management deal with an individual's attitudes that include arrogance and a sense of entitlement. We have found that the most dangerous, high-achieving advisors follow a typical behavior pattern. They are absolutely certain that they know more than you do! They rarely challenge an issue except those that may affect their way of doing business. The least amount of supervision is the most desirable. When investments go wrong, they know who the scapegoat is—they have already picked out the weakest and the most vulnerable advisor, staff member, or manager to be the fall guy.

Narcissists and Psychopaths: The Danger Zone of Management

The first rule of managing these difficult characters is to make sure that you don't take their actions and attitudes personally. They will blame you first (we call this being thrown under the bus). Both of these characters are master manipulators who can be on the attack in an instant. You must focus on their behavior and attitude and not on your feelings. For example, John wanted to reprimand Ray for an act that he considered unprofessional. He started the conversation softly, saying that he was hurt when he learned of Ray's actions. Ray, who already viewed himself as superior to John despite John's 25 years of management experience, countered that he was sorry John was hurt, but that the business had to get done and he (Ray) was the only person able to do it!

As you will see, that exchange put John in the weak position and moved him away from Ray's actions. While narcissistic characteristics can be traced to a personal, yet vulnerable, belief in his superiority, the psychopathic attitude has no doubt. He *knows* that he is superior. In either case, you, as a manager, will never break through that superior attitude. It is next to impossible. Such people are so protective of their own feelings and interests that they will do everything to not be—or feel—vulnerable.

In their book, *The New Why Teams Don't Work: What Goes Wrong and How to Make it Right,* by Harvey Robbins and Michael Finley, they state in Chapter 11, "Dealing with Difficult People," ". . . Some [individuals] are not necessarily bad people—though some (the dark angels) are truly bad. All require action on the team's part—either distancing, discipline, or banishment." Here are a few examples the authors cited:

- The addict, who acts crazy because of some personal problem
- The ogre, who acts out of antisocial rage (in our view, the narcissistic advisor, aka the peacock)
- The crook, who thinks nothing of crossing ethical lines (aka the snake)
- The fanatic, who puts achieving his objectives above all rules and policies (aka the true believer, the end justifies the means)

You say you want to fire these individuals because it's not worth putting up with their crap? Terminating any sort of big producer is confrontational, unpleasant, and potentially litigious. A big producer with an addiction may collapse from the weight of his own problems. A big producer with a narcissistic personality, driven by some dark rage, may still be an exceptional producer. A big producer who is unethical or overzealous may be doing everything he sees his models doing in the industry. So, explaining the Ten Commandments, or the Golden Rule, or any other ideal standard of living won't change them.* You have to confront his behavior and understand what makes him tick. You have to manage such people, and part of management involves containment.

Remember, we know these individuals are the most dangerous and are very much in the minority. Let's turn our attention now to the everyday superstar.

Managing the Everyday Superstar Advisor

The high achiever has a turbocharged internal engine. This individual runs hotter, faster, and harder than most advisors. Trying to slow her down won't work; her stress factor may actually be lower when the action is high. High achievers are often included in the workaholic personality type, or one who is addicted to work. Sometimes misunderstood, the word *workaholic* does not always imply that an individual actually enjoys her work, but rather simply feels compelled to do it. So, what to do?

---

*Harvey Robbins and Michael Finley, *The* New *Why Teams Don't Work*, Chapter 11.

Create the Environment

Since you already know you can't dominate or control superachievers, what you must do is create or provide an environment that allows for a healthy workplace for them. You need to figuratively check the water in the fishbowl and make sure that the water the fish are swimming in is fresh, and there are no dangerous objects or pollutants in it. You create an atmosphere where the fish can thrive. You have to identify and cull the predators that will consume the other fish in the bowl and contain the fish that behave like whales from consuming all the resources of the others.

Typically managers tend to stay out of their advisors' personal lives. In the case of the superstar, however, while you may not want to get personally involved in her life, meddle, or ask too many questions about how it may be affecting her behavior on the job, it is important to at least understand what she does after hours. You have to understand her personal life to know what motivates her and where the dangers lurk.

If there is a problem with time management at home, or the advisor does not have enough relaxation time because of having to deal with household demands or spousal duties, why not try to help by incentivizing them in creative ways. For example, instead of offering advisors event tickets as an incentive, one manager we know developed a Yellow Pages type of list of services. He included seven meals cooked by a chef, one week of a driver, and a pick-up and delivery of dry cleaning. This was unusual, of course, but much more oriented toward something that would help his advisor in his personal life, which, in turn, may benefit her work experience.

We look at the amount of time, effort, and energy that goes into the superstar advisor's public self—this is the persona that is focused on outcomes or goals. Her work efforts must have an appropriate focus and strategy from you, as the manager. To manage a superstar takes a commitment, time, and energy. What tends to happen in the life of the everyday superstar advisor is that the work-and-play balance point of her life gets knocked out of place and something has to give. So, classically, what high achievers recognize when speaking to other high achievers is that they have to consume tremendous amounts of time and energy to maintain their success. In general, the average advisor doesn't realize how much time the superstar advisor has to put into achieving her goals.

What happens to her work-home life balance? Superstars must have the appropriate balance to sustain their efforts over the long run. That means playing hard as well as working hard. Being oriented toward time away, trips, adventure. What often happens is that the superstars get lost in the routine, or day-to-day time, and forget to reconnect with family and friends. Superstar athletes, for example, have time to restore this balance because they have an off-season, but on Wall Street, where there is no off-season, the superstar advisors get so tied to their jobs, they wind up burning out as their days without a break turn into months and then into years.

If they are trying to have it all, then it requires putting an intense effort into their personal life too, but that robs them of actual downtime, as we mentioned earlier. The management battle is how to assure that these high achievers get quiet time so they can recoup, recover, *and have relationships that are not just based on achievement.* Everything is done with the highest intensive achievement-oriented mindset; that is, goals, outcomes, education, and skills. Everything becomes a demand for perfectionism; there is no room or tolerance for the problems or the hassles; there is no buffer. The super-achiever is already maxed out, so when things go wrong in her life, the buffer is not there.

Right and Wrong Ways to Deal with Entitlement and Arrogance

The tendency for someone who feels entitled is to bring that person down to size. The typical way is to confront him and try to take something away. It's a natural reaction. In your own mind, you want to punish him; it's a natural inclination. But attempts to punish usually lead to passive-aggressive behavior on your part—the bull comes charging into the room and you either step out of the way or you forget to do something important for him. You can be unaware that you are being passive-aggressive, so look carefully at any thoughts on your part to hurt the superstar advisor. Try, instead, to find out more about his interest and motivation outside of work. Ask penetrating questions such as, "What is meaningful in your life?" and "What really matters to you?" and help the superstar advisor do good work outside of work! Superstars most often will respond to a challenge, and since he believes what the general outcome will be, it is a good idea to try to find intermediate outcomes that he can participate in with others so they, too, can share their knowledge.

You may have to look for and give them alternative experiences. The best ones are assignments where you can get them to relate to kids or charities that might be consistent with their background (social areas that are of interest, like the Big Brother program, and so forth). These superstars may be much more humble relating to people in need. After all, it's better for everyone to join together for a noble cause than to punish arrogant and entitled behavior just to get even or to have a battle over control.

A Coach's Perspective on High Achievers

My (Dr. Cass) executive coaching practice is filled with top advisors who, through their weekly meetings with me, seek to hone their sales skills and become more disciplined in managing their emotional stability. Every once in a while, however, I receive an alarming phone call from a branch manager who has reached his limit in tolerating the antics of a specific top-performing advisor at that location. These branch managers often remark that they don't have the time, patience, or rapport with these top dogs to set their inappropriate or eccentric behaviors into proper alignment with the rest of the firm's culture.

Some of the most successful advisors and teams within firms are, as you know, by nature, quite demanding. These individuals, or groups, are quirky and stand out in both good and bad ways. Branch managers usually don't want to take a stance that's too strong and paternalistic with one of their top producers, as they fear the advisor will react immaturely, aggressively, or irrationally. So once a branch manager reaches his breaking point with a particular employee, rather than trade the advisor in for a more polite and obedient one, he drops the errant individual on my doorstep and asks me to get him in tune.

One particular situation comes to mind concerning a branch manager and his financial advisor, whom I'll refer to as Charlie.* The branch manager's gripe was simple. Charlie led one of the most successful teams at his firm, but his administrative assistant, partner, and management team were forced to walk on eggshells when he became overwhelmed with stress. He had an explosive temper, was

---

*Alden Cass, "How to Tame the Top Advisors," *On Wall Street* magazine, October 2006, with permission.

demanding, and became intolerant of people who couldn't keep up with his pace. One could easily hear his loud voice down the hall, especially when he was having a bad day.

Charlie had learned early on that he could get what he wanted through intimidation and loud barking. At his current firm, no one had talked to him about his problematic behavior because he was making a lot of money for them; but when his business partner pulled aside the branch manager and talked about leaving because of the relationship he had with Charlie, the branch manager had to consider taking action. This came to a head shortly afterward when Charlie's administrative assistant handed in her two-week notice. Charlie's branch manager called me that same day in a state of frustration.

Many branch managers point out that there are positive and negative traits uniformly associated with top producers. I outline the good and the bad news in the following, as well as a few ways to deal with your top dogs.

The Good News

Top producers are ambitious, disciplined, tenacious, decisive, strong-willed, independent, and goal-oriented. They take calculated risks, lead by example, and have tunnel vision when it comes to meeting the company's bottom line. These are the attributes that make them so successful and drive them to reach higher plateaus.

The Not-So-Good News

Despite these traits, there are some trade-offs. Branch managers have described their warriors as being too aggressive, offensive, stubborn, quick to anger, impatient, demanding, territorial, unaware of peoples' emotions, critical, and arrogant. Whether these advisors are complaining about not having enough money allocated to their discretionary spending accounts or about a lack of administrative support, they tend to blame their management teams and demand immediate change.

Shaping Your Top Advisors

If you're a branch manager and oversee one or more of these producers, you're probably seeking a way to have your cake and eat it, too. The reality is that you can never change someone's personality.

But you *can* teach them to understand how it affects others. Making these advisors aware of their deficits, however, must be done delicately. Here are three suggestions:

1. Have a meeting. I've suggested that branch managers set up monthly sit-downs in their offices or over meals with these advisors to maintain a dialogue about the positive aspects of their work. Keep the conversation light and unemotional. Encourage these meetings by stating that you like to have these sit-downs with only the most important advisors.
2. Disarm them with praise. By initially discussing positive behaviors, you'll prime them, allowing you to introduce constructive feedback about their more destructive behaviors. In essence, you'll be pointing out how impressed you are with their growth and production. You may even say that you'd like them to take on more of a leadership role within the firm and mentor someone. Inform them that they'll be in a position of serving as a model for others.
3. Strike while the iron is hot. The key to success is to bring up individuals' offenses as soon as they occur. Advisors will become defensive if you slam them with everything all at once. It's also essential that you explain your disappointment in their behavior and detail how it affects others.

Remember, the best way to manage your superstars is to be in constant communication with them. Their behavior is mostly aimed at keeping people away from them, so be proactive and keep them talking. You'll notice your office will be less volatile as a result. Now you'll have time to deal with the really important issues on your desk!

CHAPTER

12

Think Like a Shrink: You Are Not Alone

FIGHTING STIGMA IN THE WORKPLACE

Social stigma is defined as "severe social disapproval of personal characteristics or beliefs that are against cultural norms." Social stigma often leads to marginalization; that is, pushing someone or something to the edge to reduce any significance or meaning. Examples of existing or historic social stigmas can be physical or mental disabilities and disorders, as well as illegitimacy, homosexuality, or affiliation with a specific nationality, religion, or ethnicity, such as being a Jew, an Italian, or a Gypsy. Criminality, likewise, carries a strong social stigma.*

Mental health and illness and addiction remain a mystery to most people despite the fact that everyone's family knows of someone suffering from these conditions. According to the Canadian Mental Health Association, "Mental illness doesn't discriminate, but people with mental illness may face discrimination due to stigma, a form of negative stereotyping. . . . Embarrassment about having depression, for example, often keeps people from seeking treatment for a very treatable illness."

As a manager, you can lead the way in fighting stigma. Do simple things such as supporting stress management seminars and using

---

*Edward E. Jones, *Social Stigma: The Psychology of Marked Relationships* (New York: W.H. Freeman and Co., 1984).

your active listening skills with advisors. Your acceptance of mental illness and addiction problems as being similar to other chronic diseases (diabetes, asthma, heart disease) will go a long way to building a workplace where recovery and coping is encouraged.

Interestingly, professional athletes are familiar with managerial attitudes toward injury and illness. Athletes are a class of workers who are exposed to high-performance expectations and significant criticism and judgments if they don't perform up to the expected outcomes or standards. They have short careers and often won't last (that is, they'll be fired) if they falter. If an athlete is injured (or ill), they have to rehab on the sidelines and may be judged to be a distraction to the team if they don't stay out of the way. They are sidelined, and if the workplace conditions are wrong, they may have a serious sense of exclusion and guilt for letting the team down. These attitudes emerge despite the fact that these athletes are most often injured in the service of the team, trying to win and perform at the highest level.

So how does your advisor feel if she is sidelined? This individual may not have a broken bone or torn ligament, but may have been injured or hurt in an attempt to manage stress and perform for you and the firm. Consider ways to include the mentally ill or addicted advisor in your group. Stay connected to that individual and offer support and realistic goals on her return. Ease her back and follow up by asking for feedback. Ask such questions as, "How was the day for you? Let me know how you are doing. What's the next step that we need to take?" Remember that your advisor's problems or stressors may not stem just from work, but also from strife at home or elsewhere in her personal life. As a manager, you need to be proactive in having private conversations with any advisor whose performance or behavior has changed in an abrupt or negative way.

What You Don't Know Could Hurt . . . Well, Everybody

Approximately one in every five of your advisors and administrative staff members will suffer from a mental health or an addiction problem. In our training sessions, we emphasize the likelihood that every person in the room has a family member (or friend) with either a mental health or addiction problem or both. We are rarely surprised when people come forward to discuss their experiences with loved ones suffering from these conditions. The reality is that everyone's family is affected.

One of us (Dr. Cass), after September 11th, volunteered on Wall Street and in other areas of the financial district to work with advisors who witnessed the World Trade Center collapse. He met individually with advisors who sat in adjacent cubicles and worked in close proximity on a daily basis. He found that advisors would open up to him as an external third party (to the branch that offered confidentiality). They all reported experiencing nightmares, flashbacks, survivor guilt, and panic attacks (common symptoms of Post-Traumatic Stress Disorder). They felt anxious and vulnerable. Their colleagues, however, even those sitting at the next desk or cubicle, had no awareness they were suffering so much. The message is . . . your advisors, as close as you think you are to him or her, may be suffering. You want to listen and you want to ask questions in a supportive, sensitive way.

Challenging—and often critical—situations arise in your office where you must consider the likelihood of mental or addiction problems facing your advisors and staff. One of the most common problems is absenteeism, particularly on a Monday. It is unlikely that any length of time will pass in your office without these problems being an issue, although most of the time they will remain under the radar.

In this chapter we move from the everyday life of normal emotions, performance, and conflict into the world of mental health and addiction. You will learn to think like a shrink. In this way, you will be able to recognize problems and get the help you need before it is too late. We already have guided you through our system of understanding Bullish and Bearish Thinking, advisor mindsets and leadership styles, assertiveness, and change management. By this point, you will understand some of our shorthand so that you can quickly understand what is on an advisor's or client's mind and what some of their key characteristics are that you will have to address to assure cooperation and a healthy work relationship. So, let us now show you how to think like a shrink and be a good observer of behaviors, signs, and symptoms of impending problems, and then we'll teach you the steps you need to take to solve the problems.

Think Like a Shrink: Trained Observations

You can't see what you don't understand. As society and science change at an increasingly accelerated pace, it may be challenging to observe the most important changes in world. One of the most pressing problems in the last few years is global warming. Governments around the world are beginning to act. We have an increased sense of urgency that was relatively unknown a decade ago. Now, when you observe warming trends and devastating weather patterns, it is more likely that you will consider global warming as the explanation. You can see the threat to humankind. It unfortunately takes natural disasters and many deaths broadcasted in the news media to really get our attention and focus away from our working lives.

Similarly, in our increasingly electronic world, the exchanges among people have been forever changed. We get comfortable with e-mail, cell phones, and PDAs. Messaging is instant and expectations about a response are judged in minutes, not days. We adapt quickly to these forms of communication and start to realize how disruptions in the flow of information can immobilize our financial systems. A virus attack, identity theft, and chat rooms become part of our daily routines. We can observe these changes at work and recognize the threats to our productivity that coexist with the well-known helpful functions. ("I am more efficient; I can connect with people and global markets that were not possible five years ago.")

We experience a sense of intimacy with celebrities because of the immediacy and intrusiveness of the media. But what about our observations of the people actually in our lives? How have we accelerated our ability to observe changes in loved ones and colleagues? Do you see the changes that threaten your well-being or your family's well-being? Can you detect when significant changes are occurring with your advisors that threaten their well-being and ultimately, their productivity?

The first stage of learning to think like a shrink requires you to make observations of people, their behavior, and the ways in which they like to work. As a skilled manager, you want to get a reading on your advisors as individuals (Who are they? Do they have a support system? What do they like? Where do they vacation and with whom? What are their work habits like?) and then observe how they function as a group or team under routine conditions. For example, Harriet is a 35-year-old married woman with three children. She cares for an elderly mother and loves the arts, she arrives at work every day at 8 A.M. and leaves at 6 P.M.; she is one of the most conscientious advisors whom I have ever met. You get this baseline reading so that you will recognize changes in the team or particular individuals. You want to build up your scanning ability so that you have a Doppler-like radar system (the devices used to predict weather patterns) and a virus scan system built into your brain. You are scanning for changes in the workplace and among your advisors and staff. You are watching for threats, aberrations in behavior that serve as challenges to the productivity of your office.

Start by observing the signs and listen for the symptoms of mental illness or addiction. Signs (behaviors that you can observe) include: irritability, increased emotional reactivity, withdrawal, crying, missing days, arriving late, leaving early, avoiding clients, threatening to quit, and so on. Symptoms (changes that may be described by the advisor) include: sleep disturbance, appetite change, headaches, stress, and so on. When a person experiences a pattern of signs and symptoms indicating that he is breaking down or burning out over a period of time (usually a few weeks), a doctor or psychologist may diagnose a mental illness or disorder. Another possibility is that the advisor is under the stress of marital or family problems or behavioral issues (usually a loss of control as a result of alcohol or drug abuse, gambling, sex, making bad personal investments, or excessive shopping). In any case, you only have to make careful observations and know what to do. You want to be in a position whereby you don't have to worry about whether you did the right thing or not.

Which Drugs May Be Affecting Your Advisors?

We have consulted with some of world's top drug and alcohol rehabilitation centers. During this time, we have become well aware of the most common drugs used (and passed around) by advisors. Here is a list of the most common maladaptive stress relievers or energizers that are often purchased on the black market.

1. *Ritalin and Adderall:* Stimulants prescribed for ADHD that may be abused by workers who require prolonged focus and work hours. These drugs typically have been abused by younger traders and advisors who believe these will help them continue working into the late hours. These drugs are potentially addictive.
2. *Marijuana:* A depressant drug that is used to relax at night by many advisors who have difficulty winding down at the end of a workday.
3. *Xanax, Valium, Klonopin:* These minor tranquilizers or benzodiazapines may be used to sleep or take the edge off for those who experience high levels of anxiety. These drugs are potentially addictive.

4. *Oxycontin, Hydrocodone, Vicodin:* Opiates that are used to reduce pain legally by those who have significant physical injuries. These substances create a brain-numbing sensation for individuals who have anxiety and have a significant addictive potential.

5. *Alcohol:* This drug is a depressant, and has become a cultural norm on the Street as a relaxation option and as a social networking tool. There is a significant amount of binge drinking on Wall Street. Advisors tend to think they are under control until a DWI or DUI, or a domestic violence arrest occurs. Alcohol and cocaine, a street-drug stimulant, have approximately equal addictive potential.

6. *High-energy drinks:* The high caffeine in the popular high-energy drinks combined with alcohol can mask the effects of alcohol, making individuals less aware of how drunk they actually are, and more susceptible to making bad choices. With caffeine keeping you awake, it overrides the signals that you really are inebriated.

Mental illnesses (particularly anxiety and depressive disorders) are on the rise in Western society. Consequently, you can be certain that at some point in your management career you will have to manage an advisor with a mental health problem. Addiction (substance abuse) is not only a reality of management, but drug, alcohol, and other substance abuse is also a reality among advisors. During times of traumatic events such as catastrophe (personal and professional), war, and political unrest, substance abuse becomes a dangerous way of self-coping;* it is also a reality of management.

No one wants to be mentally ill or addicted. The culture of Wall Street appears to turn a blind eye to the abuse of alcohol. While the number of executives requiring inpatient rehabilitation seems to be on the increase, this apparent pattern *is a good thing!* It means greater recognition of the problems. These are brain diseases that often involve self-defeating, powerful habits or behaviors. If change was easy, society wouldn't be faced with billions of dollars of lost

---

*See Appendix B: "Bad Medicine for Wall Street: Alcohol Use and Other Substance Abuse Trends During War and Other Catastrophic Events." Alden Cass et al., Catalyst Strategies Group.

productivity. These losses are the result of mental health and addiction problems that very often seem invisible in the workplace. But they are not really invisible. The trained manager picks up clues and makes observations that lead to helpful interventions.

Job One: Keep Your Eyes and Ears Open

Always listen for your advisor's sense of hopelessness and helplessness. She may make comments like, "I'm not competent at this job. I can't handle the pressure. Nothing works out for me. I'm going to lose everything. No matter what I do, I seem to fail." Being observant and prepared is Job One for a manager because he needs to be alert to the major risk for suicidal behavior. These negative self-*thoughts* can be distinguished from negative *predictions* (which may be correct) about the environment, such as: "The markets are going to crash." "The bottom is going to fall out of the real estate market." "That new offering is overpriced." These judgments can be substantiated with simple questions that will serve to justify the catastrophic predictions ("The Fed is going to raise interest rates and the markets will take a hit.").

The greatest risk for a troubled advisor is suicidal thinking. Advisors are expected to be upbeat, positive, and hopeful about investing and willing to manage the risks at an acceptable level. When they are depressed, anxious, or addicted, it is important to watch for (observe) sudden changes in their mood or behavior. Settling accounts, preparing for the transfer of files, or asking about life insurance or other benefits are classic warning signs of suicidal behavior. Other signs include unexplained prolonged absences or a reduction in verbal communication. Men are more likely than women to complete the act of suicide and tend to use more lethal and aggressive methods. Single men who live alone are also at greater risk. Divorced and separated men are twice as likely to commit suicide as men who are still in a relationship.* Thus, marriage and support systems tend to reduce the likelihood of suicide. Alternatively, a troubled advisor who has been depressed for months and then dramatically improves and is cool, calm, and collected may be at greater risk for suicidal

---

*A. Kposowa, "Marital Status and Suicide in the National Longitudinal Mortality Study," *Journal of Epidemiology and Community Health*, 54 (2000): 254–261.

behavior (usually because he has decided to act on a deep sense of hopelessness).

These typical signs of mental illness or addiction take some careful observation. You have to be attuned to a change in your advisor's thinking, feeling, and behaving. Complicating the matter is denial. Most people suffering from mental illness or addiction deny that there is a problem. ("I'm fine." "Thanks for your concern, but there is nothing to worry about." "There's nothing wrong with me.") Sometimes the denial has an edge—we call it defensiveness—"You should look after your own problems before you ask me about mine." "Leave me alone—I'm fine." "Don't tell me how to live *my* life." Denial is very difficult. We advise managers to say, "I am worried about you, but I'm no expert. This is what I have noticed. You have missed three Monday morning meetings in the past three months. You seem tired and upset. I want you to get help if you need it. I'd like you to meet with someone who has experience in this area because this will help to improve your business." As a manager, it is important to show the advisor how getting help will benefit his or her bottom line. Advisors who don't like to admit to their managers about mental illness or addiction (sadly, because they see it as a weakness) often respond positively to this type of bottom-line perspective.

Blaming others (including the manager) may also serve as a denial or distraction. "How do you expect me to perform with these products?" "No one can hit these numbers." "I don't know what you are talking about." "If you had to work under these conditions or in this market, you'd have trouble sleeping, too." In these instances, emphasize the changes you have observed and ask for the same follow-up. "I have noticed you are more irritable with staff and I know that you are not yourself these days. Yes, your numbers are off your targets and I have looked over the various possible reasons. One of them is that you are under a great deal of stress."

I Learned a Little Too Late

Kalle was an experienced industry veteran who managed 22 advisors and staff in a highly productive midtown office in a large midwestern city. He took great pleasure mentoring staff and helping to celebrate his employees' milestones and successes. He was a warm and caring guy.

A close friend of Kalle (a man whom he had tremendous respect for) asked him to accept his son, Steve, as a trainee. Kalle was pleased to help. Steve joined the office and was well liked by most of the staff. One morning Kalle was confronted by a trusted senior advisor who told him that Steve was a disruptive influence. He was out with a group and started partying hard. He was cynical and made fun of some of the staff and this particular advisor. Kalle was shocked because he had known this young man for years. What was going on?

Kalle invited Steve to his office and confronted Steve. Now it was Steve's turn to be shocked. He denied any problems and wanted to know who was making the accusation. He asked for Kalle's support and asked that the issue stay between them, as he didn't want his dad to hear about the accusations. Kalle decided to drop the matter. Six months later, he and the firm were faced with two harassment charges from staff and several stunning revelations that Steve was an active cocaine and methamphetamine abuser. He had borrowed money from several advisors and some staff. He laughed at the stuffed shirt environment of the office.

The out-of-court settlement was significant. Kalle had been fooled, and looking back, appreciated that he wasn't alone. Such is the nature of addiction. Four years later, Kalle received a letter from Steve. This letter was an amends and Steve thanked Kalle for his support, apologized for his behavior, and asked Kalle to lunch. Steve was in recovery; he had paid back the money he borrowed and offered a seminar to staff and advisors on addiction. Steve had learned; so had Kalle.

This is a positive outcome for a situation that could have ended in disaster. Conflicting stories such as the one that Kalle had received from Steve, and from his advisor, should have been a warning sign that something was amiss—with Steve. This is where your careful observation and good listening skills can literally save a person's life.

A Fatal Lesson

Alan was a superstar producer. He managed more than $500 million of high net worth portfolios and he worked with a few high-profile institutional money managers. But . . . he also liked to trade. Some of his biggest clients love to call and talk stock with him. In the later stages of the growing tech bubble, Alan and his clients made so much money that he would, on occasion, take his favorite clients aboard his private Lear jet and spend a weekend in Hawaii or elsewhere, living the lavish lifestyle. Alan, a family man, started drinking and partying to excess and then took up cocaine for recreation. He was gone more than he was at home with his wife and high-school-age children, and his cocaine habit became regular routine every evening after work. Then, the unthinkable. . . .

On March 10, 2000, the Nasdaq Composite index peaked and the Great Bubble burst! What followed was financial ruin in the trillions of dollars. Alan and his high net worth clients were left virtually penniless because greed stepped in and the common sense of diversification was regarded as a fool's game. Lawsuits began to file in to Alan's office. The firm, a major wirehouse, transferred Alan and made him a branch manager. "Let's just move the problem around," his regional manager said, without giving much thought to any underlying problems that Alan might be experiencing. With his drug addiction and his guilt over losing his best clients' entire fortunes as well as his own, Alan felt he had no one to turn to. Not his wife or family, not his regional manager, and not his friends. He was shamed and downtrodden, unable to face another day. Late one Friday evening, Alan's regional manager went into the branch office to keep an appointment he had made with Alan, to discuss the low advisor morale and low production figures. The door was locked and the office was dark. He turned his key, entered and saw a shadow in the back against the wall opposite Alan's private office. It was Alan, hanging from a beam in the ceiling. The note in his clenched fist said: "I'm sorry. Forgive me."

Alan's regional manager said to his supervisors the following Monday: "If I had just noticed the signs; I had no idea. If I had asked him how he was doing, feeling, but I just assumed he was tired and overworked. Maybe I could have saved him."

WALL STREET'S HARDEST DAY

Without a doubt, it was the hardest day of my long career; 27 years have passed since that day. My job has difficult times. Counseling families after tragedies, ranging from suicide to postpartum homicide, takes an emotional toll. As a dedicated therapist, I have to regroup, reaffirm my basic values, and keep communicating to help improve the public's understanding of the human mind. Somehow, talking about the toughest times helps. Communicating is what humans do best, so when we shut down, we create an island in our minds that completely cuts us off from the world.

I have been a good therapist to many, but have failed others. I wish I could pinpoint *why* the failures occurred. I couldn't help them see that depression twists and distorts your thinking to the point that nothing in life has any meaning; couldn't counter their agony and negativism; couldn't clear that black cloud, even for a second.

This day, however, was the hardest. It was Sunday morning. I was going for a relaxing walk in a nearby wooded area when a young police officer came running up to me. "Dr. Shaw, please come with me." In my business, these words can be chilling. "One of your patients is in trouble," said the officer urgently, "and we think you can help."

Within minutes we were in his car racing, at full alert, to the sub-urban home of my client (in fact, it was a client I hadn't seen in two years), but I remembered him well. Jack was 37 years old, a success-ful broker who had built his business on years of excellent service to his clients. He had experienced a major depressive episode three years earlier, the culmination of long-term stress and unending per-sonal demand. At that time, he had succumbed to the belief that he was finished. The young officer didn't have much information about Jack's condition; he was focused on driving.

The police car was screaming through the city, but I was thinking . . . and thinking. Jack was a driven man; he loved to be in the action and hated losing. In retrospect, I never really understood all of his analogies to winning and losing. I spend part of my life as a sports psychologist, so I know about competition. Jack kept score. However Jack's competition was with himself. He had certain expectations for his performance ("I've read lots of motivational books"). He set standards ("Gotta have a goal, doc"), and was unrelenting in his self-hate if he failed to achieve them. It simply didn't matter to Jack if the market was going up or down ("There is always opportunity . . . always"). Jack also was a brutal self-critic. He was charitable with oth-ers, but if he let himself down he couldn't look in the mirror. Providing for his family was very important to him. He loved his wife. He loved his kids. But he also had an exaggerated inner drive to achieve, to succeed. He hated having to depend on anyone; he called the feel-ing "going cap in hand, like a schoolboy." I knew this reaction as a sense of dependency and a fear of not measuring up; a fear that if he didn't look after himself, no one else would.

(Continued)

Cognitive therapy is designed to attack many of these self-defeating thinking styles. In therapy, clients learn how to perform at high levels without tipping their minds into the abyss of helplessness and hopelessness that inevitably seems to follow from severe self-criticism. At his worst, Jack used to say of himself, "Buddy, you are one horse-ball of a broker." He wouldn't accept his defeats at first ("I don't make excuses, ever"). He thought I was stupid for praising effort and not outcomes ("Doc, you'd never make it in my business"). His mood could get so black. At times, I would have to use every clinical skill to break through his barrier of resentment. When a person is depressed, one can't take it personally. They are caught by their own thinking; they can't find their way out of their self-destructive maze.

But I managed to help Jack, to break his seemingly endless volleys of self-evaluation and analysis. Jack seemed to respect the cognitive therapy exercises. He liked the discipline and liked the game of challenging his biased, self-defeating thinking. He started to laugh at himself, in a good way. No bitterness, but acceptance that maybe he was a human being and not some robot. Maybe he did make a few decisions without knowing the outcome of the deal (and at times without even knowing all of the factors that influenced the deal). "There's hope, doc. I guess I could always teach this stuff."

Jack ended therapy with me on good terms. His episode lifted, he was busy, and his motivation to pursue his dysfunctional attitudes was minimal. He had been taking antidepressant medications and agreed to continue with them. My training helped me press the point as far as I could. I told Jack that he needed a better understanding of his attitudes—the all-or-none ones, the ones that fueled his fears. He had things to do, people to see. I left the door open for Jack to return as needed. I felt another bolt of realization as I heard his voice in my head: "I gotta say, Dr. Shaw; I'd never survive another depression. Thank goodness I'm better. That was the worst." Clinicians know that depression, like other recurrent disorders such as cancer, asthma, diabetes, and addiction, is a chronic disorder with at least a 50/50 chance of recurrence.

"We're getting close doctor, prepare yourself." For what? The young officer knew his job—get me to the scene, give a clear instruction. But, prepare myself for *what*?

We arrived at what looked like a fire scene. There was a fire truck, an ambulance, two police cars, and two black sedans littering the street. A serious-looking detective waved me aside. "Dr. Shaw, the situation is this: Jack Broker is a 37-year-old Caucasian male, married, three kids. He's your patient, right?" I started to explain that I hadn't seen Jack for two years. "Doesn't matter," the detective explained, "He's in the basement with a gun in his mouth, and he won't talk to anyone but you. He hasn't said anything for an hour after he told our negotiator to get out."

Mrs. Broker, whom I had met twice before, came out, completely distraught, and thanked me for coming. She told me that Jack had become increasingly depressed at the start of the summer. He told his wife that he wasn't going to call me; that he wasn't going through another episode; that she should get on with her life. Mrs. Broker is a strong and supportive person; she was usually reassuring but admitted to being so worried that she pleaded with Jack to get help.

Now, her husband was in the basement with a gun in his mouth, the black monster of depression had taken hold and there seemed to be no hope. Jack had mentioned my name to the police negotiator, early on in the conversation. Maybe I could talk to him, help him see that his wife, his three kids, and pretty well everyone who knew him loved him and cared. But first, I had to connect on his terms. I had to start where he was . . . not where I wanted him to be. His children, all under 10 years old, were playing in the neighbor's yard (*playing* is probably not the right term; *waiting* is better).

In these circumstances, global assurances filled with love and deep affection have very little effect. When an individual is depressed, they are immune to the positives, no matter how realistic they are. Love does not counter major depression—I wish it did, don't get me wrong. Loving a person who has an illness is important, but it has little or no effect during an episode of depression. What has to be understood is the extent of the person's despair and hopelessness, and the energy fueling their sense of worthlessness and self-hate. The therapist's job is to expose these dangerous mindsets and to challenge them with simple questions; to undercut the lethal mindset with a better understanding and compassion. Real and genuine compassion for the suffering.

But there was a practical problem that day. The police did not want me to actually enter the basement. He had a presumed loaded gun and they insisted I communicate with him from the top of the stairs. Therapy is a personal experience usually conducted in a confidential and private setting. This work was crisis management; the professionals who work for police departments and crisis services know all too well that the *connection* with the person is the key. How do you connect with someone from the top of the stairs?

I tried talking to Jack, but he said nothing. He didn't acknowledge my presence. With the gun in his mouth, Jack pulled the trigger.

(Continued)

I never had the chance to understand, to know what happened that day. This is one reason why I focus on the financial services industry—to help the "Jacks" of this business before others are talking downstairs to a person who is incapable of listening to them. Jack suffered. He was in agony. The psychological autopsy helped us to better understand many of his depressive experiences. The regret of not being able to help is enormous. The feeling of helplessness is crushing. If only . . . if only. What if . . . what if?

I have long accepted my fallibility as a therapist, but I am dedicated to my mission of countering the misunderstanding and stigma that I observe on a weekly basis in the financial services industry. These are the conditions that we label as mental illness and addiction; these are the conditions we know as human tragedy . . .

—Brian F. Shaw, PhD

What to Do: The Next Steps

You don't have to *be* a shrink with a black leather couch to *think* like a shrink. First, you need to ask the advisor how he is doing and what he is planning to do over the next week. What is he looking forward to? What is happening in his family's life? Listen. You may observe an emotional shift (sad, teary, blank stare) or behaviors indicating anxiety or fear (fidgeting, restlessness, agitation). In these cases, ask the advisor if he would be willing to meet you for dinner or lunch. In a casual way, encourage him over the meal to get professional help or support. Say that you are concerned for him, that you care about him and that you want to do the right thing to get help. If you are worried about addictive behavior, do not accept a simple denial. In most cases, the advisor will be afraid even if he doesn't show it. It is also important to remember that addicted individuals tend to be very manipulative, and will lie straight to your face to maintain his habit. Such people are afraid of being caught. Obtain professional advice about how to approach your advisor.

If the crisis involves a concern about self-harm, here are your critical next steps:

- Stay with your advisor or have another staff member accompany him until you can get professional help

- Call the advisor's family and ask them to support him
- Ask for help and support from your company physician or employee assistance provider

A Darker Side of the Business

Equally alarming and, in reality, much less frequent, but much more dangerous to the health of the organization, managers also have to consider the possibility of a psychopathic personality in their midst. These individuals have been labeled "snakes in suits" by Professor Robert Hare, the world's leading authority on the dangerous minds of psychopaths in the business world.* (See Chapter 11 for more information.)

If you were alarmed by the word *psychopath* in the previous sentence, you are not alone. Perhaps you thought psychopaths were serial killers and sociopathic criminals living in the underbelly of society. Surprisingly, however, only a minority of diagnosable psychopaths are violent offenders. We'll talk about these personality types so that you are fully prepared to understand the behaviors and emotions of all individuals in your office.

So, let's take a side journey down the road that is frequently not taken. In our biased and time-pressed world, a person labeled a *psycho* or a *head case* is immediately categorized and stigmatized. We wanted you to think like a shrink so that for a short time, you have considered the important but often fuzzy or scary world of mental illness, addiction, suicide, and psychopathic personality. People with psychopathic personalities are attracted to environments in which they can work independently with little supervision and make money. They aren't interested in the service aspects of the business unless there is considerable opportunity. This information doesn't really help you, but the fact that *approximately 3 percent of the industry has this type of personality* should be enough to get your attention.* A person with this personality type could be working with you, or living next door to you. Identifying this type of individual is, therefore, critical. Important note: Only a small percentage of psychopaths are violent offenders. According to Professor Robert Hare, "Wherever you find money, prestige, and power you will find them."

---

*Paul Babiak and Robert D. Hare, *Snakes in Suits: When Psychopaths Go to Work* (New York: HarperCollins, 2006).

Here is a good description of their traits:

- A psychopath has no concern for the feelings of others and a complete disregard for any sense of social obligation.
- They seem egocentric and lack insight of any sense of responsibility or consequence. Their emotions are thought to be superficial and shallow, if they exist at all.
- They are considered callous, manipulative, and incapable of forming lasting relationships, let alone showing any kind of meaningful love.
- They typically never perform any action unless they determine it can be beneficial to oneself.
- They show poor impulse control and a low tolerance for frustration and aggression. They have no empathy, remorse, anxiety, or guilt in relation to their behavior. In short, they truly are devoid of conscience.
- They understand that society expects them to behave in a conscientious manner, and will mimic this behavior when it suits their needs.
- Their manipulative skills are valued for providing audacious leadership. Some have argued that psychopathy is adaptive in a highly competitive environment, because it gets results for both the individual and for the corporations they represent.
- These individuals will often cause long-term harm, both to their co-workers and the organization as a whole, because of their manipulative, deceitful, abusive, and often fraudulent behavior.*

The skill set needed to deal with this personality type who may work in your midst is complicated. One reason for this chapter is to discuss the areas of management that are rarely discussed. Clearly, mental health and addiction problems are common, while suicide and psychopathic personality are much more infrequent.

If you suspect that one of your advisors is engaged in behavior that concerns you and you wonder about her personality and ethics, get professional advice. Don't be alone with your worries—consider

---

*U.S. Department of Health and Human Services, National Institutes of Health.

your options. No one gets fired for her personality, but it is critical that your supervision of her actions be ramped up.

The Room of Silence

You have, no doubt, heard of the adage, "Physician, heal thyself." This is easier said than done, for both physicians and for managers in financial services. We have observed prominent physicians, specialists in their fields, as patients. No one wants to be sick!!! But we all get sick at times. These physicians may be stoic and accepting, knowing what they are facing and what the treatment entails. They may be highly anxious as they lose control and have to wear those awful hospital gowns with the gaping backs.

When physicians have a mental illness or an addiction, they may be baffled about what treatment or rehabilitation is required. Perhaps not surprisingly, given medical school training, they may know more about managing leprosy or tuberculosis than drug addiction and eating disorders. Given the state of knowledge in society, we do not expect that you, as a branch manager, will be expert in your care. We only want you to recognize when you need care.

So we are going to pass on what we say to our physician and surgeon colleagues. Denial (the unwitting, unknowing refusal to acknowledge a problem) is common in all aspects of mental illness and addiction. If a colleague has a stroke, heart attack, appendicitis, tumor, hip displacement, and so forth, it is pretty obvious that he needs care. Other conditions are more subtle and mental illness and addiction fall into this latter category.

Once you have had an advice or confrontation or intervention session with one or more of your advisors, you may want to consider getting some support yourself. No, we are not trying to turn the whole office into clients. This type of personal counseling is brief and to the point. In emergency services work, it is known as "critical incident debriefing" and it is a focused review of your response and a discussion of any concerns that you may have.

When there is a trauma or shocking news (for example, a colleague commits suicide, or there are massive fraud allegations), everyone will be talking. As a manager, you want to know about the fears and worries and what to do about them. During your own debriefing session, you can get an objective view about the events as they unfold before reviewing the obligatory public relations and investor communications strategies and announcements. After challenging events, leaders are often left in their own room of silence where no one knows what to say or do.

Other Avenues of Help for You

Understanding the psychology and mindsets of your advisors, being observant of signs and symptoms of mental illness or addiction, and having to run an efficient and profitable office on top of all that can be overwhelming. In addition to your own counseling, you need a support network and resources to help you with your professional and personal challenges in and out of the office environment. Management has significant rewards and considerable challenges, but branch management (middle management) is like being in the "sandwich generation"—caught between demanding and needy children and demanding and needy parents. In fact, many branch managers are members of both groups.

Additional Support for Managers

- Counseling options (employee assistance programs; local specializing psychologists and psychiatrists; performance coaches)
- Networking with other managers at industry trade shows
- Firm-sponsored manager conferences
- Securities Industry and Financial Markets Association (SIFMA) Branch Management Development Program
- Securities Industry Institute at Wharton Annual Program (three-year)
- Leadership and support groups; for example, the Young Presidents Organization (YPO) or the World Presidents Organization (WPO)

These groups provide support and encouragement for leaders in a safe and confidential environment. Safety and trust and confidentiality are critical prerequisites for most humans to get humble, to be fallible. For many years, in medicine and in public safety, errors were buried or hidden. More recently, there is a greater willingness to acknowledge errors, and as a result, managers can come forward in a supportive, realistic environment. The fields of transplantation and cancer care in medicine are two other examples of how failures of systems can lead to success at a later time.

Hope for the Future: Remember, You Are Never Alone

When you are dealing with issues of mental health and addiction, you will no doubt enter a world of uncertainty. Your advisors and possibly their families will be afraid and defensive. You will project confidence that you will obtain the help that is needed. You will stay involved and will monitor how things are progressing. You will most likely want to consult with experienced professionals and peers who have had experience in this area.

There are many options for treatment. The sciences of psychology and neuroscience provide continuous advances in our understanding of both mental health and addictive disorders. There are more counselors and therapists with specific experience on Wall Street and in the financial industry than ever before. Interventions by experienced staff are readily available. You should never be alone with your worries about yourself or about your advisors.

The Last Word . . . The First Step

Addressing the emotional turmoil on Wall Street is not easy, and it is uncomfortable for many, but it is necessary from a mental health perspective. It also makes good business sense. Advisors who can manage emotions, who are comfortable feeling, and who can relate to clients and their colleagues through sincere communication, are more successful in the long run.

We truly believe that by sharing with the community positive ways of coping with the numerous challenges brokers and managers face on the job, ways that allow changes in patterns of thinking and behaving, and ways that provide relief, will result in the achievement of a healthy mindset. If the community will make these changes, advisors will be more likely to seek the counseling they need; and those who might not otherwise, will come forward to ask for help.

We trust that we were able to expose the warning signals and dangers of anxiety and depression, uncover the myths, offer practical solutions, and lead you back to a healthful (emotional and physical) state of mind. Our Bullish Thinking techniques, the OCEAN system of understanding leadership styles, and the descriptive processes of learning advisor mindsets and investor profiles all work with much success in coaching sessions and in real-life situations, and we believe they will help you.

It is also our hope that the advisors needing help will find the courage to identify with others who may share the same fears, thoughts, problems, and insecurities. They will discover they may need help on a professional level and, in time, doing so will no longer be a stigma. Demystifying the taboos of mental and emotional health will help advisors get over the hurdles keeping them from achieving emotional health and peace of mind.

We want to help you find your way back to the job—and the life—you love, and to lead you there in a nonthreatening, empathic, and positive manner. To give you techniques for achieving peace of mind, more tolerance, more joy in your business, and a more balanced lifestyle. We encourage you to take the first step toward healing emotional wounds that are robbing you of a calm and joyful life and a continued successful career. Open your mind. Open your heart. Ask for help if you need it. If you can do that, you will quiet the noise in your head so you can obtain the peace you so richly deserve.

Good luck. Good health.

> The truth is that our finest moments are most likely to occur when we are feeling deeply uncomfortable, unhappy, or unfulfilled. For it is only in such moments, propelled by our discomfort, that we are likely to step out of our ruts and start searching for different ways or truer answers.
>
> —M. Scott Peck (1936–2005)
> Psychiatrist, Author, *The Road Less Traveled*

Dr. Alden Cass's Landmark Research Study

CASUALTIES OF WALL STREET: AN ASSESSMENT OF THE WALKING WOUNDED

Alden Cass, John Lewis, and Ed Simco

Introduction

It has long been known that Wall Street stockbrokers are exposed to highly stressful working conditions during their pursuit of affluence, which may interfere with their overall quality of life and occupational productivity. The job description for these account executives requires them to handle a great deal of personal responsibility, and because the broker is usually paid on a commission basis, he must work to make as many trades in stocks and bonds as possible to achieve success. Also, the threat of job uncertainty due to the success of online trading, the volatility of the contemporary market, the possibility of inflation or interest rate hikes, [and] international market competition . . . has further complicated the job description for the account executive working in today's market.

The ambiguity of their on-the-job decisions, coupled with the complex nature of their profession and the likelihood of experiencing failure, has facilitated a growing trend of increased personnel turnover, absenteeism, social withdrawal, and a deterioration of employees' productivity, as well as their physical and mental health (Felton and Cole, 1963; Ivancevich and Matteson, 1980; Ganster and

Schaubroeck, 1991; Greenberger, Strasser, Cummings, and Dunham, 1989). These negative personal outcomes have proven to be very costly for firms over the past 20 years because of the rapid growth of "psychiatric injury claims" and reports of "gradual mental stress" (Lubin, 1980). Poor decision making on the buying and selling of stocks and the cost of training new employees are also speculated to be substantial costs to firms at the present time.

Ivancevich and Matteson (1980) and Cooper (2000) estimated that stress costs the U.S. economy $50–150 billion annually. A 1992 survey of 1299 full-time employees from U.S. firms pinpointed sales and service workers as being the most likely candidates of burnout (as cited in Singh, Goolsby, and Rhoads, 1994). Furthermore, the American Institute of Stress categorized the customer service worker, a position consisting of a comparable job description, as one of the 10 most stressful jobs in the United States (Miller, Annetta, Springen, Gordon, Murr, Cohen, and Drew, 1988). Consequently, a growing number of clinical psychologists have moved to organizational settings to help reduce health care costs and to facilitate interest in creating innovative stress prevention programs (Kurpius, 1985).

A paucity of research exists in the psychological and organizational literature, investigating the mental health of stockbrokers and its relationship to their success on their job, quality of life, and lifestyle habits. Speculation, as well as the findings of organizational researchers, has also intimated that stockbrokers have been overlooked as a target population for studies examining job burnout and stress tolerance (Burke, 1988), cognitive skills, job satisfaction, substance abuse, and organizational commitment. The most notable studies conducted to date in the psychological and organizational literature have investigated worker efficiency, the effects of physical and technological stressors on brokers, information processing speed, and the variables associated with increased success within the profession, respectively (Borman, Dorsey, and Ackerman, 1992; Burke, 1990; Beehr and Newman, 1978; Slovic, 1969; Ghiselli, 1969).

Because of the lack of available research conducted on the mental health, coping skills, and lifestyle habits of stockbrokers, one is left to make inferences from investigations completed on other comparable and highly stressful professions (for example, nurses, paramedics, police officers, sales representatives, lawyers, and physicians). Contemporary research on comparable professions has identified five areas of clinical concern, including high levels of job burnout, clinical and subclinical levels of depression, moderate to high levels of anxiety, stress-induced deterioration of employees' physical health, and maladaptive coping skills. Based on these aforementioned findings, it makes intuitive sense that stockbrokers may be faced with these same negative personal outcomes.

As it is well known that account executives are faced with high levels of job-related stress, the purpose of this investigation was to identify whether stress-induced clinical and subclinical levels of major depression, levels of burnout, and levels of anxiety, were present within a sample of Wall Street stockbrokers. This research sought to illuminate the extent to which Wall Street stockbrokers' job productivity (annual salary) was affected by each of the five major areas of clinical concern. We also hoped to qualitatively and quantitatively examine the coping skills and lifestyle habits that these individuals use for the purpose of alleviating job-related stress.

It was postulated that several variables, taken together, are predictive of increased job success and productivity, as defined by the participants' reported annual salary. These predictor variables are the emotional exhaustion and depersonalization components of burnout, levels of depression and anxiety, and the participants' reported number of hours of sleep per night. Furthermore, this investigation sought to differentiate which of these variables were most predictive of an increase in annual salary.

The present study used a Lifestyles Questionnaire for the purpose of identifying the various types of stress-mediating lifestyle habits and coping skills that are used by the participants. Adaptive, as opposed to maladaptive, coping skills and lifestyle habits are defined as behaviors such as exercise, proactive individual and group activities, sufficient number of hours of sleep, and less time spent engaged in work-related activities during the weekend. Maladaptive coping skills and lifestyle habits are considered to be use of cigarettes, drug use, alcohol use (more than two drinks per day), lack of exercise per week, fewer than six hours of sleep per night, lack of group activities during the week and weekend, and a refusal to take off work during times of illness.

Method

Participants

Participants were 26 male stockbrokers between the ages of 22 and 32 years old, with an average age of 26.27, who were identified and contacted to form a convenient sample. These individuals were obtained from seven of Wall Street's most prestigious brokerage houses. Race and ethnicity were not factors involved in selecting this particular sample of stockbrokers.

Location

All interviews were conducted after hours in public places located within the Wall Street district, where confidentiality of the participants could be strictly upheld and the work environment would not affect the participants' responses.

Instruments

The emotional exhaustion and depersonalization components of burnout were measured by the Maslach Burnout Inventory (MBI) (Maslach and Jackson, 1981, 1986). This is a 22-item self-report measure that also examines a third component of burnout, specifically personal accomplishment. The frequency that respondents experience feelings related to each subscale was assessed using a 6-point Likert scale. A high degree of emotional exhaustion and depersonalization was reflected in higher scores on each of these subscales. Levels of emotional exhaustion were categorized within ranges of 0–16 (low), 17–26 (moderate), and 27 or over (high), whereas levels of depersonalization ranged from 0–6 (low), 7–12 (moderate), and 13 or over (high). Maslach and Jackson (1986) estimated internal consistency using Cronbach's coefficient alpha and reported reliability coefficients of .90 and .79 for the emotional exhaustion and depersonalization subscales, respectively. Test-Retest reliability coefficients for the emotional exhaustion and depersonalization subscales were .82 and .60, respectively. Convergent validity was also obtained for the MBI, as presented in the manual.

Depression was measured by the Beck Depression Inventory (BDI) (Beck and Steer, 1987), which is a 21-item self-report instrument designed to assess the severity of depression in normal adults within one week of assessment. Respondents were required to select one of four statements for each item that best described the way they feel. Clinical score ranges were the following: 0–9 (normal range), 10–15 (mild depression), 16–19 (mild-moderate depression), 20–29 (moderate-severe depression), 30–63 (severe depression). Item number 8 was of particular interest to the investigators because it assessed the severity of self-critical thoughts and feelings related to making mistakes that the respondents had experienced. An alpha coefficient of .81 was found for 15 nonpsychiatric samples. This indicated that the BDI has high internal consistency in nonclinical populations. The Test-Retest reliability reported in the literature ranges from .60 to .90 for nonpsychiatric patients. Construct, concurrent, and discriminate validity are adequate and are described in the BDI manual.

Anxiety was assessed by the Trait items (21–40) of the State-Trait Anxiety Inventory (Form Y) (STAI) (Spielberger, Gorsuch, and Lushene, 1970). These 20 items were used to evaluate how respondents generally feel in a variety of hypothetical situations. The essential symptoms assessed by this instrument are feelings of apprehension, tension, nervousness, and worry. The higher the accumulated score on this inventory, the more severe was the anxiety experienced by the respondent. The cutoff score prescribed by the authors to differentiate those working adults (n = 1,387) who are highly anxious from those who experience normal levels of anxiety, was set at 44.08. More than 5,000 subjects were tested in the construction and standardization of the STAI. Alpha coefficients are reported to be .91 for working adults. Evidence for the concurrent, convergent, divergent, and construct validity of the STAI is present and displayed in the manual.

Clinical and subclinical levels of current major depression were determined through the use of the Structured Clinical Interview for DSM-IV (SCID) (First, Spitzer, Gibbon, and Williams, 1994). This instrument was used to make an accurate assessment of whether each participant met DSM-IV criteria for clinical or subclinical levels of current major depression. An individual responded to the verbally presented criteria regarding the presence of symptoms of depression, while the examiner coded each response as a 1 (absent symptom), 2 (subthreshold or subclinically present symptom), or 3 (threshold, clinically present symptom). This instrument has not been used within organizational settings to date, but was useful in making more of an accurate diagnosis at the time of each interview.

An individual must first have experienced within the past month, either two weeks of a depressed mood for most of the day or two weeks of markedly diminished interest or pleasure in almost all activities most of the day to be diagnosed with current Major Depressive Disorder using this instrument. If the examiner coded at least one of these first two symptoms as being clinically present (3), then the individual was required to report clinically present symptoms (3) for at least four more of the next seven items presented to them. (Please refer to DSM-IV criteria for Current Major Depression criteria A3–A9).

Thus, at least five of the presented symptoms must be coded a (3) and at least one of these must be item 1 or 2. If this requirement was met, then the individual must be coded a (3), attesting to the fact that these symptoms caused him clinically significant distress or impairment in social, occupational, or other important areas of functioning. If this requirement was satisfied, the next step was taken toward a diagnosis if a (3) is coded for criteria ruling out depression due to the physiological effects of a substance or due to a general medical condition. Finally, the diagnosis could be made for clinical levels of current Major Depressive Disorder if the individual was coded a (3) for a response ruling out depression due to bereavement. Any individual who was coded with at least one (3) for the first two items, but did not meet criteria for clinical levels of current Major Depressive Disorder, was coded as a (2), signifying subclinical levels of depression.

Relevant qualitative information about the participants was obtained by using a tailor-made Demographics Questionnaire. This questionnaire required that the participants report information regarding their age, years at their current occupation, level of education, socioeconomic status, estimated annual salary, previous occupation, number of hours in the office per day, previous psychiatric hospitalizations, level of education, and marital status. This questionnaire was used solely for this initial investigation on stockbrokers and thus, reliability and validity statistics are not currently available.

Finally, a brief Lifestyles and Coping skills questionnaire was created to determine whether these participants were using adaptive or maladaptive coping skills as a means of relieving stress. Participants were required to fill in blanks at the end of a posed question, with personal and qualitative information regarding their lifestyle habits and coping skills. Specific areas of interest were tapped through the use of this questionnaire, such as the number of hours during the week and weekends spent in individual or group activities, the types of activities used to alleviate stress, consumption behaviors (for example, alcohol, cigarette, and drug use), sleeping habits, and physical health. No reliability or validity data can be presented for this questionnaire, as it has not been used in any previous investigations that focused on this population of professionals. The readability and comprehension of this questionnaire was checked by administering the questionnaire to several adult males during a pilot investigation.

Procedure

Institutional Review Board (I.R.B.) approval was obtained before submitting the study. All subjects were treated according to APA guidelines for the ethical treatment of human subjects.

The examiner used standardized procedures throughout each assessment, and in all cases, the order of the instruments used was maintained (Demographics Questionnaire, Lifestyles Questionnaire, MBI, Trait items from STAI (Form Y), BDI, SCID oral interview). Each assessment packet was coded with a number that was assigned to the participant for the purpose of insuring anonymity. Participants completed the self-report questionnaires without the guidance of the examiner, and when they were completed, these question-naires were collected. At this point, the examiner informed the par-ticipants that they would be tape-recorded and asked to respond orally to questions about their mood within the last month (SCID, 1994). Following this structured clinical interview, participants were debriefed and informed of their right to request information regard-ing the results of the study. Participants were thanked and asked not to discuss the experience with their co-workers. The total procedure required 30 minutes in most cases, but for those not meeting criteria for either subclinical or clinical levels of Major Depression on the SCID, the procedure took only 20 minutes.

Once the data were collected, the examiner used the SPSS 9.0 for Windows program to enter it into analyses of interest such as Multiple Regression analysis, ANOVA, and descriptive statistics.

Results

Before conducting the multiple regression analysis, regression diag-nostics were performed on the data to determine the degree to which the assumptions of multiple regression were met. This analysis was also conducted to discover whether the variables, emotional exhaus-tion, depersonalization, depression and trait-anxiety levels, and the number of hours of sleep per night, taken together, could signifi-cantly predict how successful a stockbroker would be, as measured by his reported annual salary. This statistical analysis yielded results indicating that these aforementioned variables, as a group, were significantly predictive of the participants' reported annual salary ($R = .667$, $p < .05$). Together, these five predictor variables account for 30.6 percent of the variance in reported annual salary ($R2 = .445$, adjusted $R2 = .306$, $F(5,20) = 3.204$, $p < .05$).

Results suggested that only two of these five variables, depersonalization levels and hours of sleep, were independently and significantly related to the outcome measure under investigation. The Beta weights (standardized multiple regression coefficients) and squared semipartial regression coefficients (uniqueness index) were also reviewed to assess the relative contribution of the five variables to the prediction of job success, as measured by reported annual salary.

Specifically, the depersonalization variable displayed the largest significant standardized weight and the second largest significant squared semipartial regression coefficient, with values of $-.56$ ($p < .05$) and .1946, respectively. The Pearson correlation coefficient was found to be in the predicted direction, and supported prior findings that identified a negative relationship between job success and levels of depersonalization. Lower levels of depersonalization were thus moderately associated with an increase in job success or reported annual salary ($r = -.467$, $p < .05$). The findings regarding squared semipartial regression coefficients indicated that depersonalization accounted for approximately 19 percent of the variable in annual salary, beyond the variance accounted for by the other four predictors.

In addition to the negative relationship discovered with depersonalization, annual salary was expected to have a positive relationship with the number of hours of sleep per night. Contrary to prior research findings that pinpointed negative personal outcomes related to sleep deprivation, however, it appeared that the variable for number of hours of sleep was negatively related to the annual salary of the participants, as evidenced by a Pearson correlation coefficient of $-.453$. This variable also displayed a significant standardized weight at a value of $-.52$ ($p < .05$), indicating the strength of its relative contribution to the prediction of reported annual salary. The findings regarding uniqueness were also significant in that the number of hours of sleep variable accounted for approximately 23 percent of the variable in reported annual salary, beyond the variance accounted for by the other four predictors ($Sr2 = .2304$).

The results of this investigation also yielded descriptive data regarding the samples' scores on several mental health assessments (BDI, Trait Anxiety Inventory, MBI, SCID), as well as on their lifestyle habits and coping skills (Lifestyles Questionnaire). Means and standard deviations for both sets of data appear in Tables A.1 and A.2.

Table A.1:   Descriptive Statistics

Mental Health Indicators

	Mean	Standard Deviation
Emotional Exhaustion	24.92	9.45
Depersonalization	11.42	6.67
SCID Current Depression	1.81	.80
Trait Anxiety Raw Scores	41.31	7.58
BDI-Depression Raw Scores	9.69	6.86

Table A.2:   Descriptive Statistics

Lifestyles Habits and Coping Skills

	Mean	Standard Deviation
Years at current job	2.69	1.98
Annual salary*	$139[†]	$130[†]
Hours at work	10.27	1.22
Hours of work on weekends	2.42	2.02
Hours of individual activities (week)	8.46	6.82
Hours of group activities (week)	5.85	7.15
Hours of individual activities (weekends)	7.65	9.71
Hours of group activities (weekends)	9.19	7.90
Number of alcoholic drinks	1.50	1.63
Hours of exercise	5.15	5.18
Packs of cigarettes per day	1.54	.51
Drug use quantity per week	2.58	3.58
Hours of sleep	6.23	1.82
Time to fall asleep (minutes)	36.54	30.91
Days of illness	4.15	3.45
Sick day absenteeism	2.23	2.41
BDI-Item 8 (self-critical thoughts)	.96	.53

*The median annual salary for this sample was found to be $100,000.
[†]Expressed as thousands

Discussion

This preliminary investigation examined the relationship of five variables, all of which have been associated with negative emotional and physical outcomes, and their ability to predict the job success of 26 Wall Street stockbrokers. Although as a group, these five predictor variables were shown to be significantly related to the reported annual salary of the participants, it was surprising that only depersonalization levels and the number of hours of sleep variables contributed to the majority of this relationship.

Corroborating earlier research conducted by Maslach (1982), there was evidence of a significant and moderate relationship, in a predicted direction, between levels of depersonalization and the reported annual salary of the stockbrokers. It was expected that stockbrokers, who used depersonalization as an emotional buffer and to psychologically distance themselves from their clients, would report having lower annual salaries within this sales-related profession. It may be that stockbrokers, facing high levels of depersonalization, treated their clients in a predictably cold and unfriendly manner. Clients may consequently have taken their accounts elsewhere. It is, therefore, plausible that the stockbrokers may have greater earning potential if they learn to be more expressive and aware of their emotions, and begin to treat their clients in a more personal and concerned manner. It is also speculated that higher levels of depersonalization may decrease an individual's awareness of their own psychological and physical health. This lack of awareness may lead one to engage in poor lifestyle habits and use ineffective coping skills, both of which may affect an individual's ability to be productive at work, as well as affect their mental and physical health.

The second variable, the number of hours of sleep per night, was found to be significantly and negatively related to job success. These results suggest that those stockbrokers who spent less time sleeping each night are more likely to have a higher annual salary. This makes intuitive sense in that sleeping less would give a stockbroker more time to research new stocks and obtain new accounts while at work and home. Consequently, more time devoted to work and less to sleep would increase the likelihood of reaching a higher annual salary.

Contemporary literature, however, has shown that negative psychological and physical outcomes have been associated with a lack of sleep (Kahill, 1988). This relationship between a lack of sleep and negative personal outcomes validated our contention that these individuals may neglect their physical and mental health, possibly as a result of experiencing moderate to high levels of depersonalization, or as a means of pursuing affluence in an extremely volatile stock market.

The results of this study indicated that trait anxiety, levels of depression, and emotional exhaustion were not large contributors to the prediction of annual salary. This finding is intriguing in that prior research, as well as intuitive sense, would lead one to hypothesize a strong negative relationship between these three variables and an individual's success on the job. One reason for this may be that the brokers within our sample may have been experiencing high levels of depersonalization, and consequently, were not even aware of their symptoms of depression, anxiety, and emotional exhaustion for them to subscribe to in the self-reports. This finding may be worth exploring in future investigations.

The descriptive data obtained through the use of our assessment questionnaires contributed to the investigators' understanding of the current mental health, coping skills, and lifestyle habits of these 26 stockbrokers. The results reported in Table A.1 lend credence to our contention that the mental health and quality of life of stockbrokers is negatively affected by high levels of job-related stress. Most notably, the results indicated that the participants' obtained mean scores placed them in the moderate-to-high range for emotional exhaustion and depersonalization. Regarding the levels of trait anxiety on the STAI, the stockbrokers obtained a mean score that was higher than the mean obtained by the original norm group ($41.31 > 34.89$) that was composed of working adults (Spielberger, Gorsuch, and Lushene, 1970). The original STAI standardization sample was not composed of stockbrokers, suggesting that the present sample may be faced with qualitatively and quantitatively different types of job-related stressors. The results, however, indicated that the respondents for our investigation reported significant amounts of distress related to symptoms of anxiety. Finally, regarding the participants' acknowledgment of depressive symptoms, results obtained from the BDI and SCID instruments suggested that, on the average, they approached mild levels of depression and subclinical levels of current major depression, respectively.

Means and standard deviations of items on the Lifestyles Questionnaire indicated that the stockbrokers were using some maladaptive coping skills and were engaged in some risky lifestyle habits during the workweek. Specifically, these individuals were spending between 10 to 12 hours at work, smoked on average almost two packs of cigarettes, and consumed almost two drinks each day. This sample also reported, on the average, using both alcohol and some form of illegal substance at least two times. Relating to sleep patterns, these individuals on the average took almost 37 minutes per night to fall asleep, leaving them with about six hours of sleep for the rest of the night. Regarding their awareness of their physical health, these individuals reported suffering from either the flu or a virus, on the average, four times per year, and still only called in sick for work two times, indicating either the extent of their motivation or fear of not being at work. The stockbrokers within our sample also showed evidence of negativistic thought patterns, in that approximately 96 percent of them agreed with the BDI statement "I am critical of myself for my weaknesses and mistakes." Finally, these individuals chose to engage in more pleasurable individual activities (for example, jogging, fishing, masturbation) than group activities (for example, drinks with friends, going to dinner, sex, nightclubs with friends) during the week and more pleasurable group activities than individual ones during their weekends.

It was our contention that stockbrokers were a population of professionals facing high levels of job-related stress, and that this stress, if not actively mediated, would impair their mental and physical health as well as their occupational and social functioning. The results of our investigation illuminated the fact that our participants, on average, were experiencing moderate-to-high levels of depersonalization and emotional exhaustion, both of which compose two-thirds of job burnout (Maslach, 1982). These individuals were also certainly reporting a moderate-to-high level of distress relating to manifestations of anxiety, as well as mild depressive symptoms.

Although the participants reached only mild levels of depression on the face valid BDI measure, it was fortuitous that we used a structured interview (SCID) (First et al., 1994) for the purpose of identifying clinical, as well as subclinical levels of current major depression within this sample. The results indicated that 23 percent of our sample met criteria for a clinical diagnosis of current major depression and 38 percent reached criteria for subclinical levels. This finding is startling because the National Institute of Mental Health (2000) has reported that 7 percent of all men are currently diagnosed with major depression, and our sample of males contains a much greater percentage of depression than that would be expected in the general population at the present time. Thus, many of these individuals may require professional help and perhaps even medication to alleviate their distress, but they are not likely to seek the help necessary to ameliorate these symptoms.

The most astounding finding of our investigation is that despite the moderate-to-high levels of emotional distress reported by the participants, these individuals were still making on average $139,346.15 for their annual income. Even more surprising was the revelation that those brokers who reported greater impairment regarding depression, anxiety, and emotional exhaustion, as well as poorer coping skills, proved to be the most successful individuals within our sample on the basis of their annual income. In essence, these rookie brokers appear to be paying for financial success with their mental health and their quality of life.

The results of this investigation have implications for the provision of services in organizational settings to the increasing number of employees who experience clinically significant work-related stress and are at risk for mental illness, physical impairment, and burnout. It appears that stockbrokers are not using effective coping skills for the purpose of alleviating their work-related stress, and consequently, are developing the debilitating symptoms of burnout, anxiety, and depression. It is our contention that negative personal outcomes will be associated with these mental health concerns, and will consequently lead to negative organizational outcomes such as absenteeism and a decreased quality of life for employees and their families. Also, if the early warning signs of burnout, depression, and anxiety continue to remain unnoticed by stockbrokers as well as their employers, their overall productivity and commitment to the organization may wane over time, leading to an increase in turnover. This may cost brokerage houses additional money for training replacement brokers who will more than likely suffer the same fate as their predecessors.

The present investigation thus sheds light on the importance of preventing mental and physical illness from infringing on the lives of stockbrokers. It behooves the larger organizations to implement some form of stress management program at a training level for the purpose of preventing these rather costly and negative personal outcomes from affecting their employees, and eventually the growth of the organization. As clinical stress researchers, we concur with the work of Lazarus and Folkman (1984), and consequently emphasize the importance of continued organizational research on individuals and how they perceive or appraise the stressors within the working environment. It appears that a great deal of energy is currently being directed toward identifying environmental triggers within organizations that elicit stress within employees. Not a lot of research is required, unfortunately, to realize that for the stockbroker, the environmental stressor that most significantly contributes to the increased levels of burnout, depression, anxiety, and poor coping skills is the ambiguous and intangible stock market. This particular stressor cannot be eliminated from their job description, which means that a more person-centered focus is required for organizational researchers who study stockbrokers. Early interventions during training will hopefully enable these individuals to identify means to turn perceived threats into perceived challenges, and improve their overall quality of life.

References

Beck, A.T., and Steer, R.A. 1987. *Beck Depression Inventory*. San Antonio, TX: Psychological Corporation/Harcourt Brace Jovanovich.

Beehr, T.A., and Newman, J.E. 1978. Job stress, employee health, and organizational effectiveness: A facet analysis, model and literature review. *Personnel Psychology*, 31:665–699.

Borman, W.C., Dorsey, D., and Ackerman, L. 1992. Time-spent responses as time allocation strategies: Relations with sales performance in a stockbroker sample. *Personnel Psychology*, 45:763–777.

Burke, R.J. "Sources of managerial and professional stress in large organizations."1988. In *Courses, coping and consequences of stress at work*, by C.L. Cooper and R. Payne (eds.), 77–114. Hoboken, NJ: Wiley.

Burke, R.J. 1990. Effects of physical environment and technological stressors among stock brokers: A preliminary investigation. *Psychological Reports*, 66:951–959.

Cooper, C.L. 2000. Editorial: Future research in occupational stress. *Stress Medicine*, 16:63–64.

Felton, J.S., and Cole, R. 1963. The high cost of heart disease. *Circulation*, 27:957–962.

First, M., Spitzer, R.L., Gibbon, M., and Williams, J.B.W. 1994. *Structured Clinical Interview for DSM-IV*, Washington, D.C.: American Psychiatric Association.

Ganster, D.C., and Schaubroeck, J. 1991. Work stress and employee health. *Journal of Management*, 17(2):235–271.

Ghiselli, E.E. 1969. Prediction of success of stockbrokers. *Personnel Psychology*, 22:125–130.

Greenberger, D.B., Strasser, S., Cummings, L.L., and Dunham, R.B. 1989. The impact of personal control on performance and satisfaction. *Organizational Behavior and Human Decision Processes*, 43:29–51.

Ivancevich, J.M., and Matteson, M.T. 1980. *Stress and work: A managerial perspective*. Glenview, IL: Scott, Foresman.

Kahill, S. 1988. Symptoms of professional burnout: A review of the empirical evidence. *Canadian Psychology/Psychologie Canadienne*, 29(3):284–297.

Kurpius, D. 1985. Consultation interventions: Successes, failures, and proposals. *The Counseling Psychologist*, 13:368–389.

Lazarus, R.S., and Folkman, S. 1984. *Stress, appraisal, and coping.* New York: Springer.

Lubin, J. "On-the-job stress leads many workers to file—and win—compensation awards." *Wall Street Journal* (September 17, 1980), B1.

Maslach, C., and Jackson, S.E. 1981. The measurement of experienced burnout. *Journal of Occupational Behavior,* 2:99–113.

Maslach, C. 1982. *Burnout: The cost of caring.* Englewood Cliffs, NJ: Prentice-Hall.

Maslach, C., and Jackson, S.E. 1986. *The Maslach Burnout Inventory.* Palo Alto, CA: Consulting Psychologists Press.

Miller, A., Springen, K., Gordon, J., Murr, A., Cohen, B., and Drew, L. "Stress on the Job." *Newsweek* (April 25, 1988), 40–45.

National Institute of Mental Health Survey 2000, Report obtained online: nimh. nih.gov.

Singh, J., Goolsby, J.R., and Rhoads, G.K. 1994. Behavioral and psychological consequences of boundary spanning burnout for customer service representatives. *Journal of Marketing Research,* 31:558–565.

Slovic, P. 1969. Analyzing the expert judge: A descriptive study of a stockbroker's decision processes. *Journal of Applied Psychology,* 53(4):255–263.

Spielberger, C.D., Gorsuch, R.L., and Lushene, R.E. 1970. *Manual for the State-Trait Anxiety Inventory.* Palo Alto, CA: Consulting Psychologists Press.

Bad Medicine for Wall Street

ALCOHOL USE AND OTHER SUBSTANCE ABUSE TRENDS DURING WAR AND OTHER CATASTROPHIC EVENTS

Alden Cass, Joseph Santoro, Dave Moore, and Joseph Caverly

Abstract

There is a body of evidence indicating that uncontrollable traumatic events can contribute to an increased susceptibility in alcohol use (National Institute on Drug Abuse, 2002; Volpicelli et al., 1999). Research has also supported the notion that alcohol consumption and traumatic events are related, with the most pronounced increase in alcohol use following the trauma, rather than during the actual event (Volpicelli et al., 1990). As traumatic events typically elicit strong emotional reactions in humans, self-medication through alcohol use has served as a prominent coping mechanism to decrease painful affect (Epstein et al., 1998).

There is a common perception among business executives of a stigma attached to weakness or painful feelings. Business executives are consequently reticent to respond to alcohol use surveys for fear their jobs will be threatened if they are truthful in responding. A confidential alcohol use survey using the Alcohol Use Disorders Identification Test (AUDIT) and a demographics questionnaire examining participants' gender, age, income levels, marital status, company location, and type of job were conducted through the Internet to encourage truthful responding.

A total of 151 usable surveys were collected and analyzed. The majority of participants were single men under the age of 30 who do not exercise frequently and made less than $100,000 per year. To examine the findings of the current study, an analysis of variances (ANOVAs) and t-tests were performed to determine whether significant differences in problematic drinking behaviors occurred across the pre-, during, and postwar groups. Interestingly, the findings refuted the *happy hour effect* (Volpicelli et al., 1990), with significantly more problematic drinking behaviors occurring during than after the war. Also, participants from the during-war group drank more often, binge drank more, and felt more guilt and remorse after drinking.

Bad Medicine for Wall Street: Alcohol Use Trends During War

Mental health professionals universally consider alcohol and drug addictions to be severe and pervasive problems, spanning across several areas of modern society. Substance abuse affects millions of Americans each day and costs society billions of dollars per year in treatment and prevention efforts. Substance abuse has been the subject of hundreds of research studies over the years, but certain populations have been excluded from these studies. Wall Street executives have been largely underserved and ignored with respect to their mental health and substance abuse concerns. The issues of mental illness and substance abuse have also been linked to a stigma of weakness and passivity in corporate America.

The issue of substance abuse is speculated to be sidestepped or conveniently ignored by most financial services companies until an employee begins to display problems with his overall productivity, thus negatively affecting the bottom line of a company. Many employees may feel that alcohol use is part of the corporate culture for networking, making business transactions, and relaxation. Alcohol use problems are rarely talked about, and when they are, employees may feel that their jobs are in jeopardy if management were to find out. For this reason, an Internet investigation was utilized to allow these individuals to honestly and anonymously answer questions about their alcohol use in a safe and confidential manner.

The current study was developed as a result of a paucity of research available concerning mental health and substance abuse concerns facing Wall Street executives (Cass et al., 2000). The focus of this investigation is on the impact of the United States's involvement in Iraq in response to September 11th on Wall Street executives with regard to their alcohol abuse patterns and job performance. Specifically, this study examined whether the stress in anticipation of the war, during the war period, or after the declared end of the war influenced alcohol use problems among financial services executives.

Trauma and stress have been linked to the development of alcoholism and other substance abuse problems (Brady and Sonne, 1999; Crum, Muntaner, Eaton, and Anthony, 1995; Najavits, Weiss, and Shaw, 1997; Najavits, Weiss, and Shaw, 1999; Seeman and Seeman, 1992; Volpicelli, Balaraman, Hahn, Wallace, and Bux, 1999) with significant impact on multiple areas of a person's life. Alcoholism often diminishes work performance, family relationships, legal standing, and a host of other life situations that are considered to be vital to daily living. The severity of trauma and stress has been positively correlated to the likelihood of developing a substance abuse disorder (Brown and Anderson, 1991; Fullilove, Fullilove, Smith, Winkler, Micheal, Panzer, and Wallace, 1993). In general, it was found that the greater the violence experienced and the greater the number of violent experiences, the greater the likelihood of developing a substance abuse disorder. The trauma experienced both directly and vicariously by people in and around the Wall Street district on September 11, 2001, was likely a very traumatic event in their lives.

In a large survey of males, Seeman and Seeman (1992) found that drinking problems were closely related to stressful experiences. Their research indicated that such experiences did not need to be severe or chronic to produce a drinking problem. The event could be related to an occupational stressor in which the person feels powerless, and thus uses alcohol as a coping mechanism. Male participants in the Seeman study reported the most severe drinking problems developed in response to an occupational stressor of not having the freedom to choose how to fulfill their job obligations. The lack of control and freedom to choose seems to be a risk factor for the development of drinking problems in the workplace.

Crum et al. (1995) also found that the type of stress experienced has an impact on whether a person will develop a dependence on alcohol. Their study looked at men in high-strain (high demand and low control) and low-strain (low demand and high control) job situations. They found that men in high-strain jobs were more likely to develop an alcohol dependence than men in low-strain jobs. In a related study, Takeshita, Muruyama, and Morimoto (1998), found that chronic, low level, work-related stressors are associated with higher drinking levels. An example of this type of stressor would be dealing with an uncooperative co-worker or daily parking problems at the office. The employee often has limited control over the outcome of the situation and feels frustrated. This research again makes the case for control being a major risk factor in the development of alcoholism.

Volpicelli et al. (1999) have done extensive work on trauma, Post-Traumatic Stress Disorder (PTSD), and alcohol addictions. Specifically, they have investigated the role that uncontrollable trauma plays in the development of PTSD and alcohol addictions. The degree to which a person can control a traumatic event is an important factor in understanding the impact of the event (Maier and Seligmanm, 1975) and the subsequent development of PTSD or alcoholism. If a person is unable to control a traumatic event, he is more likely to act passively and fearfully in similar situations. This sets the person up for the development of PTSD-like symptoms. In response to these feelings, people often self-medicate with alcohol to avoid emotional distress related to the trauma (Volpicelli et al., 1999).

Conventional knowledge would tell us that people looking to avoid the negative emotions associated with a trauma would consume alcohol during the course of a traumatic event. However, a body of research indicated that this is not the case. Volpicelli, Ulm, and Hopson (1990), found that alcohol consumption typically increases following the trauma rather than during the trauma. They have termed this the *happy hour effect.*

As there has been a great deal of support for the happy hour effect in clinical research, it was postulated that the present unsolicited survey would indicate that executives on Wall Street would display significantly higher alcohol consumption rates during the postwar period of our time line rather than in anticipation of or during the actual infiltration of Iraq by U.S. troops. It was also hypothesized that demographic categories such as marital status and annual income would be significantly related to problematic drinking behaviors as well.

Method

Participants

Participants were unsolicited individuals who visited a web site designed for brokers and other financial industry employees. Individuals who visited the web site were asked to complete a survey regarding their drinking behaviors. A total of 155 participants completed all or part of the demographics questionnaire and survey (see the results in the following section for specific information regarding participant demographics).

Materials

A demographics questionnaire and the AUDIT (Alcohol Use Disorders Identification Test; Babor et al., 1989) were used to collect data for the current study. The demographics questionnaire included questions regarding each participant's age, gender, marital status, state of residence, workplace residence, position, income level, and amount of exercise. These were all categorically presented to the participants, who chose the category most appropriate for them.

The AUDIT is a questionnaire that was developed to examine problematic drinking behaviors. This 10-item questionnaire examined drinking frequency, amount, the influence of drinking on daily living, and behaviors related to alcohol abuse. After completing the AUDIT, participants received feedback scores to help them understand the extent to which their drinking was impairing their lives. Scores were divided into categories labeled Very High, High, Moderate, Low, and No Problem, respectively. The web site located at catsg.com was used to post the demographics questionnaire and the AUDIT.

Design and Procedure

A survey was used to collect data to determine the demographic variables and the impact the war in Iraq had on drinking behavior. Respondents were first asked to read a thorough debriefing and informed consent page, which concluded with a prompt to click a button as a form of acceptance that they understood the benefits, limitations, and threats to their confidentiality. Immediately following this acceptance, the respondents were prompted to complete a demographics survey. Once this page was completed, the participants were asked to click on a button to move on to the AUDIT survey. At the conclusion of these items, participants received an overall AUDIT score and a narrative explaining any risks or problems with drinking that their score indicated. Referrals were made to substance abuse facilities throughout the United States if an individual felt that she needed help. At the end, data were analyzed using SPSS 8.0.

Results

Respondent Information

A total of 155 individuals responded to the current survey. Of the 155 respondents, 151 provided complete demographic data and answered all of the survey questions. The 151 respondents completing the demographic data and answering all of the survey questions were included in the current study. The four respondents who were not included left several demographic and questionnaire items blank. These respondents were deemed as inappropriate to include in the current study because a total score on the alcohol questionnaire could not be computed and because of their lack of demographic information. A sample of 151 participants was considered appropriate for all of the proposed analyses (that is, one-way ANOVA, correlations, t-tests).

Demographic Information of Respondents

Demographic information was collected regarding respondents' ages, gender, salary, marital status, amount of exercise per week, occupation, and residence. A summary of the participants' responses to questions regarding several demographic variables can be found in Table B.1.

Findings Regarding Hypotheses

One-way ANOVAs and post hoc analyses using t-tests for equality of means were conducted to examine the data collected from the current study. It was found that neither of the hypotheses were supported. The happy hour effect was not found to occur. In fact, significantly more problematic drinking behaviors occurred during the war than after the war in Iraq, $F = 4.13$, $p < .05$. When examining the total score on the AUDIT rating scale, the group of participants who completed the rating scale during the war had a significantly higher total score. Also, the prewar and during-war groups were not found to have significantly different amounts of problematic drinking behaviors. The additional hypothesis that specific demographic characteristics would relate to increased problematic drinking behaviors was also not supported. Unlike previous research, salary levels and marital status did not have a significant impact on drinking behavior in the current study.

Table B.1:   Participant Response

Demographic	Category	Number of Participants	Percent of Participants
Age	18–25	28	18%
	26–30	49	33%
	31–35	11	7%
	36–40	21	14%
	40–50	24	16%
	51+	18	12%
Gender	Female	25	17%
	Male	126	83%
Marital Status	Single	71	47%
	Married	55	36%
	Divorced	25	17%
Income Level	Under 50K	32	21%
	50K–100K	85	56%
	100K–150K	17	11%
	150K–200K	6	4%
	200K+	11	7%
Amount of Exercise per week	Not at all	40	27%
	<2 hours	59	39%
	2–4 hours	33	22%
	>4 hours	19	13%

The majority of the participants were found to be single men, under the age of 30 who exercised infrequently and made less than $100,000 per year. Analysis of the additional demographic variables indicated that over 90 percent of the sample consisted of individuals working and living in and around Manhattan.

Findings Regarding Specific Drinking Behaviors on the AUDIT

Analyses were conducted to examine which specific problematic drinking behaviors were most significantly affected by being in the pre-, during-, or postwar groups. Interestingly, despite the finding that on average the problematic drinking behaviors of participants were highest during versus after the war when examining specific questions, there was only one area in which this was found to be marginally significant. How often participants drank was found to occur more frequently in the during-war than in the postwar group, $F = 2.46$, $p = .09$. Surprisingly, the during-war group was found to have more drinks containing alcohol on a typical day when they drank, $F = 6.83$, $p < .01$, and binge drank more frequently, $F = 6.35$, $p < .01$, than the prewar group. Also, the during-war group indicated that they more frequently felt feelings of guilt or remorse after drinking than the prewar group, $F = 3.93$, $p < .05$.

Discussion

This preliminary investigation examined the issue of self-medication and coping skills during times of great stress and trauma, as evidenced by the aforementioned empirically validated research on alcohol use. Specifically, the investigators sought to illuminate whether individuals working within the financial services industry in New York City would display more problematic drinking behaviors after the conclusion of the war, thus supporting the happy hour effect pattern noted in the research of Volpicelli et al. (1999). Previous research by this investigator also indicated that these individuals typically use maladaptive coping skills for the purpose of relieving stress. Also, a longstanding cultural acceptance of drinking alcohol for the purposes of relaxing, conducting business meetings, and networking has existed on Wall Street. The findings of this investigation were noteworthy in that more of the problematic behaviors relating to alcohol use were reported during the war, as opposed to after major combat operations were concluded. This contradiction with prior research can be explained by various sociocultural factors and international events that may have interfaced with our target population before and at the time of this study.

Logic suggests that the events of September 11, 2001, would affect no group more significantly than the financial services executives working on Wall Street. Many individuals physically or vicariously witnessed the traumatic attack on the World Trade Center while others survived it. Many cases of Post-Traumatic Stress Disorder were reported within the first six months to a year after this event, as would be expected from an event that was so vivid and catastrophic in nature. Specifically, there appeared to be more instances of survivor guilt, startle responses, nightmares, depression, and insomnia as a consequence of this disaster. It was speculated that prescriptions for antidepressants had significantly increased in the New York City area and substance and alcohol use problems reportedly rose drastically as well.

Media depictions of this event registered with all Americans, but likely were more salient for New Yorkers who worked on Wall Street. Graphic images of people jumping out of a burning building will probably never be forgotten by those who worked in close proximity to the World Trade Center. This was a time when Americans may have felt a strong sense of victimization and a loss of control. With each year since the September 11, 2001, anniversary, reactions appear to occur reliably, with the resurfacing of memorials and media coverage of the initial event that involved terrorism.

The findings that appear to contradict the happy hour effect may be stemming from the fact that many Wall Street workers have not fully recovered from the attacks on their security and way of life in 2001. This attack was viewed by many on Wall Street as a symbolic attack on corporate America and capitalism. When the United States officially announced it was going to attack Iraq using shock-and-awe tactics, many emotionally charged reactions were likely to be elicited for anyone who had lost a loved one, a colleague, or friend during this terrorist attack. It is not surprising that this group of individuals working within the financial services industry, a profession that has adopted alcohol use as an accepted means of socializing and conducting business, began drinking as a means of escaping these painful feelings during the attacks on Iraq. Historically, these individuals utilize maladaptive coping skills as evidenced by prior research conducted by the lead investigator who found that they reported using activities such as nightclubbing, masturbation, and drinking alcohol as a means of dealing with job stress. Demographic data indicated that the majority of the current sample spent less than two hours per week physically exercising as a means of dealing with their stress. Although this finding was not significantly related to an increase in problematic drinking behaviors, it supported prior research conducted by Cass et al. (2000), indicating that financial executives did not engage in healthy lifestyle habits.

Upon the initiation of war on Iraq, media coverage of the war spanned 24 hours a day and displayed vivid images of destruction and violence. Unlike previous war coverage, reporters were embedded in combat units, some incurring loss of life or injury. It is likely that the vivid imagery of the war, in conjunction with a reawakening of unresolved anger and guilt regarding the World Trade Center tragedy and maladaptive coping skills, may have led to the increase in problematic drinking behaviors during the war, rather than postwar, as noted in our findings. The findings that indicated higher levels of guilt and remorse for drinking and binge drinking in the during-war group is not surprising because of the likelihood that similar feelings of uncertainty, vulnerability, and guilt for experiencing painful emotions had resurfaced for individuals who find these feelings to be reprehensible. In many ways, New Yorkers have become habituated and desensitized to these vivid images of destruction and loss over the years, but more recent related events appear to bring their unresolved emotions to the surface quicker than they would be if a completely unrelated or shocking trauma were presented. Thus, the happy hour effect may still be applicable and accurate if a trauma is unrelated to any previous one.

Interestingly, it is speculated that the reasons why the prewar and during-war groups did not show significant differences in problematic drinking behaviors were because anticipation of war and war itself has historically had a positive impact on U.S. markets. Times of uncertainty, though (such as after the World Trade Center attack), historically lead to economic troubles in the United States and decimate the markets. Individuals who work as traders, analysts, or investment bankers felt some relief and hope for a struggling economy at the time the war was begun. Thus, it is likely that more market volatility existed in anticipation of war and during the war, which required that individuals working in the financial services arena needed to remain at work longer and behave in a more consistent fashion. The majority of participants experienced moderate problems related to their drinking as found by the AUDIT survey. It seems that had the prospect of war, or the actual ongoing war not existed, the sputtering economy and the bear market trends would have led to greater impairments as a result of drinking behaviors.

The secondary hypothesis regarding marital status and annual income and their relationship to alcohol use problems was not confirmed through our analysis. This may be due to factors such as having too few married participants included in the study and participants who were, on average, wealthier than would be expected if at high risk for having problematic drinking behaviors after experiencing a trauma.

The results of this investigation shed light on the importance of noticing the true casualties of Wall Street—the men and women who work within the highly stressful financial services industry. Specifically, it is imperative that corporate America begin to take alcohol and substance abuse seriously, because it has long-lasting and consequential effects on whole companies and individual employees' longevity within a firm.

Interventions like Exposure Response Prevention (ERP), support groups like Alcoholics Anonymous (AA) and Narcotics Anonymous (NA), and residential treatment for substance abuse problems are currently used as primary ways to deal with substance abuse concerns. ERP is based on the principles of operant and classical conditioning and is a way for an alcoholic to take back control over his addiction through the use of empowering self-statements and graduated exposure to the alcoholic product of his choice within a realistic context.

One must not forget that these individuals are constantly reminded of the horror of September 11th on a daily basis while walking to work. Internet studies and other support should continue to reach out to this highly reticent population of executives who hide behind a façade of confidence and strength for the purpose of not letting anyone know about their painful feelings or weaknesses. Financial executives will always fear that they will lose their jobs if they admit to a drinking problem, so it is important to continue research through the Internet for the purpose of helping these fearful individuals. Alcohol abuse is a tremendous problem that has been normalized by the culture of Wall Street and this study hopes to bring it back out in the spotlight. The current study hopes to aid future researchers in predicting alcohol use behaviors within this population if another tragedy or trauma should occur again.

A primary strength of this research design was the ability to tap into a specific target population of employees who could not be reached by handing out surveys within their work environment. The anonymity of using a home computer to fill out the survey instead of responding through a job-related one afforded us more honesty in the responses that we obtained. The AUDIT was, fortunately, usable within the public domain and is also a widely used instrument for assessing problematic drinking behaviors. Also, individuals with problematic drinking behaviors were provided with the awareness that they have a problem, along with strategies and referrals for resolving them.

Conversely, this study has limitations. A convenience sample that was collected from individuals who were drawn to our consulting firm's web site was used. Thus, anyone who was looking for help in the area of stress management or dealing with job burnout would be a likely respondent to this survey. This in itself may have superficially inflated the generalizability of our findings to the financial services industry as a whole. Also, while confidentiality was ensured in taking the survey, it is impossible to confirm the veracity of the responses given or the careers of the individuals who responded. Lastly, our sample was very homogeneous and rather small, which limits the generalizability of our findings. Future investigations should attempt to collect a larger sample of respondents, which include a wider variety of age ranges and marital statuses.

References

Brady, K.T., and Sonne, S.C. 1999. The role of stress in alcohol use, alcoholism treatment, and relapse. *Alcohol Research and Health,* 23(4):263–271.

Brown, G.R., and Anderson, B. 1991. Psychiatric morbidity in adult inpatients with childhood histories of sexual and physical abuse. *American Journal of Psychiatry,* 148:55–61.

Cass, A.M., Lewis, J., and Simco, E. 2000. "Casualties of Wall Street: An Assessment of the Walking Wounded." Directed Study Research, Nova Southeastern University.

Crum, R.M., Muntaner, C., Eaton, W.W., and Anthony, J.C. 1995. Occupational stress, and the risks of alcohol abuse and dependence. *Alcoholism: Clinical and Experimental Research,* 19:647–655.

Fullilove, M.T., Fullilove, R.E., Smith, M., Winkler, K., Micheal, C., Panzer, P.G., and Wallace, R. 1993. Violence, trauma, and post traumatic stress disorder among women drug users. *Journal of Traumatic Stress,* 6:533–543.

Lex, B.W. 1991. Some gender differences in alcohol and polysubstance users. *Health Psychology,* 10:121–132.

Maier, S.F., and Seligman, M. 1976. Learned helplessness: Theory and evidence. *Journal of Experimental Psychology,* 105:3–46.

Najavits, L.M., Weiss, R.D., and Shaw, S.R. 1997. The link between substance abuse and post-traumatic stress disorder in women: A research review. *American Journal on Addictions,* 6(4):273–283.

Najavits, L.M., Weiss, R.D., and Shaw, S.R. 1999. A clinical profile of women with post-traumatic stress disorder and substance dependence. *Psychology of Addictive Behaviors,* 13(2):98–104.

Seeman, M., and Seeman, A.Z. 1992. Life strains, alienating, and drinking behavior. *Alcoholism: Clinical and Experimental Research,* 16:199–205.

Takeshita, T., Muruyama, S., and Morimoto, K. 1998. Relevance of both daily hassles and the ALDH2 genotype to problem drinking among Japanese male workers. *Alcoholism: Clinical and Experimental Research,* 22:115–120.

Volpicelli, J.R., Ulm, R.R., and Hopson, N. 1990. The bi-directional effects of shock on alcohol preference in rats. *Alcoholism: Clinical and Experimental Research,* 14:913–916.

Volpicelli, J.R., Balaraman, G., Hahn, J., Wallace, H., and Bux, D. 1999. The role of uncontrollable trauma in the development of PTSD and alcohol addiction. *Alcohol Research and Health,* 23(4):256–262.

Bullish Thinking Monitor Log

CATALYST STRATEGIES GROUP

CATALYST STRATEGIES GROUP, INC.

BULLISH THINKING *MONITORING LOG*

WORK EVENTS Describe two situations, events, or interactions that lead to specific consequences.

1.

2.

PERCEPTION OF EVENT Stream of positive, rational thoughts, and/or self-statements

BULLISH THINKING	BEARISH THINKING	BULLISH THINKING	BEARISH THINKING
1a.	1b.	2a.	2b.

CONSEQUENCES

BULLISH OUTCOMES	BEARISH OUTCOMES	BULLISH OUTCOMES	BEARISH OUTCOMES
Physiological	Physiological	Physiological	Physiological
Performance	Performance	Performance	Performance
Emotional *(enter here)*	Emotional *(enter here)*	Emotional *(enter here)*	Emotional *(enter here)*
Sense of Control	Sense of Control	Sense of Control	Sense of Control

Blank Monitoring Log

208

Recommended Readings and Resources

Beck, Aaron T.; Rush, A. John; Shaw, Brian F.; Emery, Gary. *Cognitive Therapy of Depression*. The Guildford Press, 1987.

Burns, David D. *Feeling Good: The New Mood Therapy (Revised and Updated)*. Avon, 1999.

Copeland, Mary Ellen. *Living Without Depression & Manic Depression: A Workbook for Maintaining Mood Stability*. New Harbinger Publications, 1994.

Faupel, Adrian; Herrick, Elizabeth; Sharp, Peter. *Anger Management: A Practical Guide*. David Fulton Publishing, 1998.

Greenberger, Dennis and Padesky, Christine. *Mind Over Mood: Change How You Feel by Changing the Way You Think*. The Guildford Press, 1995.

Kassinove, Howard, Pd.D. *Anger Disorders: Definition, Diagnosis and Treatment*. Taylor & Francis, 1995.

Shaw, Brian F., Ph.D.; Ritvo, Paul, Ph.D.; Irvine, Jane, D.Phil.; Lewis, M. David. *Addiction & Recovery for Dummies*. John Wiley & Sons, 2004.

Rehabilitation Facilities

A.I.R. Alternatives
Alcohol and Drug Abuse Care Management
airalternatives.com

The Canyon
Depression Anxiety and Addiction
thecyn.com

Caron Foundation
Addictions
caron.org

Catalyst Support Services
Outpatient Case Management Services for Dual Diagnosis
catsg.com
catsg.com/support

Cirque Lodge
Addictions
cirquelodge.com

The Clinic at DuPont
Specialty Psychological and Psychiatric Services; Stress, Anxiety, Depression,
    Substance Abuse, Behavioral Health
theclinicatdupont.com

Betty Ford
Alcoholism
bettyfordcenter.org

Mountainside Treatment Center
Alcohol and Drug Addiction Treatment and Rehabilitation
mountainside.org

Sierra Tucson
Trauma/Addiction Treatment
sierratucson.com

SLS Health
Dual Diagnosis Residential Treatment
slshealth.com

Web Sites

nimh.nih.gov
National Institute of Mental Health

therapeuticresources.com
Therapeutic Resources, Inc.

depression-guide.com
Depression Guide, Inc.

catsg.com
Catalyst Strategies Group

nida.nih.gov
National Institute on Drug Abuse

Index

Available Now

ISBN 978-0-470-13770-3
Paper • 208 pages
US $19.95 • CAN $21.99 • UK £10.99

Help your advisors:
- Recognize the warning signals associated with "under the radar" stress
- Avoid job burnout and depression
- Overcome emotional and psychological hurdles to succeed in this highly competitive field

For bulk discount information, please contact Sam Testa at (201) 748-6789, or via email at stesta@wiley.com.

WILEY
Now you know.
wiley.com